Living with the Sea

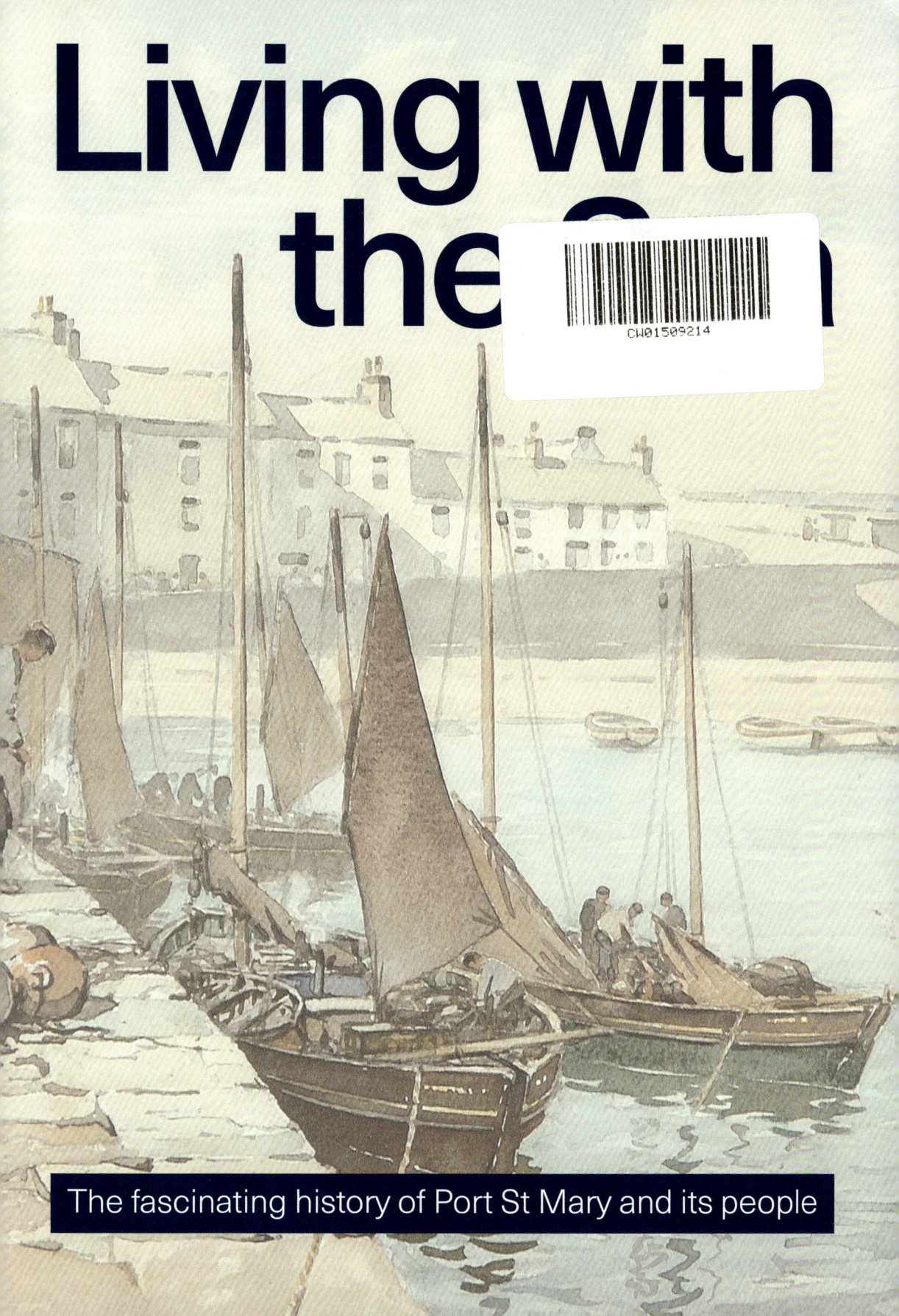

The fascinating history of Port St Mary and its people

Front cover image – painting of Port St Mary by John Ernest Aitken (1881-1957). Aitken's studio was to the rear of Lime Street in Port St Mary.

Contents

Introduction

ANGELA W. LITTLE

*L*iving with the sea conjures a host of images. Children play by the sea, swim in the sea, sail on the sea and dream of 'going to sea'. Lives depend on the sea as a source of food, of trade and commerce and as a means of travel. Fishermen, net makers and boat builders make their living from the sea. Flocks of gulls float on the sea unwittingly guiding the fishermen to where they should shoot their nets. We admire the beauty of the sea, and respect its power. The moods and state of the sea, the sky and the on-shore and off-shore weather more generally, are constant sources of conversation among those who live by the sea and by those whose lives depend upon it.

Living with the sea is part of the everyday experience of the people of the Isle of Man. The Isle of Man is a small island located in the Irish Sea at the very centre of the British Isles and is not to be confused with the Isle of Wight, located in the English Channel, off the coast of the county of Hampshire. The authors of the old Irish sagas referred to the Isle of Man by many names, the last of which was *Ellan Sheeant*, the Sacred Isle. Until the early nineteenth century the majority of the population were speakers of Manx Gaelic, a Goidelic Celtic language, derived from Old Irish. Constitutionally, the island is a crown dependency that has never been part of the United Kingdom or Great Britain. It has no representation in Westminster. Instead it boasts its own directly elected legislature that stretches back unbroken at least 1,040 years to a time when the Norse Vikings ruled. It lays claim to have been the first country in the world to give some women a vote in parliamentary elections as early as 1881. It has its own education, health and legal and fiscal systems; its own national flag, postage stamps and currency.

The island's strategic location in the middle of the Irish Sea, at the centre of the British Isles, has rendered it a crossroads of cultures. The island's heritage is steeped in a culture that is at once Pagan, Christian, Celtic, Norse, British and maritime. The sea has inspired many aspects of Manx culture – poetry and literature, folk lore, dance, art, music, religious hymns and popular songs. People sing with joy of being 'beside the sea (side)', they lament 'the wreck of the herring fleet' and, through the evening hymn, they pray for 'the harvest of the sea'. The island's most famous poet, T.E. Brown, wrote of childhoods 'care-pricked yet healed the while with the balm of rock and sea'. In Manx folk lore the herring was chosen by the other species of fish as their king. The Celtic god Manannan Mac y Lir is the son of the sea and the island's protector. Thought by some to have been a celebrated merchant who lived in the Isle of Man, Manannan was reputed to be the most famous pilot in Western Europe who could forecast the weather by studying the heavens. He was also a necromancer with the ability to envelop himself and his island in mist, making them invisible to strangers and invaders. Still that protective cloak of mist descends, often for days on end. And still, some believe in him in the way that others believe in the power of the religious Lord God to protect 'those in peril on the sea'.

Port St Mary

Our book focusses on the seaside village of Port St. Mary, in the south west of our island, and its development over the 150-year period 1829–1979. Port St. Mary is located in the Parish of Rushen (strictly, the Parish of Kirk Christ) and within the larger sheading[1] of the same name, Rushen. For many years it was referred to as 'The Port' with settlements around the harbour and on the hilly slopes nearby. In 1891 it became a village and included the rapidly developing area to the North of the harbour, around Chapel Bay. It takes its name from Keeill Moirrey or (St) Mary's Church, long since disappeared, but possibly located on the site on which the current Town Hall is situated, overlooking Chapel Bay. Over the years its name has been recorded variously – Portell Morrey, Purt le Murrey, Purt le Mourray, Purt le Maurai, Port Le Morey, Purt Noo Moirrey and Port-le-Mary. The Victorian music-hall song, 'I'm the Pride of Purt le Murra', offers yet another spelling. Today's visitors are welcomed to the Port by the signboard *Failt erriu dys Purt le Moirrey*.

The sea was a main source of subsistence and cash for many Port St. Mary families and generated employment in a range of seafaring activities. Herring fishing was the mainstay of the local economy, with the first herring houses established in 1770. 'Crofter-fishermen' went to sea to catch herring and mackerel during the 'seasons', while others engaged in trades related directly with the sea – boat builders, rope-makers, carpenters, joiners, timber merchants, net-makers and nailors. Many others supported those who lived by the sea – shoemakers, publicans and inn keepers, blacksmiths, stonemasons, grocery dealers, butchers, bakers, tailors, saddlers, schoolteachers, preachers, undertakers and sumners[2]. Through much of the nineteenth and twentieth century gangs of herring girls arrived in the Port from Scotland every year to gut, salt and pack herrings. It is said that a team of three experienced girls could gut and pack up to 1,000 herring every hour.

Before the development of roads and the railway, the sea was the main means of transportation around the island, between the island and the other British Isles and around the globe far and wide. In times of economic depression Port St. Mary families emigrated to Australia, New Zealand and North America by sea. The sea has separated and reunited the people of Port St. Mary in ways that the land has not.

The sea sustains life but it also takes life away. Many Port St Mary people have been taken by the sea in the course of earning a livelihood, fighting wars and assisting and saving others. Generations of Port St Mary families can name the ships wrecked on rocks, near and far. They recall with pride the role the Port has played in the construction of the lighthouses on the Calf of Man and Chicken Rock and the lives saved by their lifeboat and its volunteer crew. Many recall the story of the 'Brig Lily' disaster of 1852, probably the worst ever loss of life on the island's rocky coast. *En route* from Liverpool to South West Africa, the 160-ton brig was wrecked in a storm on the islet of Kitterland between the Isle of Man and the Calf of Man. Five crew drowned but the men of Port St Mary managed to save eight. The following day, a thirty-man salvage team, comprising Port St. Mary fishermen, carpenters, and shipwrights, assembled, led by Enos Lace – a Port St. Mary grocer, ship broker and sub-agent for Lloyds insurers. The men boarded the brig at 6am and smelled smoke. At 7.55am the whole of the south of the Isle of Man was rocked by a catastrophic explosion of forty tons of gunpowder. Twenty-nine men died, leaving behind twenty-two widows and seventy-two children.

> *The hearts of widows and orphans are torn in bitter anguish! Port St.*
> *Mary is in tears! Ye Christians of Mona, for the love of Christ, help*
> *these distressed ones!"* (Mona's Herald, 29/12/1852)

The sea and the land meet on the shore and the beach. But the meeting point of the sea and the land is not fixed. The 'space between'[1] the land and sea is made, washed away and remade by the semi-daily tides, sometimes gentle and calm, sometimes raging and tempestous. Over long periods of time the relentless, incoming tides have eroded the coastline. Historically, the beaches exposed by the tides provided seaweed used by farmers to fertilise the land. The carboniferous limestone beds exposed at the edge of the sea at Kallow Point were quarried. Some of the stone was used for building and some was burned in nearby kilns to create lime for farming. The sea for its part reclaims nutrients and minerals from the land it erodes. In places, the fluid 'space between' the land and the sea has become more fixed, or at least contained, by the erection of sea walls at the Promenade, Shore Road (the underway) and the Point.

But people have not always looked after the sea on which they depend. For centuries people all over the world have used the sea as a dump for waste that goes on to harm to marine life. They have also developed technology that has depleted fish stocks and destroyed the sea bed. Port St. Mary people have played their part in the process but they, like many elsewhere, are now working to protect and conserve the sea bed in closed and managed areas and to keep the beaches clean of the plastic waste that kills sea life.

Through the centuries the sea brought invaders, immigrants, migrant workers, traders and 'stranger visitors' alike. But as well as a means of travel, the sea, the beaches and the coast became a source of leisure. By the late nineteenth century the Isle of Man was attracting large numbers of holiday makers from the industrial North of England, Scotland and Ireland. Port St. Mary participated in this growing tourism industry in a major way, facilitated in part by the arrival of the railway in 1874. Her large beach was safe for swimming and sand castle making, and her coast offered walks as beautiful as they were bracing. Boarding houses and hotels were built 'along the Promenade' around Chapel Bay, to the North of the harbour. The main season lasted only 12 weeks but there were some visitors in May and September. Although the season was short, the economic benefits were significant – for housekeepers, job seekers, shopkeepers, pleasure boat owners, farmers, grocers, butchers and bakers, pub owners – and for the church and chapels whose congregations swelled. Tourism became a mainstay of the Port's economy and brought significant numbers of women into the labour market. It transformed the

Port from a 'fishing village to a holiday haunt' (IOM Examiner, 17/09/1937). In the 1960s the Karran-Quirk footpath was built as a winter works scheme. Known popularly as 'The Cat Walk' this new seaside attraction enabled tourists and residents alike to walk *above* the sea, if not *on* it! Tourism remained very important right up until the late 1970s, interrupted only by the two world wars.

During the two world wars many Port St. Mary people left the island by sea and served far and wide. Some did not return and families were left bereft. WWII would also bring many to the Port by sea and train. These were German and Austrian women and children classed by the United Kingdom government as 'enemy aliens' and housed in the Rushen internment camps in Port St. Mary and neighbouring Port Erin. Only a very small minority were Nazi sympathisers, the majority offering no security risk at all to the British war effort. Ironically, they arrived in Port St. Mary on the 29th May 1940, the very same day that three of the Isle of Man's Steam Packet vessels, the Mona's Queen, Fenella and King Orry, were sunk during Operation Dynamo,the evacuation of allied troops from Dunkirk in which eight Manx vessels participated. The arrival of 'aliens' in a village that was itself coping with the losses of war created some disquiet. Women on both sides of the barbed wire suffered enormous emotional hardships through the war years. Despite, or perhaps because of this, friendships were formed between villagers and 'aliens', many of which have endured to this day.[4]

Port St. Mary 1829–1979

How then has life changed over the 150 years of our history? In their Trade Directory of 1843 Pigot and Slater provide us with a fine introduction to the start of our story. We quote from it *verbatim*, starting with a general description of the parish in which Port St. Mary is situated.

> Rushen (or Christ Rushen) parish, in the sheading of its name, lies at the south-western extremity of the island; it is about five miles and a half in length from north to south, by an average breadth of one and a half from east to west. The church, situate four miles west of Castletown, near the centre of the parish is a plain unadorned edifice, rebuilt in 1775, and adapted to contain a congregation of four hundred and fifty persons; the living is a vicarage, in the gift of the crown. The parish school is adjacent to the church; and about a quarter of a mile to the south is a school for girls, supported by a small endowment. The central part of the district is fertile productive land, and is as well cultivated, perhaps, as any locality in England; but the north and south portions are bleak barren highlands. This parish contains plenty of limestone of the best quality, and lead ore is found at several places: *Kentraugh*, the beautiful mansion of Edward M. Gawne, Esq., about three miles from Castletown, is unequalled in the island…A noble colonnade

extends along the entire front of the edifice, upwards of ninety feet, supported by eight massive columns of the Ionic order. The lofty rooms of the interior, especially the saloon (which is eighteen feet in height, and of proportionate dimensions, with a beautiful Gothic arched ceiling), display the elegant taste of the hospitable proprietor. The gardens and pleasure grounds are delightfully laid out; and the offices and out-houses, conveniently grouped, contain all the various requisites furnished by the best judgment, and appropriate to an establishment of the magnitude to which they belong.

Port Erin (so called from the bay opening towards Ireland) is a small village and sea-port in the above parish, nearly five miles west of Castletown and 15 south-west of Douglas. The village comprises about forty dwellings, a small Wesleyan chapel, and a comfortable inn; the employment of the inhabitants is fishing and husbandry. The bay, which forms a natural square, has good anchorage; and vessels of two hundred tons burthen can come close to the rock, on the south side, in favourable weather. Breda *(sic)* Head, a bold and abrupt precipice, forms the north boundary of the bay. Port Erin is the most convenient place for taking a boat for the purpose of visiting the Calf of Man which is distant about three miles south-west.

Port St. Mary (or Port-le-Mary) is a busy prosperous village and sea-port, in the same parish as Port Erin, situated on the western side of a fine spacious bay, on the south shore of the island, four miles west of Castletown, fifteen south of Peel, and the same distance south-west of Douglas. The village consists of about eighty houses, principally erected close to the harbour, which is protected from the violence of the sea by a substantially built stone pier, two hundred and thirty yards long and eight yards broad, with a lighthouse on its northern extremity. There is a new pier about to be built on the south side of the harbour, which will furnish extra facility for loading and unloading vessels. More than eighty light vessels, from fifteen to forty tons burden belong to this little place; many of them are employed in the fishery during the season. The Carrick Reef, near the middle of the bay, is dangerous, being covered at high water. A little south of the village, on the shore, below high-water mark, is a stratified quarry of limestone, of superior quality, from which the new jetty at Douglas, and many other piers and quays, have been constructed. At Mount Gawne, about one mile on the road to Castletown, is the extensive brewery of Mr. Michael Connal.

The Calf of Man is a small Island separated from Man by a dangerous channel of five hundred yards width; its area comprehends about 570 acres, of which nearly one hundred are cultivated; and it contains one farmhouse, three cottages and two lighthouses. The occupier of the farmhouse, Mr. Shepherd has opened it as an inn, erected a corn mill, and provided a threshing machine. The surface of the Calf is uneven-in some places elevated from four to five hundred feet above the sea; and great part of the coast is composed of high rocky shire. Rabbits have multiplied here to a somewhat valuable amount, not less than from two thousand four hundred to two thousand eight hundred being annually exported.

In the main, our book covers the period 1829–1979. How life has changed for the people of Port St. Mary! The physical description of Port St. Mary and its environs above would be recognisable still in 1979, but many aspects of social, political and economic life would not. In 1829, land ownership was concentrated in the hands of one man, John Murray, the fourth Duke of Atholl. By 1979, land ownership was distributed widely. Compared with 1829, the population in 1979 was larger,[5] its residents lived longer and many more were immigrants from elsewhere on the island, the British Isles and further afield. By 1979, all were literate in English and all young people attended school up to at least the age of 15 years. Where, in 1829, no ordinary citizen had a say in who represented them in the Manx parliament, by 1867 11 Port St. Mary men were 'qualified' to vote, followed by five women in 1881. By 1979, all adults could vote. In 1829, most made their living directly from the sea and the land; by 1979, few did. In 1829 everyone attended church and/or the chapel; by 1979, congregations were small. In 1829, the majority of residents spoke Manx; by 1979, only a handful did.

What happened in between is in part a result of broader political, economic and social changes on the island and 'across the water' in England more generally. Through the late nineteenth and early twentieth centuries, the Manx government came to provide, through personal and other taxation, free education, health services and 'old age' pensions. In 1891 the Port St Mary Village Commissioners were established as a local government authority and from then on they facilitated the gradual introduction of sewers, water, gas and electricity, new housing and the extension of village boundaries. What happened in between was also a result of changes in the conditions of life in Port St. Mary and, critically, of the contribution to change by the people of Port St. Mary. The stories of some of those – from conservative and reforming politicians to political activists to those who kept alive the Manx language and culture – have been published already.[6] Our book introduces many more stories of the people who have made Port St. Mary what it is today.

Our book addresses maritime life, farming, building, roads and landmarks, education, tourism, places of worship, streets and place names, shops, pubs and internment during WWII:

In Chapter One, Mick Kneale talks about the Port's important maritime industry, recalling a time when the bustling harbour was home to fishermen, boat builders, 'gutter girls' and vessels of all shapes and sizes, including nickeys, cutters and schooners.

In Chapter Two, Nigel Crowe investigates the origins of the network of route-ways serving Port St Mary. He also identifies some of the oldest building in the district.

In Chapter Three, Catherine Clucas looks at how the upland and lowland farms around the Port developed their own individual character and kept pace with the inevitable changes within farming.

In Chapter Four, Andrew Foxon discusses the story of places of worship and sites of religious significance in and around Port St Mary. Not only are there ancient places of burial and the early keeill which gives the Port its name, but there also stories of the established church, the role of Methodism, the Beach Mission, and the turmoil of internment.

In Chapter Five, Angela W. Little charts the development of two tracks of schooling for the children of Port St Mary. She reminds us of long forgotten schools, such as the Port St Mary National School and the 'Tin Tab' school, and asks 'what *was* the 'Rushen School Crisis' all about?

In Chapter Six, Hugh Davidson shows how Port St Mary differentiated its tourism offer from Douglas, 'making no apology for its lack of bright lights, blaring music or tinselled pageantry', instead skilfully positioning itself through a combination of the old world charms of a fishing village and the freshness of a modern seaside resort – a centre for exploring the scenic and heritage attractions of the 'Beautiful South'.

In Chapter Seven, Doreen Moule records the inception of the WWII Women's Internment Camp in 1940 and its evolution into the Married Camp in 1941. The questions on the lips of the local people were: 'Enemy Aliens? Who are these people? Why are they here and where have they come from?'

In Chapter Eight, Staffan Overgaard and John W. Qualtrough walk us through the streets and roads of Port St Mary, tracing the origins of their names. Some names are very old, some are in English and Manx, some followed the fashion of their day – and some have no names at all.

In Chapter Nine, Staffan Overgaard and John W. Qualtrough take us on a tour of eighty locations which housed shops, occupied by 250 shopkeepers in the last 120 years. The true number of shopkeepers are most likely much higher – the residents of Port St Mary were very industrious.

In Chapter Ten, Pamela Crowe shares her memories of Millennium Year 1979 – a colourful celebration which marks the end of the period of our history of Port St Mary.

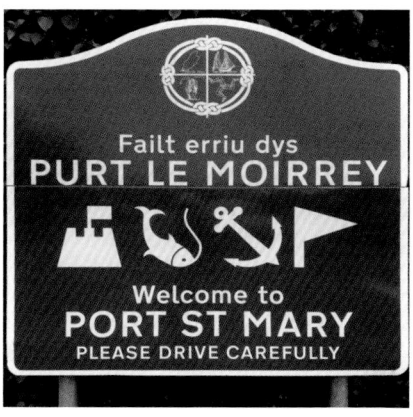

The Authors

CATHERINE CLUCAS

Catherine was born and bred in Port St Mary, descended from Cubbons Master Mariners of Port St Mary, skippers of *The Progress*, reputedly the last Manx-built schooner and connected genetically to Clucases all over the world. She attended Rushen Primary, Castle Rushen High School, University College Isle of Man and the Centre for Manx Studies. Catherine has always had an interest in history, family history, languages, reading and a love of books, films, art and music. She has worked for Manx National Heritage in various roles since 1989. In 1991 she became one of the first Manx Registered Tour Guides (Blue Badge Guide). Other roles have included being the first leader for Mooinjer Veggey Playgroups, and SESO at the Bunscoill Ghaelgagh; assistant librarian on the Mobile Library; secretary of the Gaelic Broadcasting Committee; and a heritage trust coordinator. Catherine currently works as a peripatetic Manx Language teacher and freelance researcher.

Catherine has a MA in Manx Studies, was a shortlisted poet at the Strokestown International Poetry Festival, past recipient of the Constance Radcliffe Heritage Award, and written lyrics for two Manx entries for the Pan-Celtic Song Contest. She was a founder member of Possan Straiddey street performance group and Labyrinth, Manx history in action players and a Manx storyteller. Catherine is a regular volunteer for various events, including the Isle of Man Walking Festival and Festival Interceltique Lorient, assistant librarian for Isle of Man Family History Society and is one of the organisers of the Oie Voaldyn Manx May Fire Festival (www.oievoaldyn.com). Her current areas of research include the descendants of the men killed at the Brig Lily disaster in 1852 and the social impact of the disaster on Port St Mary; folklore and customs; branches of the Clucas family; and tracing her Irish ancestry.

'I am delighted to have contributed to this snapshot of the Port St Mary story, there are a lot more stories to collect and tell yet.'

NIGEL CROWE

Nigel Crowe was born in Douglas and raised on the ancestral farm in Baldwin. Like many of his relatives, he has a great love of music and presently sings in a local a capella group. At the age of thirteen he was introduced to the world of genealogy by an American relative and subsequently went on to become a founder member and officer of the Isle of Man Family History Society. After five years as a Manx civil servant, Nigel studied and took his degree in property management at Reading University. After working in Shropshire, he returned to Manx shores to complete his qualifications and continue his professional career at a long-established firm. After some twenty-five years, he was awarded his fellowship by the RICS, retiring as a director of his firm some time later.

His wider interest in local history was encouraged by the late Robert Curphey and he has served a term as president of the Isle of Man Natural History and Antiquarian Society. His current research centres on landscape, urban and architectural history. He is working towards an account of the origins of the Island's landscape. Nigel's professional expertise and historical interests, like his Manx ancestry, have extended to all parts of the Island. His mother's family – Clagues and Kinvigs – originated in the south and he also descends from the Watterson family of Ballarobin, Malew, and previously of Corvalley and Glendown, Rushen.

'Until now, landscape history has been an untold story in the Isle of Man, along with urban morphology. Understanding the roads and streets is a necessary first stage in unscrambling the complex evolution of our countryside and settlements. I have tried to make it my mission to raise awareness of these issues, and the South will have a valuable role in helping us work out the significance and value of our man-made landscapes.'

PAMELA CROWE

Pamela was director of a wholesale and retail booksellers and newsagents for twenty-five years. She was elected to Tynwald, the Isle of Man parliament in 1996, where she served for thirteen years in various roles, including Minister for Local Government and the Environment. She is now a fundraiser for charity and a keen researcher. Pamela has written three books – *Manx Scenic Cookbook, Rhymes of Mann, Rhymes of Scotland*, and was one of the authors of *Friend or Foe?*, the definitive history of the Women's WWII Internment Camp in Rushen.

'I married Graham in 1964 and his family was one of the largest in the south of the Island - Crowe/Cregeen/Keggin. When the Examiner Shop, the Port St Mary newsagent, came up for sale we were encouraged by the family to purchase it, despite the fact that I was in hospital having a baby (Fiona). We bought the business and converted the guesthouse above to a family home. My retail training was at John Lewis and I thought I would miss the bright lights of the "city", but instead I loved every minute of living in Port St Mary. The Millennium of Tynwald in 1979 was a truly memorable year in the Port.'

PROFESSOR HUGH DAVIDSON MBE

Hugh Davidson and his family have strong links with 'the beautiful south' of Rushen. Two Davidson brothers helped fellow Scotsmen build the first two Calf of Man lighthouses in 1818 and stayed on. And for many centuries the Quayles on his mother's side farmed the lower slopes of South Barrule near Grenaby. Hugh was educated at St Mark's School and Cambridge where he studied economics and law, later qualifying as a barrister at Grays Inn. He had a long career in business, starting with Procter & Gamble, working in twenty-five countries, and co-founded Oxford Strategic Marketing.

He has written many books on marketing, some on family history, and was Visiting Professor of Marketing at Cranfield University School of Management for twelve years.

On returning to the Isle of Man, Hugh moved from business to social entrepreneurship with his wife, Sandra, founding the H & S Davidson Trust in 2004 and Rushen Heritage Trust in 2014. On the Island, the H & S Davidson Trust co-funded The One World Charity Challenge for ten years in partnership with the Manx Government, and an inter-generational schools initiative, the Tell Me Project. Overseas, the H & S Davidson Trust co-funded and worked on joint ventures with Save the Children and Oxfam in Vietnam, India and Bangladesh, enabling more than 60,000 people, mainly very poor women and girls, to transform their lives by trebling their income and dramatically increasing their empowerment. Hugh has lived in many places including Oxford, Toronto and New York but prefers the Isle of Man.

'Although I was brought up in Douglas, my mother, who was born in Castletown, had many relatives in the "beautiful south", and it was always a treat to visit Port St Mary. It originated as a fishing village and in the late nineteenth century had more than 100 fishing boats, second only to Peel on the Island. Tourism started relatively late, in the early part of the 20th century, centered on Chapel Bay, while fishing continued around the piers and the port. The two activities complemented each other, since the atmosphere of the old port, and sea trips with dramatic scenery, appealed to visitors. Port St Mary has always had a strong community spirit with many activities in summer and winter, often influenced by the sea. Visitors enjoying the beauty of the place and friendly atmosphere may chat with locals, but unlike them do not live with the sometimes angry mood of the sea in winter. I greatly enjoyed the process of writing the book with so many interesting and enthusiastic colleagues, ably led by Staffan Overgaard and editor John Quirk, with John Qualtrough helping everyone with his memories and amazing collection of more than 160,000 items about the village. I hope the book will be read both by people on the Island and in other seaside towns and villages around Britain.'

DR ANDREW D. FOXON

With a background in archaeology and prehistoric technology, Andrew has more than forty years' experience in the interpretation and museums sector in Orkney, Edinburgh, Glasgow, Hull and in the Isle of Man, where he worked as Head of Professional Services for Manx National Heritage. He has lived in Port Erin since 1997 and is an active member and steward at Port Erin Methodist Church.

In 2013 Andrew set up Go-Mann Adventures (www.go-mannadventures.com) offering guided walks, tours and outdoor skills training in the Isle of Man. He is a Manx Registered Tour Guide (Blue Badge Guide) and a Hill and Moorland Leader. He is also Deputy Commandant of the Isle of Man Civil Defence and instructs in map reading, navigation, hill skills, search, safety and survival, as well as a range of other topics.

'The idea of helping in a group project to research and write about the story of Port St Mary was an interesting and intriguing one to me. Since I was focusing on one theme, I felt there was a risk that I saw that theme in isolation from the rest of the story, but I

found that all these different threads are interwoven and that the links between people, places, activities and events kept leading to new ideas. This has been an interesting project and one I hope readers will find equally interesting.'

MICHAEL KNEALE

Port St Mary born and bred, Michael has a life-long interest in the sea, messing about in boats and sailing from an early age, even running a commercial angling boat while still at school and learning to dive when Donald the dolphin was living in the bay. He joined Port St Mary volunteer lifeboat crew in 1970. His parents established the 'Manesca' shellfish processing firm in 1960, in which all the family played their part. Michael crewed on the company's scalloper *Petit Raleur* for a couple of years, then took over as manager ashore. In 1980 he rebuilt the old smokehouse into a modern unit and ran it up to 1997. In 1998, he accepted the RNLI's invitation to become a full-time coxswain at Port St Mary Station, retiring aged 65 in 2017.

He has built, sailed and raced dinghies, yachts and dayboats since the mid-1960s and, like his father Philip, served on almost every committee of the Isle of Man Yacht Club for more than forty years. He now continues to sail his individual style of gaff and lug rigged boats. His mother, Angela, had a hectic twenty-five years as the Island's French Honorary Consul looking after the many Breton trawlers working around the Irish Sea and beyond. When she took a job in Brussels, Michael took over the role just as these fleets were declining through the 1980s. He has an abiding interest in the local old sailing vessels, their rigs and the men who worked them, and his research continues.

'The maritime chapter is a brief overview of the huge amount of information available on the subject. I hope it leads readers to dig deeper into whatever aspects are of particular interest. The number of stories yet to be discovered and recorded is vast.'

PROFESSOR ANGELA W. LITTLE

Angela is Manx born and bred, having grown up overlooking Port St Mary bay in the 1950s and 1960s and been educated at Rushen Primary School where her father was headmaster 1953-74, and Castle Rushen High School. Her mother was very involved in village life through the Ladies Lifeboat Committee, Mount Tabor Church and the Women's Institute. Angela continued her education 'across' at the Universities of Surrey, London and Sussex before embarking on a career in international education that has taken her to schools and universities worldwide. In 1987 she was the youngest ever woman appointed to a Professorship at the University of London, where she held the Chair of Education and International Development until her retirement in 2010.

A former President of the British Association of International and Comparative Education, she is currently a Fellow of the Academy of Social Sciences, Trustee of the United Kingdom Forum for International Education and Training and Patron of the Ceylon Workers' Education Trust (www.angelawlittle.net). In 2013 she returned to live on the Island, where she is currently a Board member of Culture Vannin and the United

Nations Association, a keen walker with the Manx Footpaths Conservation Group and student of Manx Gaelic.

'I was delighted to have been invited to join the Rushen Heritage Trust project on the history of Port St Mary. Being brought up in a place generates local knowledge based on personal experience. This project has generated knowledge that goes far and beyond the personal. It has opened my eyes to the economic, social, political and educational conditions that have shaped the lives of the people of Port St Mary over generations and to the role played by so many in the shaping of those conditions. It has raised many questions, provided some answers and leaves many more to be found in the future.'

DOREEN MOULE

Born in Wolverhampton, Doreen grew up in the Black Country and trained as a teacher in Birmingham, where she taught in a primary school from 1970 to 1999, with responsibility for the development of the English curriculum. In 1999, she was fortunate enough to secure a teaching position in the Isle of Man, where she taught for almost ten years, this time with responsibility for Mathematics. Doreen and her partner moved to Rushen in 2004 and four years later she retired.

'Having read Connery Chappell's book, Island of Barbed Wire, *as an introduction to the subject of internment on the Island and become fascinated, my colleagues and I in the Internment Team have gone on to produce two exhibitions which attracted a total of approximately 6,000 visitors. Since then, we have produced a book,* Friend or Foe?, *about the women's internment camps, and the research, the outcomes and the continuing links being forged with descendants/families of the internees continues apace.'*

STAFFAN J. OVERGAARD

Corporate branding and campaign activities have been Staffan's signum for most of his professional life, either as a manager, project leader or copywriter. He started Candor Diagnostics in 2012, which serves as a medical diagnostic company. Staffan is Swedish and Overgaard is Danish which equally is his DNA.

He is interested in learning Manx Gaelic and using it as a gateway to Manx culture; Celtic and Viking influence of the Isle of Man; Nordic languages, and hopes to learn Icelandic and Faroese; Viking sagas of Snorre Sturlasson and others; and telling heritage stories with modern digital tools.

'I've enjoyed being chair for our Living with the Sea *project. At the start we gathered together as a team and chose subjects that we were interested in. I chose place names, which has been an interest of mine for a long time. I decided to restrict it to street names, otherwise the scope would have been too wide. I hope that readers will, when reading about Port St Mary, see that the stories told could be of any small seaside village in the British Isles.'*

JOHN W. QUALTROUGH

John was born in February 1935 in High Street in Port St Mary, at what was his father's and previously his grandfather's shoe shop. He was educated at Rushen School at the Four Roads and King William's College. After building radio sets as a hobby, John started an apprenticeship with T.H. Colebourn as an electronics engineer before doing National Service with the R.A.F. as a wireless mechanic on a Nightfighter Squadron in Germany. After two years he returned to Colebourn's, being appointed service manager in 1964, a position he held until his retirement in 1998.

John married Beryl Karran in 1959 and lived in Royal Avenue, Onchan, for eighteen years before they moved back to the Qualtrough family home in Queens Road, Port St Mary after his mother passed away. John and Beryl have three children, six grandchildren and two great grandsons.

John has always had a keen interest in photography and had a darkroom at home, but he has many other hobbies – ballroom and old-time dancing, sailing, fishing, vintage motorcycling, hill walking, local history, and cruise holidays.

'I was pleased to be involved with Living with the Sea. *I feel that any knowledge of our past and local history should be recorded and passed on for future generations. I have always been willing to share my knowledge and photographs with anyone who is interested – the more information and photographs that are around, the better chance that knowledge has of surviving. If not, it will be lost with the passing of time. People walk around the Port, not realising the history they are passing by. My knowledge was gained largely by spending time talking to the older generations, studying old documents and, of course, living in the village most of my life.'*

L-R: William Samuel Cubbon, unknown visitor, Billy McGain and James Clucas at the stern of the schooner Lily Garton *from around the 1890s.*

Rigs:
D = Dandy,
L = Lugger,
N = Nickey,
Nb = Nobby,
K = Ketch,
Cr = Cutter,
Sl = Sloop,
H = Half-decker,
O = Open boat

1. Smack or Cutter

2. Dandy 'Lugger'

3. Nickey

4. Nobby

Cutters, Luggers and Nobbies

CHAPTER 1

MICHAEL KNEALE

Since time immemorial, the sea has been both a transport highway and a source of food. Except for the Viking period, little is known about the size and type of craft used around the Irish Sea until the 18th century. Most local working craft were then relatively small open boats, 20 to 24 feet on the keel, usually built where they could easily be launched. They were mostly used for potting and long-lining, turning to netting herring from July to September. From the late 16th century, boats from England, Ireland, France, Holland, Spain and Portugal came annually to join the Irish Sea herring fishery. During the early 1800s, many cutter-rigged 40 to 60-foot 'smacks' were trading around the Irish Sea, even going as far as the Mediterranean and the Baltic with cargoes of salt or smoked herring, returning loaded with wine, fruits, timber and grain. They also acted as 'fresh buyer-smacks' for the herring fleet, taking catches from the smaller fishing boats at sea to land ashore for barrelling or curing.

The Isle of Man is well-placed for shipping, with nearby fishing grounds, and local boat-builders were quick to adopt the best features of the variety of craft to be seen in home waters. From the early 1800s, thousands of vessels were plying their trades whether it be freight, passengers, mail, fishing, revenue cutters, pilots, naval ships and even the occasional smuggler or pirate.

Prior to the building of the inner pier, Port St Mary was just a rocky bay, sheltered from the prevailing south-westerlies but with very little suitable ground to dry boats out every tide in all wind directions. Derbyhaven had much more space and was considered a better bay at the time, although not much better sheltered. Much trading and fish processing took place here – the (now) stone-built herring houses were producing salted barrels, or red herrings and kippers for export, long before any at Port St Mary.

Port St Mary pier was built in response to the demand created by trading and fishing activities, with development of the port and surrounding area accelerating through the 19th century.

Trading boats sailed far and wide, often at great risk to vessels and crew. Returning to the 'home port' was, for many long-distance traders, a rare event. Others regularly carried home coal, wood, grain, salt, cement and stone – and then shipped out barrels of salted herring, kippers, fresh fish, limestone, slate, farm produce and ore from the many productive mines.

For centuries, the number of coastal shipwrecks and boats vanishing without trace was enormous, leading to calls for infrastructure improvements to aid navigation and reduce commercial and human losses. These were gradually built, often in the wake of tragedy, with rocket brigades and lifeboat stations established to try to help those in trouble near the shore. Many vessels continued to be overwhelmed by weather, foundering in the wider seas and oceans, particularly the earlier open or half-decked fishing boats and later trading schooners plying their trade further afield.

Baie ny Carrickey – Manx for Bay of Rocks – is very appropriate, for the port's close approaches and, through the 19th century, the new lighthouses, refuge towers, piers and breakwaters were a great improvement.

Major nearby shore infrastructure works

1812	Port St Mary pier built – lantern 25ft above MHW, visible 9M
1818	Calf of Man twin lighthouses built
1826	Lifeboat station established at Castletown
1827	Crane erected on pier to load limestone into Smacks and Schooners
1842-43	Derbyhaven breakwater built
1848	West Quay built (still called the 'New Quay' by some)
1859	Thousla wooden tower and refuge cage built
1869-74	Chicken Rock lighthouse built
1875	Chicken Rock light established 1st January. Calf lighthouses abandoned
1880	Langness lighthouse established
1882-86	Alfred Pier built
1885	Lifeboat station established at Port Erin
1892	Alfred Pier extension completed
1895	Carrick tower and refuge cage built
1896	Port St Mary lifeboat station built – slipway surfaced within two years
1905	Thousla refuge replaced with a concrete tower with cross top-mark
1916	Raglan Pier completed at Port Erin
1922	Castletown lifeboat station closed
1940s	Brick smokehouses built behind Lime Street replacing earlier wooden ones
1950 appr.	Concrete jetty completed over Bealevayer (Boolavur)
1958-60	Alfred Pier widened/stabilised creating the 'Duckpond'
1968	New Calf of Man lighthouse established
1975	IOM Yacht Club built on site of TA Miller's former boatyard, Lime Street
1979	Land reclamation from inner pier to the lifeboat slip to create boatpark

For this story, we are focussed on Port St Mary but every working port in the British Isles was equally involved in ship and boat-building with all its ancillary trades, fishing and fish processing and cargoes of all types constantly coming and going. In Manx ports and creeks, hundreds of vessels were packed into the available space. At Peel for instance, the fishing fleet and boat-building was double that of Port St Mary because the river created a large natural harbour and there was more usable land reclaimed along its banks for associated activities. Douglas and Ramsey also had very busy shipyards occasionally building very large vessels – for example the Euterpe/Star of India at Ramsey.

The following lists include those boats having Port St Mary as their home port according to either the registers, other contemporary records, memories or the research done by Captain Harry Watterson in the late 20th century. Official records are reasonable from 1869, although there are a few anomalies. Note that fishing vessel registered numbers are recycled, so when a boat is lost or sold away, its number can be reallocated, sometimes almost immediately. Where there are gaps, it's because we have not yet been able to confirm the exact detail. Research continues. The vast majority of these boats will have been built at Port St Mary but, unfortunately, the Fishing Vessel Registers only record a vessel's 'home port', unlike the Shipping Registers, which include the name and place of the builder and/or shipyard. However, we do know that those listed here represent probably only half the boats actually produced in the port, many for the likes of Port Erin, Derbyhaven and other Manx ports. Some were constructed for off-Island buyers too. Small boats, punts and skiffs were also built in great numbers as tenders to the larger fishing boats and for inshore longline and lobster fishing.

It's worth reminding ourselves that all this work was done without power tools or hydraulics or any of the handling equipment we take for granted in the 21st century. This was all hard graft: ships to load and unload, huge timbers to cut, shape, drill and bend. Imagine the work in lengthening a schooner, for instance! Rigging, nets and sails were all finished by hand, never mind the sailing of these heavily canvassed boats and the struggle of herring and mackerel fishing, followed by the huge effort ashore to process, preserve, pack and ship it out.

The rigs illustrated are by no means fixed and many hybrids were, no doubt, tried out to improve handling, performance or allow deck space for differing fishing methods. The cutter rig (or often sloop rig with a single foresail) was used on small fishing boats, replacing the 'square-sails' based on Viking design common in the 18th century, especially after the wreck of the herring fleet at Douglas in 1787. It was also used on large smacks (up to 70-foot) acting as herring 'fresh buyers' at sea during the season and as general cargo vessels, regularly going as far as the Baltic and Mediterranean. The dandy rig developed from the smack by reducing the mainsail and adding a relatively small standing lug mizzen. The Manx confusingly called these boats 'luggers' on the strength of the standing lug mizzen but they were really dandies. A dandy is generally defined as having the mizzen about a third the size of the mainsail. The term lugger tended to be later used for the larger vessels – up to 60-foot – and dandy for those under 50-foot but the local names were rather interchangeable.

With main and foresails dropped, the small mizzen helped the dandies to lie head wind while riding to the mile-long drift-nets. This idea was copied from the smaller Cornish luggers seen at fishing grounds around the Irish Sea and south of Ireland from the mid-1860s. Indeed, the Manx were so impressed with the sailing qualities of the Cornish luggers, that they commissioned their own, increasing their size and called them Nickeys. It seems that there were so many Cornishmen called Nicholas, they were collectively known as Nickeys – and the name was applied to the Manx version of the Cornish luggers.

The first Nickey for the Isle of Man, *CT65 Zenith*, was built in the mid to late-1860s at Kilkeel by Cornishman William Paynter who soon moved to Port Erin and continued building boats.

These boats were true luggers, rigged with a dipping lug on the foremast and a standing lug on the mizzen and built quite a bit bigger than the Cornish boats. Manx Nickeys were mostly over 50-foot overall and the Cornish luggers up to 40-foot. A big advantage of the un-stayed foremast was that it could be lowered while riding to the nets to reduce the boats' rolling. Nickeys sailed closer to the wind than the smack rig and were faster to get catches ashore, especially at the mackerel fishing South of Ireland where the grounds could be up to forty miles out.

As can be seen from the following lists, many Nickeys were very quickly sold to Ireland. The Cornish and Manx had taught the Irish how to fish the mackerel commercially in the first place and, with British Government assistance, the Irish developed their own fleets to join in the bonanza. A demand the Manx builders were, no doubt, very happy to satisfy.

The history of the various fisheries, particularly herring, is well documented elsewhere (see Sources of Information) but it's worth noting the effort the Manx put into the mackerel fishery out of Irish ports along the south and west coasts. Not all the mackerel was salted – much of it was boxed up fresh, mixed with ice shipped in on schooners from Norway and shipped out on steamers, mostly to Milford Haven. During the mackerel season, many of the Port St Mary carpenters also worked aboard the Manx-owned 'factory' hulks lying in Crookhaven making the wooden fish boxes on site.

Port St Mary Nickeys preparing for the season in the 1880s.

Manx fleets also sailed north as far as the Shetlands to fish herring along with the Dutch, Scottish and English, creating much work ashore for the travelling gutter girls, in addition to the necessary shipment of empty barrels, salt and supplies to small fishing ports. The filled barrels were then shipped to markets far and wide – all under sail.

By the late 1880s, the building of Nickeys and Schooners at Port St Mary was all but over and local fishing went into a period of decline. Crews willing to continue fishing were ageing and some converted their boats to Nobby rig, which was easier to handle. When going about (tacking), the Nickey's main lug was dipped, lowering it down far enough for the yard to be up-ended on deck to take the weight and the sail worked forward, around the mast with the sheet detached, then re-hoisted. The yard and sail were very heavy, especially when wet and it took a huge effort by all but the helmsman to work the sail round.

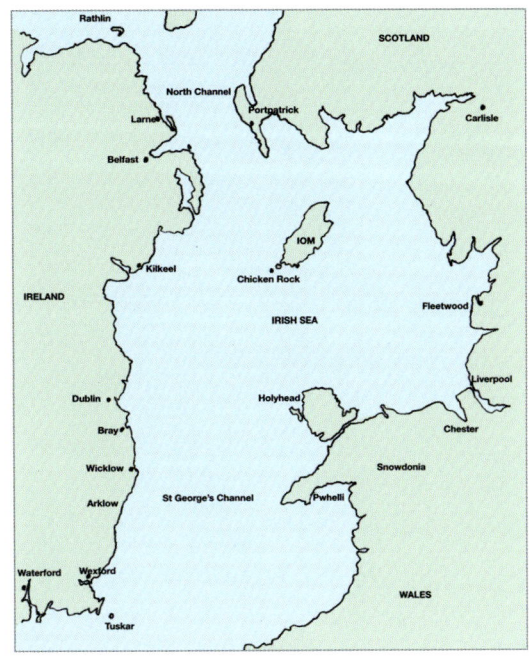

The average proper Nobby was under 40-foot on the keel and only a few were built at Port St Mary, but many were produced in Peel right up to WWI. The standard Nobby had standing lug mainsail and mizzen, plus two foresails and bowsprit, but they didn't have the all-out sailing power of the Nickeys. However, the ease of simply tacking without having to dip the standing lug sails was a great advantage, allowing a smaller (or ageing) crew to sail efficiently.

Date	Vessel Name	FV No.	Rig	Built	Built at	Keel (feet)	Fate	Cert. Cancelled	Comment
1869	Acorn		D	pre 1869		38	Sold to Belfast	1877	
	Alma		D	pre 1869		40	Sold to Cork	1874	
	Arctic		D	pre 1869		41	Sold to Dublin	1874	
	Beehive		D	pre 1869		39	Wrecked at Howth	1870	
	Bee		D	pre 1869		40	Sold to Belfast	1876	
	Bethel		D	pre 1869		41	No longer fishing	1871	
	Blossom		D	pre 1869		36	Broken up	1876	
	Busy Bee	CT 8	D	pre 1869	PSM	43	Sold to Galway	1901	Broken up 1911
	Careful	CT 68	D	pre 1869		38	Broken up	1882	
	Chance		D	pre 1869		40	Sold to Belfast	1879	
	Clipper		D	pre 1869		38	Sold to Belfast	1873	
	Comet	CT 21	D	pre 1869		41	Sold to Belfast	1873	
	Cuba		D	pre 1869		38	Broken up	1878	
	Cygnet		D	pre 1869		43	Sold to Dublin	1878	
	Daisy	CT 7	D	pre 1869		40	Sold to Isle of Bute	1883	
	Dart	CT 17	D	pre 1869		40	Sunk off the Calf	1872	

Schooners in Port St Mary harbour, thought to be from around 1900.

Date	Vessel Name	FV No.	Rig	Built	Built at	Keel (feet)	Fate	Cert. Cancelled	Comment
1869	Dolphin		D	pre 1869		43	Sold to Douglas	1874	
	Dove		D	pre 1869		36	Sold to Donaghadee	1872	
	Ebenezer		D	pre 1869		41	Sold to Kinsale	1870	
	Edith		N	pre 1869		43	Sold to Dublin	1876	
	Favourite		D	pre 1869		41	Sold to Donaghadee	1873	
	Foam		D	pre 1869		40	Sold to Peel	1876	
	Freedom		D	pre 1869		40	Sold to Howth	1870	
	Glance	CT 18	D	pre 1869		42	Sold to Skibbereen	1882	
	Gleaner		D	pre 1869		41	Sold to Cork	1877	
	Hunter	CT 40	D	pre 1869		41	Sold to Skibbereen	1883	
	Jane		D	pre 1869		40	Wrecked at Port Erin	1884	
	Jennys	CT 24	D	pre 1869	The Howe	36	No longer fishing	1891	Launched at Chapel Beach
	Joseph	CT 100	L	pre 1869		43	Built for Malahide	1874	
	Kate	CT 39	D	pre 1869		42	Sold to Skibbereen	1885	
	La		D	pre 1869		37	Sold to Caernarvon	1873	
	Laurel		D	pre 1869		38	Sold to Kilkeel	1875	
	Lily		D	pre 1869		41	Sold to Dublin	1875	
	Neddy		D	pre 1869		42	Sold to Arklow	1873	
	Ocean Bride		D	pre 1869		44	Sold to Dublin	1873	
	Olive		D	pre 1869		41	Sold to Clogher Head	1874	
	Otago		D	pre 1869		43	Sold to Skibbereen	1878	
	Pearl	CT 102	N	pre 1869		35	Wrecked at Orkney	1870	
	Pet		D	pre 1869		41	Sold to Skibbereen	1874	
	Phoenix		D	pre 1869		36	Broken up	1872	
	Pilgrim		D	pre 1869		40	Sold to Cork	1874	
	Prince of Orange	CT 44	D	pre 1869		40	Sold to Belfast	1879	Decked 1870
	Rechabite		D	pre 1869		37	Sold to Portavogie	1871	
	Rising Star		D	pre 1869		44	Sold to Beaumaris	1873	
	Rose		D	pre 1869		38	Sold to Caernarvon	1872	
	Ruby		D	pre 1869		41	Sold to Arklow	1872	
	Scud	CT 25	N	pre 1869		43	Sold to Cork	1882	
	Sibyl		D	pre 1869		44	Sold to Kinsale	1876	
	Snaefell		D	pre 1869		41	Sold to Dublin	1875	
	Speedy		D	pre 1869		39	Sold to Dublin	1872	
	Star	CT 45	D	pre 1869		39	Sold to Isle of Skye	1883	
	Swift	CT 4	D	pre 1869	PSM	44	Sold to Bantry Bay	1891	Record run Chickens to Kinsale 21 hours
	Tartan		D	pre 1869		43	Sold to Balbriggan	1872	
	Undine		D	pre 1869		43	Sold to Skibbereen	1880	Decked 1870
	Unity		D	pre 1869		39	Sold to Belfast	1871	
	Venus		D	pre 1869		39	Sold to Peel	1873	
	Victor	CT 34	D	pre 1869		40	Sold to Drogheda	1882	
	Violet	CT 56	D	pre 1869		42	Sold to Isle of Skye	1882	
	Vixen		D	pre 1869		37	Sold to Ballycotton	1872	
	William Milner		D	pre 1869		40	Sold to Skibbereen	1876	

Date	Vessel Name	FV No.	Rig	Built	Built at	Keel (feet)	Fate	Cert. Cancelled	Comment
1869	Zebra	CT 10	L	pre 1869	Newlyn	45	Broken up	1922	Castletown boat
	Zenith	CT 65	N	pre 1869	Kilkeel	44	Lost by fire off Glandore	1895	First IOM Nickey - built by Cornishman Paynter
	Zephyr	CT 28	D	pre 1869		39	Sold to Donaghadee	1879	
1870	Alpha	CT 19	N	1870	PSM	45	Sunk - collision S of Ireland	1903	First Nickey built on IOM.
	Ariel		L			45	Sold to Cork	1878	
	Euphemia		D			44	Sold to Dublin	1877	
	Eva		D			44	Sold to Dublin	1878	
	Faithful	CT 77	N	1870	Newlyn	45	Broken up	1917	After grounding behind PSM breakwater
	Hero	CT 49	N	1870	PSM	45	Sold to Union Hall	1912	
	Sappho		D			44	Sold to Dublin	1879	
1871	Annie	CT 83	N	1871	PSM	45	Broken up	1908	
	Eden	CT 79	N	1871	PSM	45	Broken up	1902	
	Emma	CT 78	L	1871	PSM	45	Broken up	1911	
	Excelsior	CT 47	N	1871	PSM	47	Sold to Skibbereen	1915	
	Harry	CT 82	N			45	Sold to Cork	1882	
	Honey Comb	CT 57	D			44	Sold to Skibbereen	1882	
	Linnet		D			44	Sold to Dublin	1877	
	Onward		D			45	Sold to Cork	1875	
	Primrose	CT 84	N	1870	Penzance	45	Derelict at Glandore	1910	
1872	Alert	CT 58	N	1872	PSM	45	Broken up	1900	
	Egret	CT 46	N	1872	PSM	45	Broken up	1903	Originally a Castletown boat
	Honey Bee	CT 85	N	1872	PSM	45	Broken up	1902	
	Hopeful		L			45	Sold to Cork	1876	
	Isaline	CT 87	N	1872	PSM	45	Broken up	1903	
	Majestic	CT 26	N	1872	PSM	45	Broken up	1906	
	Seek	CT 50	N	1871	PSM	45	Wrecked at Kingstown	1892	Wrecked on delivery trip
1873	Aleeder		L			43	Sold to St Ives	1874	
	Herald	CT 88	N	1873	PSM	44	Converted	1890	Converted to carry coal to the Calf
	Nile	CT 16	N	1873	PSM	45	Broken up	1912	
	Sensation	CT 14	N	pre1873	Penzance	46	Sunk South of Ireland	1899	Run down by SS Louisianan
1874	Amazon	CT 23	N	1876	PSM	47	Broken up	1907	
	Dove	CT 41	N	1874	Penzance	43	Broken up	1927	Oak construction
	Shah	CT 1	N	1874	PSM	47	Sold to Kinsale	1905	
	XL	CT 20	N	1874	PSM	47	Sold to Kinsale	1905	
1875	Anna	CT 33	N	1875	PSM	46	Broken up	1914	Built on the West Quay
	Black Hawk	CT 38	N	1875	PSM	48	Broken up	1910	
	Cidan		L			48	Sold to Scotland	1886	
	Sylph	CT 59	N	1875	PSM	47	Broken up	1905	
1876	Amy	CT 32	N	1876	PSM	47	Broken up	1911	

Date	Vessel Name	FV No.	Rig	Built	Built at	Keel (feet)	Fate	Cert. Cancelled	Comment
1876	Catherine	CT 3	N	1876	Liverpool	47	Sold to Liverpool	1902	Later sailed to America
	Ceres	CT 42	N	1876	Kilkeel	46	Broken up	1923	Cornish builder, Paynter
	Edith	CT 5	N	1876	PSM	46	Broken up	1923	
	Elate	CT 22	N	1878	PSM	47	Wrecked on PSM Point	1908	
	Eleanor	CT 63	N	1876	PSM	47	Sold to Skibbereen	1903	
	Fox	CT 2	L			46	Sold to Portavogie	1880	
	Lizzie	CT 12	N	1878	PSM	47	Sold to Penzance	1888	Broken up 1909
	Maggie	CT 15	N			46	Sold to Douglas	1884	
	May Queen	CT 29	N			47	Broken up	1906	
	Milky Way	CT 36	N	1876	PSM	47	Broken up	1915	Last CT regd boat to Lerwick in 1906
	Mistletoe	CT 37	N	1876	PSM	47	Sold to Skibbereen	1906	
	Zetetic	CT 35	N	1876	Penzance	46	Broken up	1902	Castletown boat
1877	Ben my Chree	CT 64	N	1876	Penzance	46	Sold to Glandore	1915	
	Elizabeth	CT 53	N	1877	Port Erin	47	Broken up	1911	
	Ellan Vannin	CT 75	N	1877	PSM	47	Sold to Beaumaris	1908	
	Emily	CT 2	N	1877	PSM	47	Broken up	1902	
	Hark		D			44	Sold to Dublin	1888	
	Harmony	CT 66	N	1877	PSM	47	Sold to Dublin	1918	
	Harriet	CT 86	N	1877	PSM	47	Broken up	1931	
	Heno		L			48	Broken up	1900	
	Jack	CT 54	Sl			38	Sold to Liverpool	1883	
	King Orry	CT 89	N			48	Sold to Skibbereen	1881	
	May Lily		L			47	Wrecked	1878	
	Mystic	CT 73	N	1877	PSM	46	Sold to Cork	1911	
	Nonpareil	CT 13	N	1877	PSM	46	Sold to Dublin	1909	
	Sunbeam	CT 91	N	1877	PSM	49	Broken up	1914	
	Victory	CT 69	N			46	Sold to Tralee	1885	
	Willie	CT 43	N	1877	PSM	47	Broken up	1923	
	Zeal	CT 80	N	1877	PSM	47	Broken up	1908	
1878	Aimée Holme	CT 90	N	1878	PSM	47	Sold to Dublin	1888	
	Bessie	CT 67	N	1878	PSM	47	Broken up	1906	
	Cedar	CT 9	N	pre1875	Cornwall	52	Broken up	1911	
	Celestine	CT 111	N	1878	PSM	47	Broken up	1917	
	Dancing Wave	CT 52	N	1878	PSM	48	Sold to Tralee	1894	
	EM	CT 48	N	1879	PSM	47	Sold to Skibbereen	1900	Castletown boat
	Hart	CT 61	N	1871	PSM	41	Sold to Dublin	1888	
	Hive	CT 27	N	1877	PSM	47	Broken up	1903	
	Honey Guide	CT 96	N	1878	PSM	48	Broken up	1928	
	Hope	CT 103	N	1879	PSM	47	Sold to Baltimore	1906	

Date	Vessel Name	FV No.	Rig	Built	Built at	Keel (feet)	Fate	Cert. Cancelled	Comment
1878	Isabella	CT 105	N	1878	PSM	47	Broken up	1907	
	Isabella Dodd	CT 51	N	1878	Port Erin	47	Sold to Lerwick		Built by Paynter
	Jenny Lind	CT 31	N	1878	PSM	47	Broken up	1922	
	Lottie Radcliffe	CT 104	N	1878	Port Erin	47	Broken up	1909	
	Majistatic	CT 98	N	1878	PSM	47	Broken up	1908	
	Mellona	CT 81	N	1878	PSM	47	Sold to Skibbereen	1906	
	Mizpah	CT 99	N	1878	PSM	47	Sold to Limerick	1906	
	Nellie	CT 93	N	1878	PSM	47	Sold to Limerick	1887	
	Nelson	CT 92	N		Port Erin	46	Sold to Cork	1883	Builder - Paynter
	Onward	CT 76	N	1878	PSM	47	Broken up	1910	
	Osprey	CT 30	N	1870	PSM	47	Sold to Baltimore	1900	
	Otter	CT 62	N	1878	PSM	46	Wrecked	1890	
	Pearl	CT 102	N	1879	PSM	47	Stranded at the Orkneys	1889	Sold at Kirkwall
	RSG		L			33	Sold to Douglas	1895	
	Sarah & Anne	CT 94	N	1878	PSM	47	Sold to Maryport	1890	
	Sunshine	CT 74	N	1878	PSM	48	Broken up	1907	
	Susan	CT 70	N	1878	PSM	47	Sold to Newry	1912	
	Thomas		Sl			28	Broken up	1882	
	Topaz	CT 95	N	1878	PSM	47	Broken up	1912	A Castletown boat
	Wesley	CT 71	D						
	Wizard	CT 101	N	1878	PSM	47	Broken up	1915	
	Zetland	CT 97	N	1878	PSM	47	Sold to Glandore	1910	Broken up 1913
1879	Bonnie Lass	CT 11	N	1879		40	Wrecked on Valentia Is.	1910	
	Edwin	CT 113	N	1879	PSM	48	Broken up	1920	
	Harvest Home	CT 115	N	1879	PSM	47	Sold to Skibbereen	1905	
	Maggie Parks	CT 121	L	1879	PSM	48	Sold to Portavogie	1899	
	Mary Jane	CT 112	N	1879	PSM	47	Broken up	1915	
	Pet	CT 106	N	1879	PSM	48	Later rigged as a Nobby	1927	Broken up
	Sarah Gale	CT 117	L			49	Sold to Skibbereen	1881	
	Satyr	CT 108	N	1879	PSM	45	Sold to Cape Clear	1892	All Irish crew
	Speedy	CT 114	L	1879	PSM	48	Wrecked at Baltimore	1899	
	Stephen	CT 110	N	1879	Port Erin	47	Broken up	1909	
	Sweethome	CT 116	L	1879	PSM	47	Sold to Union Hall	1892	
1880	Cruiser	CT 118	K	1880	PSM	47	Sold to Rosscarbery	1914	
	Expert	CT 55	N	1880	PSM	47	Broken up	1935	Last PSM boat to Kinsale 1919. Record Chickens to Fastnet 28 hours in 1894.
1881	Annie Jane	CT 21	N	1881	PSM	47	Broken up	1914	Last Nickey built at PSM
	Clementine		D			46	Sold to Cork	1881	
1883	St John		D			45	Sold to Skibbereen	1884	

Date	Vessel Name	FV No.	Rig	Built	Built at	Keel (feet)	Fate	Cert. Cancelled	Comment
1883	Faith	CT 51	N						
1884	Mona	CT 117	D	1884	PSM	49	Sold to Howth	1905	
	Puffin	CT 7	D	pre1884	Peel	38	Sold to Wexford	1894	For a time, supply tender to Bahama Bank light vessel
	Swift	CT 120	Cr	1884	PSM	37	Converted to yacht	1886	
	Vivid	CT 6	Sl	1884		49	Sold to Kingstown	1888	Became coastal trader
1885	Annie		D	1885	PSM	46	Wrecked at Glandore	1897	
	Ben Ledi		D			22	Broken up	1899	
	Gertrude		D			32	Sold to Ramsey	1885	
	Manx Queen	CT 40	K	1885	PSM	47	Sold to Skibbereen	1918	
1886	Alice	CT 54	K	1886	PSM	49	Sold to Douglas	1900	
	Bonnie Jane	CT 39	D	1886	PSM	49	Sold to Wick	1897	
	Confidence	CT 25	D	1886	PSM	50	Sold to Ramsey	1900	Trawler
	Isabella	CT 105	N			48	Broken up	1907	
	Jane	CT 6	K	1886	PSM	47	Wrecked at PSM	1899	
	Queen Bee	CT 18	D			49	Sold to Fenit	1902	
1887	Mayflower	CT 28	K			56	Sold to Castletown	1892	
1888	Dido		L			25	No longer fishing	1891	
	James & Mary	CT 56	Sl	1885	Lerwick	39	Broken up	1899	
	Reaper		K			50	No longer fishing	1890	
1890	Fisher Lass		L			31	Sold to Inverness	1892	
	Island Lass		D			27	Sold to Peel	1900	
	Majestic		L			46	Sold to Cork	1911	
1895	Pride of the South		L			28	Sold to Kinsale	1902	
1896	Edith		L			47	Broken up	1923	
1900	Lilly	CT 4	D	1900	PSM	38	No longer fishing	1954	Name change to Lilian 1933
1902	Elsie	CT 6	N	1890	Peel	37	Sold to Wicklow	1909	
	Flossie	CT 15	D	1902	PSM	36	Wrecked in the Sound	1915	
1905	Cissie	CT 7	Nb	1901	Peel	39	Sold to Newry	1911	
1907	Violet	CT 24	O	1907	PSM	17	No longer fishing	1949	
	Manx Maid	CT 14	O	1888	PSM	17	No longer fishing	1932	
	Manx Lass	CT 52	O	1885	PSM	19	Broken up	1929	
	May	CT 56	O	1896	PSM	18	No longer fishing	1924	
	Cornish Lass	CT 57	O	1892	PSM	17	Broken up	1926	
	Careful	CT 58	O	1900	PSM	18	No longer fishing	1911	
1910	Maria	CT 68	O	1900	PSM	18	Wrecked	1913	
	Jenny	CT 79	Nb	1910	PSM	41	Sold to Northern Ireland	1928	
1912	Maud	CT 89	O			17	Broken up	1928	
	Myrrh	CT 23	O	1915	Douglas	18	No longer fishing	1948	
	Ivy	CT 81	O		PSM	15	No longer fishing	1916	
	Village Maid	CT 99	O	1900	Douglas	15	No longer fishing	1916	
	Lhannan Shee	CT 20	C	1898	CT	23	No longer fishing	1916	

Date	Vessel Name	FV No.	Rig	Built	Built at	Keel (feet)	Fate	Cert. Cancelled	Comment
1912	Amy	CT 102	O	1900	PSM	14	No longer fishing	1919	
	Pansy	CT 107	O		PSM	14	No longer fishing	1922	
	Jane	CT 109	O		CT	19	Broken up	1919	
	Iota	CT 122	O	1090	PSM	16	No longer fishing	1932	
	Mannin	CT 126	K	1896	London	35	Wrecked	1918	
	Marjorie	CT 127	O	1907	PSM	18	no longer fishing	1912	
1915	Ornament	CT 92	O	1915	PSM	15	No longer fishing	1923	
1919	Georgie	CT 6	O		PSM	15	No longer fishing	1931	
	Village Maid	CT 7	O	1900	Douglas	15	No longer fishing	1928	
	Express	CT 17	D	1900	Banff	60	Broken up	1928	
	Dolly Grey	CT 11	Sl			22	No longer fishing	1916	
	Flora	CT 16	D	1864	Rothes-ay	35	No longer fishing	1935	
1920	Scud	CT 13	O	1907	PSM	19	No longer fishing	1913	
1922	Kitterland	CT 38	O	1921	PSM	16	No longer fishing	1912	
1925	Janet Cain	CT 3	Nb	1901	PSM	40	Broken up	1930	
1929	Three Brothers	CT 19	H			20	No longer fishing	1948	WS Cubbon, Athol Street
1930	Faithful	CT 8	Sl			35	Sold to Douglas	1937	
	Roma	CT 10	K		Peel	28	No longer fishing	1949	G Baines, Manchester
1931	Sunshine	CT 13	H			22	No longer fishing	1928	
1932	Mona	CT 5	O	1904	CT	17	No longer fishing	1932	
1933	Mannin II	CT 31	O		PSM	15	No longer fishing	1934	
1934	Maple Leaf	CT 11	O	1888		18	No longer fishing	1937	
1935	Lennie	CT 17	O			14	No longer fishing	1961	L Hills, Park Road
1936	Argo	CT 28	Sl		Ramsey	23	Sold to Ramsey	1947	formerly Nippy LL 30. W Jackson, Promenade
1938	Mabel	CT 36	H	1924	Birken-head	19	No longer fishing	1950	W & F Kneen, Park Road
	Anna	CT 37	O			12	No longer fishing	1949	H Halsall, Lime Street
	White Heather	CT 42	H			25	No longer fishing	1946	J Quine, Victoria Road
	Venture	CT 46	H	1936	Eye-mouth	30	Sold to Whitehaven	1944	Mrs MK Kelly, Rocklands
1939	Two Sisters	CT 1			PSM	30	Sister-ship: Fisher Lass		W Watterson, Port Erin
	St Mary	CT 3	H			30			Mrs MK Kelly, Rocklands
	Margaret	CT 6	H	1931	Glasgow	26	No longer fishing	1945	
	Vervine	CT 7							F Watterson, Port Erin
	Iris	CT 9	O	1931	Fal-mouth	16	No longer fishing	1945	R Crellin, Four Roads
	Ever Ready	CT 12							WE Cregeen, Station Hotel
	Dawn	CT 14	O			16	Broken up	1949	J Maddrell, Bay View, Road
	Myrrh	CT 23							RW Coole, Cronk Road
	Violet	CT 24							E Quirk, Lime Street

Date	Vessel Name	FV No.	Rig	Built	Built at	Keel (feet)	Fate	Cert. Cancelled	Comment
	Manx Maid	CT 32	O		Ramsey	17	No longer fishing	1949	JJ Kneen, Lime Street
1939	Glee Maiden	CT 34							J & T Woodworth, Port Erin
	Jean	CT 35							JE Crebbin, Port Erin
	Girl Daisy	CT 45							A Buchan, Port Erin
	Agnes	CT 71							R Kneen, Park Road
	Gimmagh	CT 83							JE Crebbin, Port Erin
1940	Rip Van	CT 47	Sl	1936	CT	29	No longer fishing	1947	
	Trivane	CT 51	O		PSM	13	No longer fishing	1947	
	Ivy	CT 52	O		PSM	15	No longer fishing	1947	
	Cushag	CT 54	O	1919	Ireland	13	No longer fishing	1945	
	Leprechaun	CT 56	O	1940	PSM	18	No longer fishing	1951	
	XL	CT 57	H		Liverpool	20	No longer fishing	1950	
1941	Florence	CT 61	O			17	No longer fishing	1949	
	Bonny Lass	CT 68	O	1900	PSM	13	No longer fishing	1946	
	Alice	CT 80	O	1926	PSM	16	No longer fishing	1948	
	Kathleen	CT 86	O	1941	PSM	14	No longer fishing	1946	

For a flavour of the fishing under the later days of sail, we have the following notes from the late Captain Harry Watterson in conversation with Tom Costain in 1973:

Tom (born 1901) served as cook for the 1913 season on the Honey Guide, CT 96. She was a Nickey, still rigged as such, though she had an engine fitted in about 1912 (when Tom was eleven years old). This engine was not a great success, giving lots of trouble. On such conversions, the propeller shaft was to port and forward of the rudder. The shaft bearings frequently ran hot, for which the cure was buckets of water! The engines were supplied by Knox at Douglas. At this time, probably half a dozen boats had engines, including the Harriet, CT 86.

The crew in 1913 was Big Will Watterson of the Howe, skipper, Tom Collister – Joey's father, Jimmy Faragher of Ballakilpheric, Edmund Maddrell of Glen Chass, Tom Corrin of Cregneash, John Hudgeon of Fistard and Tom Costain as cook. Excluding Tom, the crew's average age was around sixty. By this time, such a high average age was normal.

The smaller 'seventy' (made of 70 yards of cotton) was used instead of the big fore-lug (up to 195 yards of cotton) but it was still heavy work dipping it, usually taking all hands except the man on the tiller, though it could just be managed by fewer. Neither her staysail nor topsail was ever rigged in Tom's time.

The punt was still carried and was useful for landing poor catches. They would anchor off and send the punt in with the catch. On busy days with good catches, boats would take their turn alongside the breakwater to land and then move out to anchor.

The four sweeps were still carried and occasionally used but not for long pulls. Tows sometimes occurred and on one occasion that season, the Glen Maye towed the Honey

Guide round Langness, from fishing round the back. Becalmed periods weren't frequent – the longest recalled was two days off Chicken Rock.

The hull was still tight and little pumping was required. She no longer carried tarpaulins, battens or wedges for battening down as she only fished local waters.

Many steam drifters and trawlers were operating out of Manx ports by this time, mostly Scottish, with some Irish and others from as far away as Yarmouth and Lowestoft. A lot of the old fleet had been laid up in Port St Mary by this time while others were chartered by Southern Irish men for the season, returning to lay up for the winter. By 1913, the established closing event of the regatta was the burning of one of the old boats. Tom recalls seeing this two or three times before the Great War, so it can be assumed that this rather sad custom was established about 1910. Plenty of tar and other inflammables were stowed onboard. Anchored in the middle of the harbour, at the close of the regatta she would be set alight and sometimes burn all night. Most boats ended their days broken up – the Honey Guide was broken up in Port St Mary.

Nearly all the catches of 1913 were landed at Port St Mary, with a few landings in Douglas when fishing round the back of Langness. No catch was dumped through lack of wind or malfunctioning engine. No Irish men were taken as crew on Manx boats at this time.

Miller's yard was still in operation and Nobbies were probably being built. They were the last sailing boats built – smaller than the old Luggers or Nickeys, being under 40-foot as opposed to around 50-foot.

Like all her class, the Honey Guide's capstan could be turned by a geared wheel engaging at the top, the hand wheel being vertical. The anchor cable was 4 or 5-inch rope (40mm diameter), either manila or tarred hemp. Her punt carried no sails at this time. Her foremast was landed on a cradle at the aft end of the cabin roof on the centre-line.

In heavy weather, it sometimes required two men on the tiller or the use of relieving tackle but they were not normally heavy boats to handle and even the cook was given his chance at steering. Tom recalls, still very green, being given the tiller off Langness and told to keep her steady while the rest went below for their meal. Running free, he succeeded in gybing accidentally, an event marked by the clatter of plates below. There was no table in the cabin, indeed there was no room for one and meals were eaten with the men sitting on the lockers running fore and aft inboard of the lower bunks.

Big Will Watterson, the skipper, was not only big but very heavy and, as custom dictated, his bunk was above the cook's. One night, while lying to her nets, the Honey Guide was rolling heavily as usual and the skipper's bunk collapsed onto a startled Tom, now trapped in his bunk by the closed sliding doors on the inboard side, the paneling outboard and the skipper and wreckage on top. In the midst of this chaos, Big Will asked anxiously 'Are thou alright boy?'

The skipper also smoked the clay pipe favoured by all – a model with a drain at the bottom of the bowl, known as a Lerwick pipe. At the tiller in a breeze, he frequently had difficulty getting the pipe alight, whereupon Tom would hear 'Are thou there, boy?' And he'd have the pipe handed to him for lighting below. This was not his favourite job, especially if the motion was lively and his stomach in a doubtful condition. Perhaps, being *inexpert at lighting pipes at the tender age of thirteen was the cause but only minutes would pass before Big Will would say 'Boy, it's gone out on me' and the drill would have to be repeated.*

Like all boats of her class, she rolled heavily while lying to the nets if any sea was running and seasickness was not unknown. The absence of bilge-keels was no help in either respect.

With the stove and boiler in the cabin, the cook's berth in the forward starboard lower bunk was a very warm one. The sliding bunk doors provided not only privacy but a heat shield! On the outboard side, the bunks were paneled, not open to the frames. While when new, the cabins had been varnished, by this time many years had passed since any paint or varnish has been applied.

One of the staple meals was herring broth, which consisted of two dozen herrings boiled with a pound of onions – potatoes were sometimes added. A bucketful of buttermilk was also carried for each night's fishing.

Whatever pumping was required was usually done after the nets were shot.

If the fishing was good, big money could be still made in these boats. Tom recalls a week when each man's share was £75 and the cook £50. Willie Qualtrough of the High Street was the owner up to 1918 and apt to be reluctant to pay such high wages, so promptly suggested the crew leave it over for another week!

The Port

Reports from the 1840s indicate that there were about eighty Port St Mary based vessels, mostly small fishing boats and some larger trading smacks up to fifty tons. During the late summer herring season, almost 300 fishing boats, many from Cornwall, joined the local fleets producing more than 30,000 barrels of salt herring for export each year. Cornish boats laid up in Castletown harbour at weekends.

The port must have been very busy through these decades. Records show at least three full-time boat-building concerns, five blacksmiths, a nail-maker, limestone quarries, lime kilns, sail-makers, riggers, ropeworks, paint stores, net-makers and fish curers ashore. Add to these the hundreds of fishermen and sailors on their various vessels, it's no wonder the port boasted several grocers, butchers, bakers, pubs and general stores. Supplying the huge fleets of boats and their crews was a good earner for local traders. Horses and carts were used for moving all kinds of goods and people, adding greatly to the general activity, especially in the summer when the visitors arrived with their requirements. The port must have been buzzing.

Construction of the West Quay allowed vessels to get alongside another wall and increased space ashore for boat building and temporary freight holding – later a salt shed was erected there, eventually becoming a coal store.

In 1860, the fishing fleet comprised eighty-six small half-decked Dandies registered at Castletown. By 1880, only eighteen of these boats were still working locally but the fleet numbered 114, of which eighty-seven were now the fast dipping-luggers called Nickeys, most built locally from about 1869. In 1886, the fleet had reduced to 104 boats and the 1887 launch of the ketch Mayflower marked the end of big boat-building in the port except for a few of the smaller Nobbies.

The 1870s peak in the building of Nickeys and Schooners coincided with the construction of several aids to mariners, most important of which was the Chicken Rock lighthouse.

Calf of Man and Chicken Rock lighthouses

The Chicken Rock, half a mile southwest of the Calf, almost covers at high-water springs and extends to 740 square-metres when exposed at low-water.

At the beginning of the 19th century, Trinity House and the Northern Lights Board (NLB) were each asked to investigate the probable costs and dues to be levied on ships passing a suitable light and the Association of Shipowners asked the NLB to undertake the work and to construct lighthouses on the Isle of Man as necessary.

An Enabling Act was passed by Parliament in 1815 and in 1818, lighthouses came into operation at the Point of Ayre and two on the Calf, placed so that their transit was in line with the Chicken Rock.

Sixty years later, the NLB approved a recommendation to build a light tower on the Chicken Rock itself and authorised their engineers David and Thomas Stevenson to proceed. The tower was built in the tradition of the established Stevenson towers on Bell Rock (completed in 1811, the oldest lighthouse in the British Isles, built on an isolated reef twelve miles east of Dundee) and Skerry Vore (completed in 1844, built on an isolated reef ten miles south-west of Tiree in the Hebrides).

A contract was made for the supply of granite from quarries at Dalbeattie and a builder named Hunter was engaged to prepare the stones. Workmen were hired and the Clyde deep-sea tug 'Terrible' was purchased to act as a steam tender.

Work on the rock began in April 1869 and by autumn, the pit for the tower's foundations had been excavated.

Port St Mary was very lively with the extra activity and many small vessels arrived laden with rough granite blocks from Dumfriesshire. A tramway was laid between the pier and the Lime Street yard to move the blocks on bogeys (trolleys). Immense steam cranes were erected for moving the blocks and the chink of the masons' iron mallets and ring of the blacksmiths' anvils was heard all day long.

Between 1869 and 1873, no less than 100 men were employed in the project ashore in various capacities.

Rough blocks were cut and dressed and, on an adjusting platform, stone was fitted to stone and course to course before being shipped to the rock. At the same time, all the internal fittings were prepared to be fixed later.

Work on the rock varied according to the tides and weather – sometimes for under an hour, sometimes for six or seven hours, the thirty-five men engaged worked the seasons from April to September.

1869　　Pit complete
1870　　Landing crane erected and nine lowest courses built

1871   Balance crane set up and fourteen more courses built, reaching 32'8" in
height

1872   Powerful steam crane erected and forty-seven courses laid

1873   96th (final) course of the 143' tower fixed on 6th June.

The 1078 individually shaped stones are bound together by dove-tailing, joggles, clamps, bolts, ribbon-band joints and the most tenacious cement available. Joiners and others engaged in the final interior fitting were busy through 1874.

At the rock, workmen were accommodated aboard the '*Terrible*' fitted out as a barrack, for use when the tides were early or late. All the food for the 'rock-men' was cooked on board and carried to them on the rock.

The tug towed two 25-ton lighters out to the rock when stones were needed and carried the men to and fro. For landing people, the ship had two large boats and every man was given a cork life-belt, which they were compelled to wear every time they entered a boat, no matter the state of the weather. This rule also applied to every visitor.

On 31st December 1874, three keepers left the Calf stations and took up residence in the new tower and from dusk, the light flashed out from the Chicken Rock. The NLB built an apartment block in Port St Mary to house the keepers' families previously living on the Calf.

Port St Mary lifeboat was called on many times over the decades to carry food and water to the keepers when the weather prevented the usual tender operating and occasionally taking off sick or injured personnel.

After the 1960 Chicken Rock lighthouse fire, the NLB converted the light to automatic operation and decided to build a new powerful lighthouse and fog signal on the Calf, not far from the original abandoned pair. This was completed in 1968. A small helicopter was used to take the 800 tons of material out to the Calf during construction.

Port St Mary lifeboat standing by, waiting for the tide, at the Chicken Rock lighthouse fire of 1960.

Schooners

The trading schooners (including some ketch and smack-rigged vessels) were the mainstay of cargo transport until small steamships became efficient enough to compete on price. There were probably thousands of similar craft sailing from almost every small port in the Western World. Until the late 19th century, none had engines and were at the mercy of the elements. Small steam tugs were used to assist them to manoeuvre inside the busier harbours where available. Large steam-powered ships were already used for passenger and mail services but sailing cargo vessels able to access smaller ports continued to have a useful function – and at much lower cost. The most regular cargoes were coal, salt, grain, timber, fish, farm produce and a lot of stone in the form of ores and building material. All but one of the Port St Mary schooners needed ballast to maintain stability when empty, so even without a commercial cargo, they had to load a great deal of weight just to sail to their next port. Local stone of various types was probably quickest to obtain and load. Many paths and roads around Port St Mary are made of slabs from all over the British Isles and a fair amount of Irish soil came our way as ballast too.

This poem from Ambrose Maddrell gives a nice insight into the schooners. Ambrose was born in 1899 at Glen Chass and, like many of his generation, left school aged twelve to go as cook on a Nickey. However, much of the wider information and stories on which he based his many poems were related to him by John Gawne of Fistard, who was born in 1881 and did sail with the fishing fleets to the Shetlands and Kinsale. Ambrose died very young in 1949.

Purt le Moirrey Schooners

From the Western Isles to the Baltic, from Shetland round the lan'
From Pentlands down to Wearside, our vessels often ran
Around the Clyde and Mersey, or Bristol Channel way
Our Purt le Moirrey schooners went trading in their day.

We boasted some fine vessels and they numbered quite a few
But their names are now forgotten like many of their crew

A puffer, centre, steam drifters on the right against the harbour, nickeys in the foreground and a ketch left of the nickeys.

'Twas grand to see them sailing, yards square and running free
P'raps making for the harbour, their folks once more to see.

Sometimes between the 'deadmans' they'd tie up tier on tier
Their canvas set and drying, if the weather it should clear
You might see one discharging, another loading grain
While the clank of pawl and windlass meant 'under way' again

Arriving or departing or lying snug in tiers
We miss them from the harbour and think of former years
When round the watch-house daily, their skippers would parade
Discussing freights and sailings, or passages they'd made

The lore about the schooners, we learned in early days
Old mates recalled the passing of the Vixen and the Wave
We knew the Jilt and Emu, of the Meta we'd all heard
Then last of all Enigma, a ship we all knew well.

From Glasgow fully laden, bound south with precious freight
The Jilt ran down the Channel, the year, one, nine-o-eight
A heavy gale of wind she met, close by the Cornish lands
Mylchreest had made his final trip, along with all his hands.

But our harbour is now empty, for the days of sail are gone
And should you meet a schooner-man, perchance you may find one,
He'll tell the story proudly, though his eyes be full of tears
Of the Purt le Moirrey schooners and the glory of past years.

Every schooner, smack and fishing boat will have had endless adventures and stories to tell and there's a lot of detailed information available in other studies and publications.

The *Progress*, for instance, was the first schooner built by Joseph Qualtrough at Castletown in 1878, having moved his long-established boat-building yard from West Quay, Port St Mary. This schooner features in many photos of West Quay, as it lay alongside there for years before finally being broken up in 1948. Apparently, the 'salted' timber was still in good enough condition to be re-used building small yachts. Another photograph shows the *Progress* high and dry on Conister Rock in Douglas Bay and she once got jammed alongside another vessel in a lock on the Caledonian Canal, blocking all traffic for two weeks and causing a huge, very expensive traffic jam in that busy waterway.

Another local schooner, the *Jilt*, illustrates some of their problems. Built 1861 by Edward Edgar 'in the quarry alongside Keggen's death house', according to a contemporary record, this 80-foot, 94-ton clipper was to be called *Manx Cat*. Incidentally, John Gawne of Fistard relates that the locals couldn't understand Edgar's English accent! However, when it came to launch the schooner, presumably on the

Port St Mary schooners mid-1800s to WWII							
Vessel	ON	Built	LOD	Built at	Masts	Tons	Comment
Agnes Glover regd CT 1912	88711	1883	87	Tarleton, Lancashire	3	81	Sold on to Kilkeel when the Jessie Sinclair was bought. Wrecked at Holyhead 1928
Alfred & Emma regd CT 1881	27691	1861	66	Pembroke Dock	2	66	Profitable schooner that did not require ballast. Registration transferred to Barnstaple 1901
Bessy regd CT 1871	44430	1862	69	Castletown	2	44	Topsail schooner carrying mainsail, topsail, boom foresail, stay foresail and jib. Sunk by enemy action 1918
Bethel regd DO 1863	45461	1867	25	Port St Mary	2	25	Dandy rigged vessel. Broken up Kirkudbrightshire 1909
Capricorn regd CT 1893	868	1855	64/79	Aberystwyth	2	67	Lengthened at PSM 1893 Wrecked at Caernarvon 1913
Claymore regd DO 1885	7891	1850	92	Lymington	2	84	Fast schooner. 12-foot draught meant the rail was level with PSM pier when dried out. Formerly the Duke of Bedford's schooner/yacht. Registration transferred to Southampton 1886
Emu regd DO 1857	45471	1865	57	Douglas	2	51	Strongly built schooner for carrying ores from Laxey, similar to Goldseeker, Kangaroo and Yarra Yarra. Lost with all hands off NW Ireland 1895
Enigma regd DO 1857	3874	1845	74	Calcutta	2	77	All teak vessel, including spars. Originally a slaver. First vessel in the Karran fleet. Lost with all hands Solway Firth 1922
Esther regd CT 1909	70177	1875	101	Fleetwood John Gibson	3	123	Skipper owner Walter Cowley previously had the William Berey. Wrecked near Gunfleet Sands, Essex 1918
Goldseeker regd DO 1873	67283	1873	76	Douglas	2	82	Strongly built schooner for carrying ores from Laxey similar to Emu, Kangaroo and Yarra Yarra. Transferred to Annalong owners 1908. Broken up Bideford, Devon 1953
Harkaway regd CT 1881	44425	1862	58/79	Port St Mary J Qualtrough	1,2,3	48/61	Originally a smack (single mast). Twice lengthened at PSM gaining a mast each time. On one occasion at Arklow, an Irish wit observed 'she was a long time growing'. Total wreck 1929

Port St Mary schooners mid-1800s to WWII						
Vessel	ON	Built	LOD	Built at	Masts	Tons	Comment
Jessie Sinclair regd CT 1906	62968	1871	88/128	Fraserburgh	2	123	Lengthened 20' at PSM, consequently lacked beam. (Sister-ship to Mary Sinclair, built Ardrossan 1876). Lost by fire off Llandudno 1921 – fire started in recently fitted engine
Jilt regd DO 1861	29601	1861	80	Port St Mary	2	94	See separate notes on this schooner. Lost with all hands off Trevose Head, Cornwall 1908
Kangaroo regd CT 1874	45476	1867	83	Douglas	2	83	Strongly built schooner for carrying ores from Laxey, similar to Emu, Goldseeker and Yarra Yarra. Sunk by enemy submarine 1915
Kate regd CT 1874	63499	1874	83	Port St Mary	2	59	Profitable schooner, skipper Thomas Kinley of Lime Street. Sold to Kilkeel granite merchant 1911. Sunk in Mersey following collision 1915
Lilly Garton regd PL 1873	63918	1872	74	Port St Mary J Qualtrough	2	68	Built the same shape as Margaret Garton except much lighter and faster to carry fish. Broken up at PSM 1913
Lilly Miles regd DO 1874	67285	1874	74	Port St Mary	2	77	Skipper owner Walter Cowley later bought the William Berey, then the Esther. Wrecked on Longstone Rock, Farne Islands 1899
Lydia regd CT 1868	54905	1867	65	Castletown	2	55	Transferred to Liverpool register 1876
Lyra regd CT 1876	72597	1876	80	Port St Mary Gale	2	72	'Salted' construction. Bound Runcorn to Dublin with a cargo of salt, she intended to call in at PSM but was wrecked on the Carrick 1888
Maggie regd DO 1855	21990	1855	77	Peel Graves	2	89	The Star, Wave and Maggie left the Baltic together. Maggie was lost with all hands in the Pentland Firth along with the Wave 1885. Star took shelter at the Shetlands and survived.
Margaret Garton regd CT 1888	63921	1877	74	Port St Mary J Qualtrough	2	67	Freddie Gale of Ballafesson was killed at PSM, falling from the rig when a foot-rope carried away. Wrecked at Strangford 1944
Meteor regd CT 1865	47282	1865	76	Port St Mary	2	85	Missing presumed lost in the Bay of Biscay 1883
Monkey regd DO 1869	14243	1839	63	Glasgow	2	81	Schooner similar to the Emu. Wrecked in the Baltic 1888
Northerner regd CT 1874	22525	1858	59	Aberdeen	2	47	Schooner similar to the Ocean Gem and engaged in the same trade. Transferred to Beaumaris. Foundered 1885

Port St Mary schooners mid-1800s to WWII						
Vessel	**ON**	**Built**	**LOD**	**Built at**	**Masts**	**Tons**	**Comment**
Ocean Gem regd CT 1864	47281	1864	70	Castletown	2	51	Schooner employed in the general cargo trade between Liverpool and PSM. Registration transferred to Dumfries 1891
Progress regd CT 1878	78217	1878	77	Castletown J Qualtrough	2	77	Broken up at the West Quay, PSM 1948
Reaper regd CT 1868	60262	1868	54	Port St Mary	2,3	40	Lengthened at PSM gaining a third mast. Coal carrier for Joseph Hudgeon's PSM yard. Lost with all hands, off Rockall 1897
Sarah Blanche regd DO 1891	95756	1871	130	Paisley, Scotland	2	99	Fast schooner, occasionally carrying the mail for the Steam Packet in bad weather. Transferred to Ramsey register 1923
Star regd DO 1857	14386	1857	62	Peel	1	62	Smack rigged vessel. In 1885 Star, Maggie and Wave left the Baltic together and encountered heavy weather. Star took shelter at the Shetlands. Wrecked on the Skerries, Anglesey 1894
Venus regd CT 1877	72599	1876	75	Perth, Scotland	2	71	Wrecked at Port Mooar, IOM 1929
Violet regd CT 1866	54904	1866	65	Castletown	2	50	Lost off Dundalk 1895
Vixen regd DO 1851	24336	1851	74	Peel Graves	2	93	Peel schooner built to take Manx gold prospectors to Australia – included here because under PSM skipper John Sansbury (father of JJ Sansbury), vessel foundered off the Calf 1864
Wave regd CT 1875	72596	1875	73	Port St Mary	2	65	Lost with all hands in the Pentland Firth along with the Maggie 1885
William Berey regd DO 1871	45480	1871	70	Douglas	2	72	Crew taken off vessel by PSM lifeboat 1905 – aground on Creg y Chreel while loaded with turnips for Liverpool. Registration transferred to Kirkwall 1908
XL regd DO 1874	67284	1873	74	Port St Mary	2	66	Regd CT 1892. Rigged as a ketch 1901. Foundered off Ballantrae 1930
Yarra Yarra regd DO 1870	45477	1870	66	Douglas	2	63	Strongly built ore carrier like Emu, Goldseeker and Kangaroo. Total wreck at Port Erin 1914

north-east side of Boolavur, it slipped off its blocks and wouldn't budge. Eventually, the ship was persuaded into the sea and re-named the *Jilt*, because her reluctant launch was considered an unlucky omen.

The *Jilt* is unusual in being first registered with no less than twenty-four shareholders. Every registered vessel has sixty-four shares and generally between four and eight people are named even if there is a majority 'owner'. A vessel would often be shared between 'an owner', plus the builder, skipper, timber supplier, sailmaker, netmaker, blacksmith, fish buyer and various investors.

It's interesting to see the variety of occupations listed for the *Jilt's* original shareholders – the majority probably had a direct hand in building or providing materials to assemble the schooner and William Duke was likely the first skipper (or perhaps his son, Dick) – the only mariner mentioned.

EXTRACT FROM THE REGISTER:			
Name	**Address**	**Occupation**	**Shares**
Thomas Qualtrough	Port St Mary, Isle of Man	Harbour Master	9
John Cleary	Liverpool	Licensed Victualler	5
James Turnbull	Rushen, Isle of Man	Shoemaker	5
John Watterson	Port St Mary, Isle of Man	Sailmaker	4
William Duke	Colby, Isle of Man	Mariner	3
Matthew Goile	Ballacorkish, Isle of Man	Mining Agent	3
William Ketts	Surby, Isle of Man	Mining Agent	3
Jonathan Clarke	Kentraugh, Isle of Man	Servant	3
William Sansbury	Port St Mary, Isle of Man	Nailer	3
Thomas Lace	Port St Mary, Isle of Man	Ropemaker	3
John Turnbull	Liverpool	Ship Carpenter	2
John Quayle	Port St Mary, Isle of Man	Farmer	2
John Cubbin	Port St Mary, Isle of Man	Inspector of Schools	2
Thomas Elliott	Colby, Isle of Man	Nailer	2
Thomas Sansbury	Jurby, Isle of Man	Joiner	2
William Quayle	Port St Mary, Isle of Man	Blacksmith	2
Joseph Qualtrough	Port St Mary, Isle of Man	Carpenter	2
Thomas Taubman	Port St Mary, Isle of Man	Timber Merchant	2
William Qualtrough	Douglas, Isle of Man	Blockmaker	2
John Crebbin	Port St Mary, Isle of Man	Joiner	1
William Shepherd	Port St Mary, Isle of Man	Butcher	1
James Cooil	Port St Mary, Isle of Man	Carpenter	1
Robert Gelling	Port St Mary, Isle of Man	Joiner	1
William Gawne	Liverpool	Tailor	1

As an indication of the kind of life the schooner men led, we have an extract from the *Jilt* skipper's log of a particularly dreadful charter – on the face of it, a simple thirty mile delivery from Tralee (just south of the River Shannon) to Cahersiveen (just behind Valencia Island) on the west coast of Ireland; thirty nautical miles at, say, three knots would take ten hours, even at two knots it should have been less than a day's sail.

SCHOONER JILT

Captain Thomas Sansbury
January 8th 1879
Sailed from Tralee with grain.

January 9th
First part of the day clear, wind East, moderate. All drawing sail set by 4pm.
Later, wind hauling Southerly and freshening.
Double reef taken in the mainsail at 5pm, wind now increased to gale force with heavy squalls and vessel began to settle down in main hatchway.
Cargo shifted, so cut away the boom foresail and staysail.
Vessel righted herself with a slight starboard list.
7.30pm sea rising fast, shipping heavy seas in the starboard waist, which stove in the small boat and washed it off the hatch. Deck now constantly full of water and we had to break down a deal of the bulwarks to clear the heavy water off the deck.
At 10pm, we cut the fore topmast backstay to try to ease the vessel but the mast would not break off, so went aloft to cut away the yard and sail thinking every moment was our last.
Latter part of the day, blowing to complete hurricane with heavy showers. Pumps attended at every chance but making little water. Ship straining a little.

January 10th
Throughout the 24 hours, wind blowing at hurricane force from the sou'sou-east. Vessel running before it, course nor'nor-west at about 6 knots under bare poles. Decks constantly full of water and everything movable now gone off the decks.
Portion of the cabin skylight stove in and washed away and cabin now half-full of water. Steering by the sea. No fire and nothing to eat the whole of this day.

January 11th
Hurricane continues but with heavier showers, which put the sea down a little. Still keeping the vessel before the wind and sea. Barometer now 29 and steady.

January 12th
4am – a little less wind but the vessel is now a complete wreck around the decks. Barometer 29.5 and rising fast. First part of the day strong SE and overcast. Later, wind comes from away from the north-west strong to gale. Now heading East downwind under reduced sail – and it's looking like a very dirty night.
Consulted mate and crew about heaving some cargo overside for the safety of the ship and all concerned.

2.30pm Took off aft hatch and commenced jettisoning grain overside by buckets. Could not prevent water getting down the hatch but many tons of grain jettisoned.

Vessel continued to battle with the elements until-

January 15th

Now one week since departure and we had our first sight of land since sailing. It was Tiree island.

The same night, reached an anchorage in Tobermory, north of the island of Mull, after being driven 800 miles by the severe gales – and 400 miles out into the Atlantic Ocean. Crew and myself completely done up with fatigue.

The cargo was damaged but the agent told us to complete the charter and carry on to Cahersiveen.

January 29th

Two days out – forced to take shelter in Belfast Lough until January 31st.

When again we proceeded, we were blown about the Irish Sea by a succession of gales.

February 11th

Off the Chicken Rock with another dirty night coming up, so thought it prudent to anchor in Port Erin bay, close inside the breakwater for safety.

February 18th

Proceeded again but was driven back into Port Erin to shelter from Easterly gales and blinding snowstorms.

February 21st

Sailed again and good weather then prevailed, South about Ireland passing Cape Clear and Mizen Head

February 25th

Picked up the Cahersiveen pilot and berthed the same day.

Thus, 47 days to voyage 30 miles.

The *Jilt* was eventually lost with all hands during a gale off Trevose Head, Cornwall in 1908. The two Manxmen aboard were skipper Mylchreest and the mate Percy Lawson, aged twenty, from Fistard.

Two-thirds of the schooners listed here were shipwrecked or foundered, most losing all hands in the process. They were exposed to the violence of the elements without any form of weather forecast, sailing in vessels that could not get upwind to any significant degree. The ships, rigs, sails and cargoes were heavy and the crews very small, usually three men and a boy, but this was how freight was carried, often very far afield – and some were lost very close to home.

The *Lyra* was wrecked on the Carrick in 1888, watched by a crowd on Port St Mary Point. A local rowing boat crew tried to help but couldn't get near the wreck owing to the breaking seas washing over it. The Port Erin and Castletown lifeboats were horse-drawn to the Big Mill and Strandhall respectively and launched to save those that had managed to hold on (the skipper, Francis Petherick, a Cornishman who lived with his family in Port St Mary, had been lost overboard when she struck). Seven years later, in

1895 a metal tower with a refuge cage was built on the reef using railway lines; it still serves today with a light indicating an isolated danger.

It was only one year after the wreck of the French schooner *Jeune St Charles* on Thousla in 1858 that a wooden tower and refuge was built on that reef. Washed away in 1905, it was replaced with a concrete tower topped with a wooden cross (and later a light). The cross is now displayed ashore below the Sound Café overlooking Kitterland and Thousla. The story of this wreck and the determined local rescuers is the subject of The Thousla Cross, a booklet published by Rushen Parish Commissioners.

Six years earlier, the 1852 wreck of the brig *Lily* on Kitterland and subsequent explosion of the cargo deprived the port of twenty-nine men, most of them carpenters, mariners and associated tradesmen, who had been engaged to salvage what they could. This accident not only left twenty-two widows and seventy-four orphans (plus four as yet unborn), it also affected the whole work of the port – the loss of so many skilled men must have been sorely felt for years, both ashore and afloat.

The sole survivor of the explosion, James Kelly, a Port St Mary fisherman, married with three children at the time, was badly scarred. His fourth child, William became the first coxswain of the Port St Mary lifeboat in 1896.

20th century

The peak activity in the last half of the 19th century tapered away by WWI.

By 1900, only eighty-one boats remained and in 1910 the number had shrunk to forty-three – only two of the old fishing boats survived into the 1920s.

From about 1910, new boats were fitted with an engine at build and a few of the older ones remaining had engines retro-fitted. Smaller boats retained either a gaff or standing lug mainsail and a jib, many with a small engine too.

The relatively small boats registered between WWI and WWII showed little or no local investment in even medium-sized motor fishing vessels – and the schooners were superseded by steam and motor ships.

Between the wars, the port remained as busy as ever, the seasonal herring fishing conducted at first by UK (mostly Scottish) and Irish steam-drifters and later ring-netters, so the seasonal salting and curing continued apace. There was a continuous traffic of small cargo ships bringing in coal, timber, salt, cement, steel, stone, barrels and all the general needs of trade and commerce. The breakwater gave shelter to all kinds of ships, including fishing boats, naval and passenger vessels. Through the 1960s and 70s, many Breton trawlers working mostly south of the Chicken Rock were regular visitors to the port with injured crew or in need of ice or repairs.

There were several smoke-houses in the vicinity of Port St Mary and Port Erin from the mid-19th century, supplying kippers for export and to the increasing number of holidaying visitors. These were wooden structures, which inevitably fell into disrepair. In the 1940s, two brick-built smokehouses replaced wooden ones above Creg y Leech behind Lime Street and the last commercial kippering in Port St Mary was in 1979 at what was Manesca Ltd at that time. Kippers are back-split herring – originally cured and hot-smoked (ie: cooked) to preserve the fish long-term but later cold-smoked

'Gutter girls', pictures from around the 1930s.

(uncooked), more for the taste than preservation. Fish is bought and sold by weight, including kippers, and when fish is smoked it loses much of its water content ie: weight. Through the 20th century, Manx kippers were and are produced using a dye (FK2) to give them their distinctive colour and smoked so as not to dry them out too much, which is why they now have to be chilled or frozen to keep.

Machines to both split herring and smoke kippers under better control developed during the 20th century and were extensively used at the Peel yards (the one exception being T. Moore's, which retains the traditional smoking method). These machines save a lot of labour and speed things up, but no large automatic smoker was installed in Port St Mary.

Here's a first-hand account of work in the smaller of the two Port St Mary 1940s smokehouses from Yvonne Kneen (née Leece) written in 2017:

The Boss, Joe Jack Bridson known as 'Daddy Bridson', lived with his wife and two sons, George and Matty, in Tynwald Street, Douglas. His wife was a staunch Catholic. What brought him to Port St Mary, I don't know.

I started working for him in 1945, at the ripe old age of fifteen and a half and quickly learned to split and tenter herrings, pack kippers etc.

Our factory, at the back of Lime Street, was a very old wooden structure. Prior to 1944, it was tenanted by Willy Nichols, a well-known greengrocer and fishmonger, with a shop in Bay View Road (now Diane's hairdressers). The Harbour Board owned the building and they re-built it in brick 1946-47. Richard Kneen's factory across the yard was built in 1941, opening in 1942 during WWII. At first, it was a semi-detached pair of smokehouses with Johnny Curtis from Peel in the Lime Street side and Denis McAvoy in the seaward

One of the kipperhouses built in the 1940s.

half. Curtis gave up the tenancy and Richard Kneen took it on and when McAvoy gave up, Kneen took over both and knocked through doors upstairs and down between them to make it into one.

We started work at 6am packing kippers from the previous day's fish – home for breakfast 8 to 9am, then back to wait for the lorries bringing the herring from Peel – the boats rarely landed at Port St Mary at this time.

Our lorry was blue, Kneen's was green and we'd be scanning across the bay to see which was first coming down Fisher's Hill. Then it would be – How many cran have we, and how many have the Kneens – and who will finish first?

There was always rivalry between their staff and ours. Richard Kneen acquired a splitting machine and that put paid to the competition. The only thing against the splitting machines was that they frequently left in the silver swims and if these weren't removed by the tenterers, the kippers would quickly go bad. The tenterers were the ones who hung the split herring over the tenter hooks on the sticks (this is where the expression to be on tenter hooks comes from), prior to being smoked. Of course, the fish had been washed and put through the brine – or as we used to say 'the salt' – a huge vat of salted water with a small amount of dye. The length of time the fish were left in the brine was a big secret between us and the opposition: too long and the kippers would be too salty; not long enough and they wouldn't keep. So, whatever our timers said, for instance – in at 11am, out at 12.15, would really mean 12.30, an extra fifteen minutes but known only to us, in case any of the opposition came to look at our clocks.

After we'd finished splitting and gutting, we'd help with the tentering and passing the 40-inch long tenter sticks up to George in the kilns ready for smoking. We'd usually finish 4 or 5pm depending on how many cran we had. Then I'd come back about 5.30 to do the parcel post for an hour and a half or so, for which the Boss paid me £2 overtime on top of my weekly £5 wage. My mother had the £5 and I kept the £2. I had nine siblings and in such a large family, every penny counted.

We had the same four Irish women each year, all strong Catholics – and two Irish lads, Gussy McLoughlin and Richard Coogan, also locals Kettle (Peter Quirk) and Jackdaw (Alan Sansbury), Marjorie Grace (née Halsall) and Neild Squires – the older brother of Miss Daisy Squires, the very firm postmistress of the day – and of course the boss's son, George, our foreman, a nice quiet man and his brother Matty, who I think was only with us for two seasons (he was living in Lancashire, coming home for the herring season) – and the Boss who loved to spend his lunchtimes and evenings in the Albert Hotel.

When I was seventeen and a half, I was made forewoman, much to the annoyance of the older more experienced women but it was only because of the extra hours I put in – and the fact that at the end of the season, when all the staff were paid off, I was kept on throughout the year. Daddy and George Bridson would go home to Douglas, having lodged all summer at Nanny Floyd's house, Ivydene on the New Quay.

I would be left to clean the hundreds of tenter sticks, which had accumulated loads of grease and bits of fish over the season – a horrible job – scrape, scrape, scraping didn't do the hands much good either, catching my fingers on the sharp hooks.

In between, the Boss would arrange with Harry Faragher in Douglas (our main kipper buyer) to send down whatever white fish (cod etc) he had left over at the weekend for me to fillet and put through the brine and smoke, maybe three or four boxes a week. I'd have to climb up and down in the kiln with the fish on the tenter sticks, then make the three fires about a yard and a half apart. They would be about the size of a dustbin lid and a foot high, wood shavings and a good spade-full of sawdust on the top – no way Health and Safety would allow anyone do that on their own these days, but it didn't bother me at the time.

The Kneens did more than us in the winter and Johnny (Kneen) was their night smoker – we only had a night smoker for the summer season. So, if during the winter nights, the wind changed, Johnny would come round to my back bedroom window throwing stones to wake me up. I'd have to get up and change the kiln shutters, otherwise, the fires would roar, the fish literally cook and fall off the sticks. I'd have to be up early in the morning to climb the kilns again, bring down the fish and get it packed, then ring the railway station for Louis Collister (the lorry driver) to come and collect the fish to put it on the train for Douglas.

Daddy Bridson would send my wages (£4 in winter) down by train at the weekend and Louis would bring them down to me.

Going back to the summer – we would be at the bench splitting away with the windows and shutters all open and the visitors watching in amazement at how fast we worked but occasionally the Boss would start singing rude songs in a loud voice – like 'Roll me over in the clover, lay me down and do it again' – and the visitors would go away in disgust. But there was method in the Boss's madness. He knew that we would be showing off, seeing who could split the fastest in front of the visitors but in doing so, we'd maybe split the herrings at the belly – or at the tail, making it look like two tails, or leave in the silver swim – all of which would end up as seconds; no good for business, selling them off cheaply.

Occasionally, Mum would want me home for the day, to help out with my younger siblings and I'd have to say 'Oh no, sorry Mum – Daddy Bridson couldn't do without me', to which she would reply 'Young lady, if you were to drop dead today, there would always be someone to replace you. Never think you are indispensable'.

However, in December 1949, I told the Boss I was leaving to get married. He said 'OK, Titch (my nickname), well, I think it's time I retired anyway'. He gave his notice to the Harbour Board, ending his tenancy the week after I left. He was well into his 60s mind you.

I enjoyed every minute of my time there. Happy days. Some forty-four years later, after my husband David had died, I married John Kneen, a first cousin of Richard Kneen. George Bridson married a lovely Irish lady called May, who only recently died aged ninety. Like his Dad, they lived in Douglas all their lives.

Bridson's kipper factory was taken over by David (Mick) and Peter (Kettle) Quirk as a fishermen's store in the 1960s.

Scallop fishing

Scallop fishing developed slowly from the 1940s with investment in boats and processing facilities growing rapidly from the late 1950s when a market for fresh and frozen scallop meat in Belgium and France was pioneered. In the 1970s, a market in the USA for frozen queenie meat was also established, allowing local boats to work from home year-round, some also fished herring during the season. The port had three major shellfish processing companies through the 1970s: TB Croft (Terry Croft) on the Alfred Pier, Manesca (Philip Kneale) in Richard Kneen's old smokehouse from 1960, and Seafresh Ltd (Henry Goldsmith), behind what was Jimmy Hampson's paper mill off Loch Road. The factories created welcome flexible work for many mothers with kids at school, women who had previously worked splitting herrings for the smokehouses, along with students and young people in the summer.

The expanding fishing fleet dredging for shellfish created a big demand for steel gear and Vincent Blake took over the workshops behind what was Creer's, then Jones', then Archer's general store at the top of Athol Street, to make dredges, bellies and towing pipes. He developed specialist scallop dredges in the 1960s and queenie gear in the 1970s, the design of which was constantly refined as time went on. Just like in the days of sail, the Peel, Douglas and Ramsey fleets also went to the same fishing and improvements to gear and fishing methods were rapidly adopted by all. The gear makers at Peel were Leece and Havercroft at this time and no doubt there was much competition in developing the most effective dredges, tailored to the size and power of the various boats, along with the grounds they tended to fish.

PORT ST MARY FISHING VESSELS WWII TO 1979			
Registered	Vessel	FV No.	1st local owner
1940s	Maid of Erin	CT 116	WC Watterson
	Mevania	CT 117	W Kneen
	Teddy	CT 21	W Jackson
	William Herdman	RV	Liverpool University
1950s	Adraia	CT 30	J Cunningham
	Michael J	CT 9	J Cunningham
1960s	Magdalene Ann	CT 33	H Goldsmith
	Margaret	CT 53	J Clague
	Fenella Ann	CT 27	J Cunningham
	Manx Maid	CT 19	WC Watterson
	Golden Sceptre	CT 46	P Woodworth
	Friendly Isle	CT 52	N Sansbury
	Island Maid	CT 47	J E Gawne
	Village Maid	CT 51	WC Watterson
	Golden Promise	CT 49	RA Buchan
	Gay Star	CT 25	WC Squibb
	Rebena Belle	CT 63	WA Cregeen
	Peep o' Dawn	CT 65	DA Quirk
	Wanderobo Warrior	CT 66	N Ewing
	Zulu Warrior	CT 69	N Ewing
	Homarus	CT 38	Lord Percy

Above: A harbour scene circa 1930s, landing herring – each boat had to bring a sample of their own herring to the auction.

Below: A herring auction, circa 1930s.

	Masai Warrior	CT 71	N Ewing
	Heather Maid	CT 81	WC Watterson
	Matabele Warrior	CT 73	N Ewing
	Cuma	RV	Liverpool University
	Michael J	CT 93	G Summers
	Erin's Hope	CT 97	DA Quirk
	Dawn Maid	CT 99	WC Watterson
1970s	Friendly Shore	CT 20	N Sansbury
	Vervine	CT 17	R Watterson
	Maureen Patricia	CT 18	H Watterson
	Petit Raleur	CT 68	PC Kneale
	Conmoran	CT 87	PC Kneale
	Elkhound	CT 55	R Wout
	Mathilde	CT 100	TB Croft
	Elizabeth C	CT 23	H Goldsmith
	Spaven Mor	CT 77	DA Quirk
	JTS	?	G Summers
	Island Lass	CT 134	JR Williams
	L'Equinoxe	CT 136	JT Cregeen
	Frey	CT 137	G Summers
	Our Venture	CT 107	J Callister
	Zuider Kruis	CT 128	Algrie Ltd
	De Bounty	CT 73	I Geldart
	Catherine A	PL 72	D Spadoni
	Jacob Johannes	CT 54	H Goldsmith
	Pescado II	CT 122	H Goldsmith

There are always many strong characters involved in the maritime trades afloat and ashore and just about everyone will have had a nickname (or two). Just some of the Southside nicknames are quoted in the following ditty – sung to tune of Widdecombe Fair, compiled by Angela Kneale in November 1972.

My Man, My Man will you lend us some gear?
All along, down along, out along lee
For we want to go fishing for scallops and queens, with
Mick and Kettle, Alibo, Orbs and Shackter
Jungle Jim, Scats and Flash, Jeemolad
And Old Uncle Billy and all, And Old Uncle Billy and all

And when will I see again my precious gear?
All along, down along, out along lee
By Friday soon or Saturday noon, with
Trunks and Kipper and the Rover, Swy and Sherbie
Man from UNCLE, Cuffs and Wiley, Bill and Ben
And Hughie-the-Smock and all, And Hughie-the-Smock and all

On Friday My Man climbed atop of the pier
All along, down along, out along lee
And he seed his gear about to disappear, with
The Professor, Ilks and Dumplings, Snuffs and Softie
Chall and Woodie, Possie, Doddie, Omo, Yogi
And Jack-the-Crab and all, And Jack-the-Crab and all

He asked the shore people to get back his gear
All along, down along, out along lee
And they tried their best without favour or fear
Double-O and the Duke, Tweet and Snooker
Gnome and Granny, Stew-the-Brew, Jen-the-Wren
And old Murph-the-Surf and all, And old Murph-the-Surf and all

But still, My Man couldn't fish back his gear
All along, down along, out along lee
So we called out the lifeboat, which put straight to sea
With Hicksey and Nermi, Podger and The Cleat
Cheyenne, the Kneale brothers, Mighty Mouse
Soup King, Will Cubbon
And Derrick McCutcheon and all, And Derrick McCutcheon and all

My Man/Honk	Henry Goldsmith	Chall	Gordon Challenor
Mick & Kettle	David & Peter Quirk	Woodie	Peter Woodworth
Alibo	Alec Watterson	Possie	Billy Postlethwaite
Orbs/Buck	Raymond Buchan	Doddie	Colin Simcocks
Shackter	Norman Sansbury	Omo	Jack ? (Douglas)
Jungle Jim	Ken Harrison	Yogi	George Summers
Scats	Dennis Maddrell	Jack the Crab	Jack Crebbin
Flash	Harry Halsall	Double-O (as in 007)	Derek Ogden
Jeemolad	Ronnie Martin	The Duke/Dip	Dennis Parker
Old Uncle Billy	Billy Martin	Tweet	Malcolm Cockburn
Trunks	Eddie Kneen	Snooker	Jimmy Corkill
Kipper	Derek Kneen	Gnome	Robin Martin
Joe Rover	Tony Beck	Granny	Phyllis Swales
Swy	Philip Maddrell	Stu the Brew	Stu Lowe
Sherbie	Norman Leece	Murph the Surf	Brian Murphy
Man from UNCLE	Don Singleton	Hicksey	John Gawne
Cuffs	Henry Watterson	Nermi	Norman Quillin
Wiley	Will Watterson	Podger	Ronnie Hudson
Bill & Ben	Vincent & Chris Lamont	The Cleat	Colin Carine
Hughie the Smock	High Watterson	Cheyenne	Alan Quillin
The Professor	George Drinkwater	Kneale brothers	Bo & Mick Kneale
Ilks	Alan Cregeen	Mighty Mouse	Walter Leece
Dumplings	Roy Watterson	Soup King	?
Snuffs	Ken Christian	Fraites	Will Cubbon
Softie	Jerry Watterson	Mac	Derrick McCutcheon

Lifeboats

The RNLI established Port St Mary lifeboat station in 1896 'in view of the number of shipwrecks in the area', completing the boathouse at a cost of £845.

Seventy-two years earlier, in 1824, Sir William Hillary had arranged for a new lifeboat at Douglas under his newly formed 'National Institution for the Preservation of Life from Shipwreck', which later become the RNLI.

Two years later, in 1826, following the drowning of three Castletown fishermen rescuers along with six of the crew of the RN 18-gun brig 'Racehorse', wrecked on Langness, Sir William had a lifeboat station commissioned at Castletown. In 1896, the station had a new boat-house (now a private home at the top of the outer harbour slipway) built at the same time and using the same design and materials as the new Port St Mary station.

There are many examples of selfless locals doing their best to save shipwrecked people, a significant number of incidents occurring around the south-west end of the Island. There are many hazards and strong currents between Douglas and Port Erin, including the Calf Sound where sailing vessels were vulnerable – the brig *Lily* in 1852 and the French schooner *Jeune St Charles* in 1858 are prime examples. Before Radar and electronic navigation aids, steam and motor ships still had great problems in fog, for instance the *Clan McMaster,* wrecked on Thousla in 1923.

On completion of Alfred Pier (breakwater) in 1886–1892, Port St Mary harbour was greatly improved, with sheltered boat-launching and 24-hour access for deep-draughted boats. Much of the fishing and coasting traffic that had been using Castletown transferred to Port St Mary. Between a shortage of available crew and the limited launching at the drying harbour, the RNLI decided to close the Castletown station in 1922.

Further impetus to placing a lifeboat at Port St Mary arose from rescues in Carrick Bay performed by the Castletown and Port Erin lifeboats.

In 1888, the schooner *Lyra* was wrecked on the Carrick. Both the Castletown and Port Erin lifeboats were horse-drawn to launch at sites around the bay. In 1895, the *SS Nar* of King's Lyn grounded near Kallow Point and the Port Erin lifeboat was again dragged across to be launched. Also, in 1895 during the 'Big Snow', SS *Vigilant* went ashore on the Cronnags (under Kentraugh) in a white-out. A local 'shore' boat rescued half of the crew and the Castletown lifeboat landed the rest. The Port St Mary rescuers received much praise and were awarded medals.

When the Port St Mary station was established, the RNLI did suggest that the Port Erin station might be surplus to requirements and could be closed. This idea met with fierce local opposition and the RNLI agreed that the treacherous seas and currents around the Calf could easily prevent a lifeboat getting around to a rescue on the 'other side'.

In those days, all local lifeboats were on carriages and could be horse-drawn to other launch sites They were only driven by sails, oars and the strength of their crews. Most emergencies were close to shore, as it was only by direct observation that a vessel could be seen to be in trouble or signalling to that effect. Dragging lifeboats to alternative launch sites seems to have ended during WWI. Presumably, there were fewer horses available to hire at short notice when motor vehicles became the norm, although the first motor lifeboat at Port St Mary only appeared in 1936.

An annual blessing of the Marianne lifeboat at Kallow Point, circa 1920s.

Above: Each year the lifeboat – pictured is James Stevens (1896–1917) – was pulled up and down High Street, with the crowd encouraged to part with pennies by the bucket rattlers.

Below: Six of the nine SS Vigilant rescuers. Back row L-R: Thomas Kermode, John "Joey" Keig, Paul "Tonkin" Kelly and Robert Cain. Front kneeling: Willy "Itty" Coole and Teddy "Nipper" Kneen. Not pictured: Capt. Edward Mylchreest, Tommy Doran and Lewis Taylor.

At first, lifeboats were basically very large, self-righting rowing boats, replaced later with low speed but capable motorboats, then to faster modern craft. In 1976, the latest Arun class lifeboat *Gough Ritchie* was made station boat at Port St Mary. Compared to 47' Watson, the 54' Arun was like the Starship Enterprise!

The first D-class Inshore Lifeboat (ILB) was placed at station in 1966, complementing the service of the larger All-Weather Lifeboat (ALB).

The 5-metre inflatable with a 40 horse-power outboard was capable of 20 knots with a crew of two or three. It could quickly be launched to nearby emergencies, especially those in shallow water where a smaller boat is necessary.

Although ILBs may seem less impressive than the larger lifeboats, they are, in fact, the real workhorse of the RNLI, responding overall to more shouts than the ALBs, at a fraction of the cost.

Between 1896 and 1979, Port St Mary lifeboats launched on nearly 400 effective services – and at least as many false alarms, hoaxes and where others coped before the lifeboat arrived.

The changing of the guard, with the Gough Ritchie replacing the Colby Cubbin No.2 lifeboat.

Leisure sailing

The sailing and racing of pleasure yachts and oared boats is recorded at Port St Mary from the mid-19th century, with the annual regatta results reported in minute detail in the local press. Members of the organising committees and their titles were published

PORT ST MARY LIFEBOAT OFFICERS

	Coxswains		Second Coxswains
1896 – 1916	William Kelly	1896 – 1902	Harry Taylor
1916 – 1927	Edward Kneen	1902 – 1916	Edward Kneen
1927 – 1936	Teddy Quirk	1916 – 1927	John Kneen
1936 – 1951	Georgie Kelly	1927 – 1937	Richard Kneen
1951 – 1974	John Gawne	1937 – 1955	William Kneen
1974 – 1987	Norman Quillin	1955 – 1965	Stanley Hudson
		1965 – 1973	Will Cubbon
		1973 – 1976	Alan Quillin
		1976 – 1987	Johnny Williams
	Mechanics		Second Mechanics
1936 – 1955	Jimmy Clugston	1965 – 1981	Derrick McCutcheon
1955 – 1987	Norman Quillin	1976 – 1986	Tony Kneale

PORT ST MARY STATION BOATS

	Official number	Ops. number	Name	Class	Propulsion	Max speed knots	Max range miles
ALBs							
1896	401		James Stevens No.1	35' self-righter	10-oared pulling		
1917	556		Marianne	35' self-righter	10-oared pulling		
1936	785		Sir Heath Harrison	36' Liverpool	Single petrol engine	7	100
1948	753		Civil Service No.5	46' Watson	Twin petrol engines	8	150
1956	930		Colby Cubbin No.2	47' Watson	Twin diesel engines	8	195
1976	1051	54-06	Gough Ritchie	54' Arun	Twin diesel engines	19	250
ILBs							
1966		D-81	unnamed	D-class	Outboard motor	20	
1973		D-209	Frederic Moor No.1	D-class	Outboard motor	20	

PORT ST MARY BRANCH OFFICIALS

	President	Chairman	Hon. Secretary	Treasurer
1896	Rev T Kneale	Thos. Qualtrough	Capt. Jas Kissack	
1897	Rev CH Leece	"	"	
1900	EB Gawne	"	"	
1902	"	"	John Moore Jnr	
1910	Sir W Wragg DCL	Charles W Leigh	Dr Stanley Williams	
1912	Thomas Qualtrough	"	"	JC Dickson
1916	"	JC Dickson	Charles W Leigh	FW Briscoe
1919	JR Connal JP	Edwin Qualtrough	"	"
1921	Maj Gen Dunsterville	F W Lawson JP	"	"
1923	JJ Lucas	"	"	F Groves
1924	JR Connal JP	"	Alf Moore	FW Briscoe
1926	FW Lawson JP	Charles W Leigh	HC Stafford	"
1928	"	"	Capt FB Phillips	PE Cowley
1930	"	Capt W Cowley	"	"
1931	"	JJ Qualtrough JP	"	"
1932	"	"	Robert G Quayle	HB Jones
1933	"	"	"	Robert Kneen
1935	"	"	"	PE Cowley
1937	"	"	Lt Frank Crebbin	WC Kelly JP

1938	"	"	R G Quayle	"
1939	"	J Gilbert Shimmin	"	"
1940	"	"	GD Kinghorn	RR Coffey
1941	"	Wilfred E Kelly	RG Quayle	"
1946	"	"	WR Bridson	WC Kelly OBE JP
1947	E Murray Gawne	"	"	"
1949	F W Lawson JP	"	"	"
1956	JR Corrin MBE JP	Herbert Clegg	"	"
1963	"	HW Brown	"	"
1966	"	JA Clugston	"	"
1969	"	"	"	Stan W Keyes
1970	"	AR Jones	John Hudson	"
1972	LJ Cowley	"	"	"
1973	"	KJ Fulton	"	"
1974	"	"	"	Peter Keig
1975	"	Brian Doughty	"	"
1977	"	Philip Kneale	"	"
1979	"	"	"	W Neil Crowe

PORT ST MARY LADIES' GUILD – CONVENED 1933				
	President	**Chairman**	**Secretary**	**Treasurer**
1933			Ann Roberts	
1943	A Kelly		"	
1952	E M Clucas MD JP		"	Lilian J Cowley
1960	E Cannell	W R Bridson	"	"
1963	"	"	May Maddrell	"
1969	Lilian J Cowley	"	"	Winnie Little
1973	"	Margery Clugston	"	"
1978	Winnie Little	"	Dorothy Mylchreest	Mrs Marshall
1979	"	"	"	Pat McKaig

along with the names of all the boats, their owners and the races in fine detail – courses, position of the marks and timings around each of them. Most of the boats were built and owned at Port St Mary or Castletown.

Port St Mary regatta was such an important regular feature of the season that in the 1950s, Percy Qualtrough (Head of Victoria Road School, Castletown) even wrote the lyrics to a song about some of the characters involved – sung to the tune of 'The Pride of Purt Le Murra':

Purt Le Murra Regatta

1. When they houl' the bay regatta, no event could be much batta
    For it's organised so wonderfully gran'
    We've got Wilfie there as chairman an' Jimmy Clugston there man
    An' we've Willy Raisbeck there to lend a han'

There's Freddie Gawne and Gilbert Shimmin, lookin' after the yachts and swimmin'
There's Richard Kneen to keep them in command
Frank keeps count of every florin that is spent by Stanley Corrin
Oh you could not find their equal in the land
Chorus:
In the land, in the land, oh you could not find their equal in the land
Frank keeps count of every florin that is spent by Stanley Corrin
And you could not find their equal in the land

2. For the rest of the committee, you'll agree it is a pity
That we cannot mention all the faithful band
But, included in our panel, there is banker Ashton Cannell
Who contrives to keep our overdraft in hand

And there's bombardier Teddy, who is standing at the ready
To fire at the Commodore's command
An' when he fires, my, what a stir, all the gulls on Boolavur
Fly a-screamin' over to the Chapel strand
Chorus:
To the strand, to the strand, fly a-screaming over to the Chapel strand
When he fires, my, what a stir, all the gulls on Boolavur
Fly a-screamin' over to the Chapel strand

Regatta Day 1920s.

3. On a day set by for racin', you will see us all a-chasin'
    On the pier and round the harbour workin' hard
    An' you'll see Commodore Gelling, an' it's like there is no tellin'
    You'll see Gilbert with the flag and scoring card

    An' the Kneen boys never failin' to put marks out for the sailin'
    An' Doug Bashforth with the timin' watch in hand
    And there's bombardier Teddy always standing at the ready
    To fire at the Commodore's command
Chorus:
    His command, his command, to fire at the Commodore's command
    When he fires, my what a stir, all the gulls on Boolavur
    Fly a-screamin' over to the Chapel strand

4. When the yachts are busy sailin', the shore critics will be wailin'
    Of how little, chaps like us do understan'
    An' if you're standin' near them, it's quite certain you will hear them
    Say it's time to put her on the other han'

    As morning sunshine mellows, you will see the dear oul' fellows
    In some nice and sheltered spot of vantage stand
    Oul' John Josey in some corner, tellin' how he sailed the Lorna
    Givin' vivid demonstrations with his hand
Chorus:
    With his hand, with his hand; givin' vivid demonstrations with his hand
    Oul' John Josey in some corner, tellin' how he sailed the Lorna
    Givin' vivid demonstrations with his hand

5. Since JR first showed his paces in the Marion, first of Aces
    Quite a few have tried to take her colours down
    Maids Margaret, Meryl, Mary, Maxine all from Port St Mary
    An' Madge and Margery from Castletown

    There's the latest plan to best her, Harry Harrison's Genesta
    And the Maureen, which the owners sold away
    Since she left the undertaker, for a Douglas master baker
    Now you'll hardly find her equal on the bay
Chorus:
    On the bay, on the bay, now you'll hardly find her equal on the bay
    Since she left the undertaker, for a Douglas master baker
    Now you'll hardly find her equal on the bay

6. I take part in all the races, when they sail the Uffa Aces

Oh, what time and patient skill it does demand
I can't tell how long it took us, to catch up on Willie Clucas
When he's flyin' all the sail that she can stand

An' it nearly drives me potty trying to run with Frank and Wattie
If they chance to get the spinnaker in hand
In the struggle to discover, Frank says – take the damn thing over
An' throws the bloomin' halyard from his hand
Chorus:
From hand, from his hand, an' throws the bloomin' halyard from his hand
In the struggle to discover, Frank says – take the damn thing over
An' throws the bloomin' halyard from his hand

7. When we houl' the fund for sailors, what a boon it is for tailors
Oh, what wealth and style and cut there is displayed
All the ladies looking smashin', dressed in quite the latest fashion
All the quay looks like a mannequin parade

See the men like lighthouse keepers in their sailor hats and reefers
An' with ducks an' yachtin' slippers on as well
When I see the poor rig mine is, by the skipper of the *Inez*
For there's no doubt, Henry boy, you're looking swell
Chorus:
Lookin' swell, lookin' swell, for there's no doubt, Henry boy, you're looking swell
When I see the poor rig mine is, by the skipper of the *Inez*
There's no doubt, Henry boy, you're looking swell

Notes to the above song:
JP (Percy) Qualtrough - lyric writer. Head of Victoria Road, School Castletown .
Wilfie Kelly - Port St Mary school-master
Jimmy Clugston - coal merchant, assistant lifeboat mechanic
Willy Raisbeck Bridson - Hon Sec of Port St Mary lifeboat for 46 years. Died aged 107
Freddie Gawne - Port St Mary harbour-master, father of John (Hicksey) Gawne
Gilbert Shimmin
Richard Kneen ('Uncle Richard') MHK, MLC,
Stanley Corrin - starter for the Ace racing off Port St Mary harbour (using .45 revolver)
Ashton Cannell - banker
Teddy Collister (Bombardier) (Edward Raisbeck Collister), cobbler and journeyman
Commodore (HR) Gelling - IOM Yacht Club
Kneen brothers - Lime Street Kneens
Doug Bashforth - metalwork teacher
John Josey (JJ) Sansbury – his parents were lost with the 'Vixen - sank off the Calf.
JR Corrin – built the first local Ace (Maid Marion, No. 22) just before WWII
Harry Harrison - builder of Ace 184 Genesta – completed in 1951
Frank Moore (the undertaker - see also Frank and Wattie)
Arthur Quirk (the Douglas master baker)

Willie Clucas (sail-maker)
Fred Watterson (Wattie) – built an Ace for Harry Turnbull
Henry Kelly – lawyer, owned the Inez- one of the class of gaffers replaced by the Aces.
Fund for sailors = King George Fund for Sailors

National 18' 'Aces' mentioned:
Maid Marion 22, Maid Margaret 197, Maid Meryl, Maid Mary 183, Maid Maxine 131, Maid Madge,
Maid Margery 191, Maid Maureen 198 - became Ace of Clubs with Arthur Quirk and Genesta 184.

From the 1950s, more locally owned and visiting leisure craft started to make their presence felt, culminating in the 1979 Tall Ships Rally – part of the Manx Millennium celebrations.

In 1979, there wasn't a yacht marina anywhere around the North Irish Sea, so the facilities at Port St Mary were no better or worse than most other ports but had the advantage of a breakwater accessible at all states of the tide and a benign inner harbour for boats able to dry out. Douglas and Peel also had similar breakwaters but tended to be busier with commercial traffic and fishing vessels, making Port St Mary a favoured destination within a day's sail of North Wales, Northern Ireland, Merseyside and Lancashire ports.

Isle of Man Yacht Club

The club was founded 4th October 1910 at a meeting of a group of enthusiastic gentlemen from the south of the Island, held in the Station Hotel, Port St Mary. Meetings and social events were organised in the various local hostelries. The first yacht race was held 11th June 1911 – from Castletown to Port St Mary and back. Ladies were permitted to become members in 1912. By December 1913, the club was affiliated to the YRA (now RYA).

The inner harbour at Port St Mary circa 1960.

Apart from the very detailed annual regatta press reports, early club sailing records are patchy. Yachts were in two broad classes: 18 to 21-foot and 21 to 24-foot. Many club members were residents of the Wirral and Merseyside. Fifty members' yachts were listed 1910 to 1914 but only seven appeared to have raced.

1914 to 1918, club affairs were put on hold. In the aftermath of WWI, the club re-formed in late 1919, centred on the Fort Anne Hotel in Douglas. However, there was little enthusiasm at this depressing time and the club went into hibernation in 1927.

Between WWI and WWII, racing seemed to revolve around the 28-foot and 18-foot classes.

On 28th October 1946, in the wake of yet another World War, four members of the old club convened a meeting at the Bay View Hotel, Port St Mary. There had been another sailing club – the Port St Mary YC in the interim, which was absorbed into the new Isle of Man Yacht Club – most of the new committee had been members of both clubs anyway.

In 1947, with more than 100 members, the club rented part of Compton Buildings (now demolished) at the top of the inner harbour as its HQ.

The 1950s quest to purchase a better HQ ended when The Anchorage, a substantial but dilapidated five-storey property on the High Street, was secured in 1958.

A huge amount of voluntary work was put in and the new clubhouse (and bar) officially opened on 31st July 1959. Membership increased to 300 by 1960, the club's Jubilee year and a lease was taken on Gawne's Yard in Lime Street for winter boat storage, which was bought outright in 1969. The continuous spending to keep The Anchorage in reasonable order eventually persuaded most members that a new clubhouse, built on the recently acquired old boat-yard site was the best option. Building began in 1974 and the new club HQ was opened on 31st May 1975. In 1978, membership peaked at

Prize winners pictured at celebrations to mark Isle of Man Yacht Club Golden Jubilee in 1960. (IOM Yacht Club)

Taken at the 1972 Isle of Man Yacht Club annual dinner – Standing: Peter Curtis, Neil Crowe, William Cain, Donald Newby, Richard Sellwood, Stuart Collister, Brian Peyton, Dr Steve Baker, Daphne Quillin, Ted Killey, Ron Hook. Sitting: John Martin, Mrs Irving, Clifford Irving, Commodore Philip Kneale, Angela Kneale, Mike Macpherson, Pam Macpherson, and Commodore of Ramsey Yacht Club, Peter May and his wife.

650. (The building was extended over the winter of 1980/81 to its present footprint).

After 1946, the old 18-foot class evolved into the 'Ace Class' – ie: the wooden National 18-foot designed by Uffa Fox in 1938. Fourteen of these were built and raced regularly from 1950 and the 28-foot class vanished by 1952. The Aces dominated club racing but a handicap class for the many new smaller dinghies developed in the 1960s.

Races had always been started from the end of the inner harbour but demand for proper windward starts and courses led to the club buying a suitable committee boat in 1967 – an old Cheverton Champ now affectionately known as the *Yellow Peril*.

Through the 1950s to 1970s, the club regularly hosted finishes and starts for visiting yachts in Irish Sea races to and from UK and Irish ports, encouraging the development of a local fleet of capable offshore yachts. The 1979 cruiser programme included yacht races to Holyhead, Ardglass, Whithorn, Portpatrick, Strangford and Belfast Lough in addition to the local area, plus a full National 18-foot and dinghy racing schedule.

The club hosted the full National 18-foot Class championship in 1969 while still based at the Anchorage and again in 1976 from the new clubhouse.

Other events hosted over the years include Folk-boat Rallies, Ruffian 23 and E-Boat championships and probably the largest single sailing event organised was the Manx Millennium Tall Ships Rally in 1979.

The club became a RYA Training Centre soon after moving to its present site and runs a wide range of courses for all ages and abilities. The training section is active year-round but especially April to July, the sail-training for juniors absorbing a huge amount of voluntary effort from members and parents.

IOMYC FLAG OFFICERS 1910 -1979

Date	President	Commodore	Vice Comm.	Rear Comm.	Secretary	Treasurer
1910-11		Horace Mayhew	JR Connal	E Bromley	CW Leigh	JC Dickson
1911-12		"	E Bromley	D Thompson	"	"
1912-13		"	"	NG Murray	"	"
1913-14		Sir William Cain	"	"	CC Buckler	"
1914-15		"	"	RD Farrant	"	"
1920-21		FN Tomson	RD Farrant	M Turner	JF Crellin	"
1922-23		"	"	"	"	J Cubbon
1923-24		"	"	JC Dickson	"	"
1924-25		"	"	"	"	"
1925-26		RD Farrant	JC Dickson	HR Gelling	"	"
1926-27		JC Dickson	HR Gelling	HP Kelly	"	"
1927-28		"	"	"	"	"
1946-47	EM Gawne CP	HM Peacock	JW Jackson	CP Vereker	SC Stacey	JJ Miller
1947-48	"	"	"	H Turnbull	JR Corrin	T Cross
1948-49	Capt HM Peacock	H Kelly	H Turnbull	JP Qualtrough	"	JJ Miller
1949-50	"	"	HR Gelling	L Douglas	"	"
1950-51	"	HR Gelling	L Douglas	JR Corrin	TH Corlett	"
1951-52	"	"	JR Corrin	JD Qualtrough	"	"
1952-53	"	"	JD Qualtrough	FM Cubbon	"	"
1953-54	"	"	"	"	"	"
1954-55	"	FM Cubbon		JR Corrin	"	"
1955-56		"		"	"	"
1956-57		"			"	"
1957-58		"			AN Quillin	"
1958		"	JD Qualtrough	JR Corrin	"	"
1959		"	H Clegg	JP Lomas	"	"
1959-60		"	"	"	"	"
1960-61		"	"	"	"	"
1961-62		"	"	"	"	"
1962-63		"	JP Lomas	EC Killey	"	"
1963-64		"	"	"	"	"
1964-65		"	"	"	"	"
1965-66		"	"	PC Kneale	"	"
1966-67		JP Lomas	MB MacPherson	"	"	"
1967-68	Rev FM Cubbon	"	PC Kneale	J Blackburn	"	"
1968-69	"	"	RC Watkin	"	"	"
1969-70	"	JE Martin	J Blackburn	MB Macpherson	"	"
1970-71	"	"	"	"	"	JS Quirk
1971-72	"	PC Kneale	JE Martin	"	"	"
1972-73	"	MB Macpherson	HE Brewis	SH Cubbon	"	"
1973-74	"	Lt Col HE Brewis	SH Cubbon	BT Peyton	"	"
1974-75	"	"	"	"	"	"
1975-76	"	SH Cubbon	BT Peyton	N Roberts	"	"
1976-77	"	"	N Roberts	R Hook	"	"
1977-78	"	"	"	"	"	"
1978-79	"	N Roberts	R Hook	PNA Curtis	"	"

Figure 1:
Port St Mary –
A Constellation
of Settlements.
(Base mapping for
Figs 1–3 courtesy
of MNH)

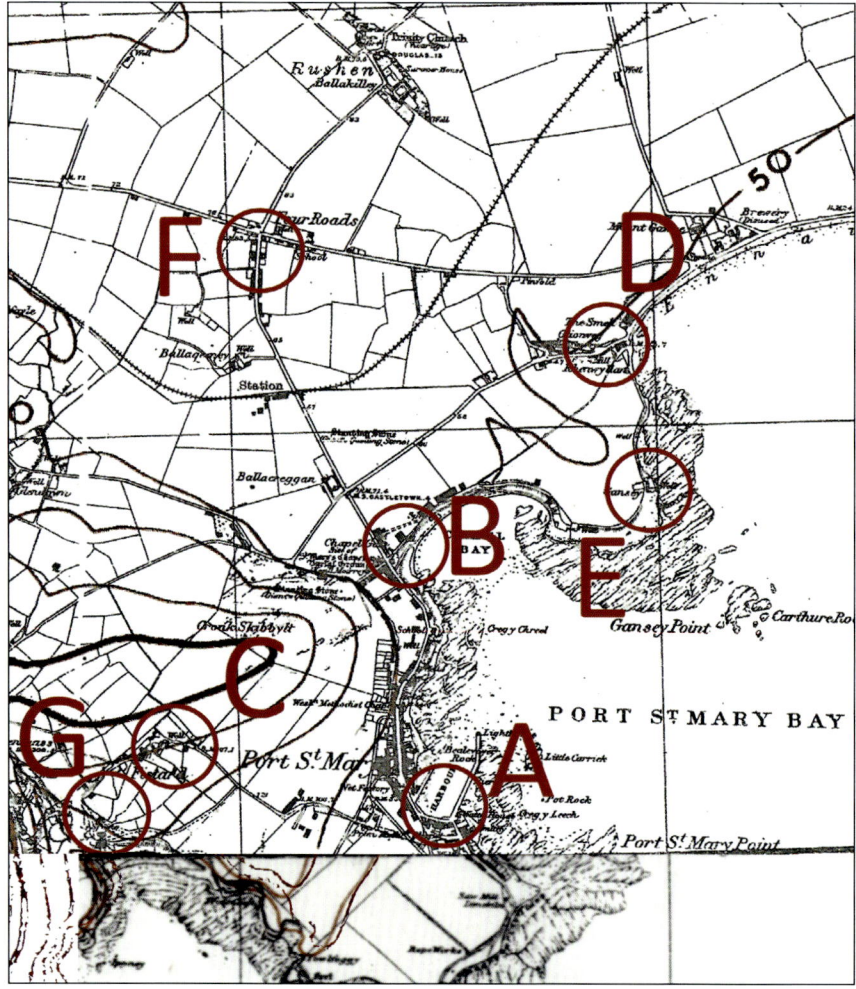

A: The Port – The natural harbour which was originally uninhabited being first used to locate buildings for fish processing and safe-keeping of items for export. It gradually attracted trade and settlement to become the most populous part of the village by 1841. The Drainage District (preceding the local authority) was initially restricted to this area.

B: Chapel Gate – A location which was close to the original chapel of St Mary with its burial ground and holy well. It was also situated on the ancient approach southwards along the coast. In 1869 there were only three cottages here. Later, a promenade was constructed and building plots laid out at the Lhargan.

C: Fistard – Area of medieval settlement which gave its name to the 'treen' or land division which stretched from Port St Mary harbour almost to Cregneash. By 1869 it had become a hamlet. In 1905 the Village Commissioners extended their boundaries to include Fistard, Four Roads and Gansey.

D: Rhenwyllan – Site of a medieval farm and a more recent mill which gave their name to this coastal area nowadays often referred to erroneously as Gansey. In the 1700s a site just to the north of here (the old smelt) began to be used to process metal ore from the nearby mines.

E: Gansey – A coastal peninsula which for a long period comprised only two or three houses and cottages.

F: Four Roads (of Ballaqueeney) –Area of farmland intersected by carriage roads which gradually attracted ribbon development. The *Draft Development Plan* in use in the 1970s envisaged the eventual merger of the two port settlements with a new civic centre near Four Roads.

G: Glen Chass – The narrow, almost inaccessible glen draining into Perwick Bay, also the name of one of the farms in Fistard treen. Lead was discovered here in the 18th century.

The Roots of a Landscape

CHAPTER 2

NIGEL CROWE

In this chapter we focus on routes local to Port St Mary we use every day, looking at each of them both as a physical feature, and as an historical source, in its own right. One at a time, we try to turn back the clock, and mentally undo changes made over the years, which have gradually led many of our roads and streets to look much the same. We then concentrate on unusual features which may point us towards their origins. Sometimes we discover an aspect of the road so distinctive that it qualifies as a *smoking gun*. As the history of these routes is unpredictable, we are sometimes carried further back than our book's official starting date of 1829. When this happens, we leave scope for future research.

Using the new approach described above does not mean ignoring more traditional geographical theories. We still need to remember the main role of routes in linking together valuable natural resources, settlements or man-made facilities.

Some colourful personalities were attracted by the development possibilities of the port. They encountered opposition in their attempts to catch rising markets – not the institutionalised opposition of public authorities or the best efforts of amenity organisations taking advantage of planning procedures. Rather, opposition, often deeply entrenched, was pursued through the courts by landowners.

The physical setting

The village district of Port St. Mary evolved from a scatter of tiny settlements around the north-eastern arm of the Mull peninsula, where there were several bays or inlets with nautical potential. None of these was regarded as safe or satisfactory in all weather conditions until it became possible to make improvements. The south-eastern tip of the peninsula (including the present harbour) is separated from the rest of the Island by Cronk Skybbylt, an eastern projection of the Mull Hill, creating a favoured, gently south-east facing hillside. Due to a geological fault, the headland at Kallow Point was formed of carboniferous limestone, exploited for a time for agricultural and building purposes. For centuries the fishing season brought activity to the haven, which was also well-placed to provide access and services to the Calf of Man. In the eighteenth century, lead and copper deposits were discovered and worked in Glen Chass, a valley just to the west. North of Cronk Skybbylt the landscape flattens out, bordered by a sheltered cove, Chapel Bay, commemorating the site of a lost medieval church which helped to name the village.

The Fishing industry prospered mightily, based on improving harbour facilities, spreading its benefits among the allied ship building and chandlery trades. They left behind them handsome warehouses and workshops. This was followed by a tourist boom which bequeathed its legacy of distinctive parades of guest houses now sought

Road – An ordinary line of communication between different places, used by horses, travellers on foot or vehicles (1596).

Street – A comparatively wide road in a town or village running between two lines of houses or shops.

after as residences, along with a few larger hotels. Other economic boosts, some real and others illusory, were promised from the extraction of stone and minerals and the attractions of the area as a health resort or retirement haven. Now perhaps the market has returned full circle to recognise the maritime attractions of the harbour again. The area lacked a sufficient water supply, and local entrepreneurs had to look to the Southern Uplands above Colby for a reliable source.

Landholding

By the 1820s the nature of landholding on the Isle of Man had become well understood and was gradually moving towards the position which existed in England and Wales. Manx farms were effectively either owner occupied or tenanted at a market rent. The 'Customary Tenure', although important for legal purposes, had little everyday significance. The Act of Settlement of 1703 embodied an agreement between the Lord of Man and his tenants and has been the basis of land tenure ever since. The terminology then in use involved *quarterlands* or fragments of such, on which *lord's rent* was paid to the Duke of Atholl as manorial lord (after 1828 the British Crown). Lord's rents were low in real terms, because their monetary amount had been fixed permanently in 1703. Distinctions between areas of land where rent had always been paid to the Lord of Man, and those previously belonging to the Bishop or the Abbot of Rushen, were of purely historic interest and made no difference to the day-to-day occupation of the properties. Another obsolete term, *treen,* referred to an area of land larger than the individual farms. There might have been ten or twenty treens in a parish. Intacks were areas of former wasteland which had been taken into use for which a modest lord's rent was payable. In 1869, a comprehensive volume *Woods's Atlas* was published which included the names of landowners and the description of their property in terms of the land tenure. Ever since the Act of Settlement, provision existed for the registration of all deeds and mortgages affecting property and this continued until the recent establishment of the Land Registry.

Background to Manx roadbuilding

Until the first Village Commissioners were elected[i] the ultimate responsibility for road matters in the district rested with the Highways Committee, established by an Act of Tynwald in 1753. The Committee became the Highway Board in 1874. The Parochial Surveyor of Highways organised matters locally, directing the farm workers, small-holders and crofters who made up his workforce. Each farmer and crofter had to contribute their quota in days of compulsory labour each year; the bigger farmers also had to lend equipment. This workforce could be used for building new roads or bridges, improving existing routes or for repairs. The Committee had charge of allocating the funds raised annually from licencing of public houses and dogs, and from rates levied on town-dwellers. They appointed the Surveyor-General of Highways, usually an experienced military man, who took an Island-wide view of highway requirements.

In the early 1700s there were no roads capable of carrying wheeled traffic. When Bishop Wilson arrived in 1697, he had to take to horseback to get to Bishopscourt. His possessions would have followed by packhorse, anything too heavy for this would need

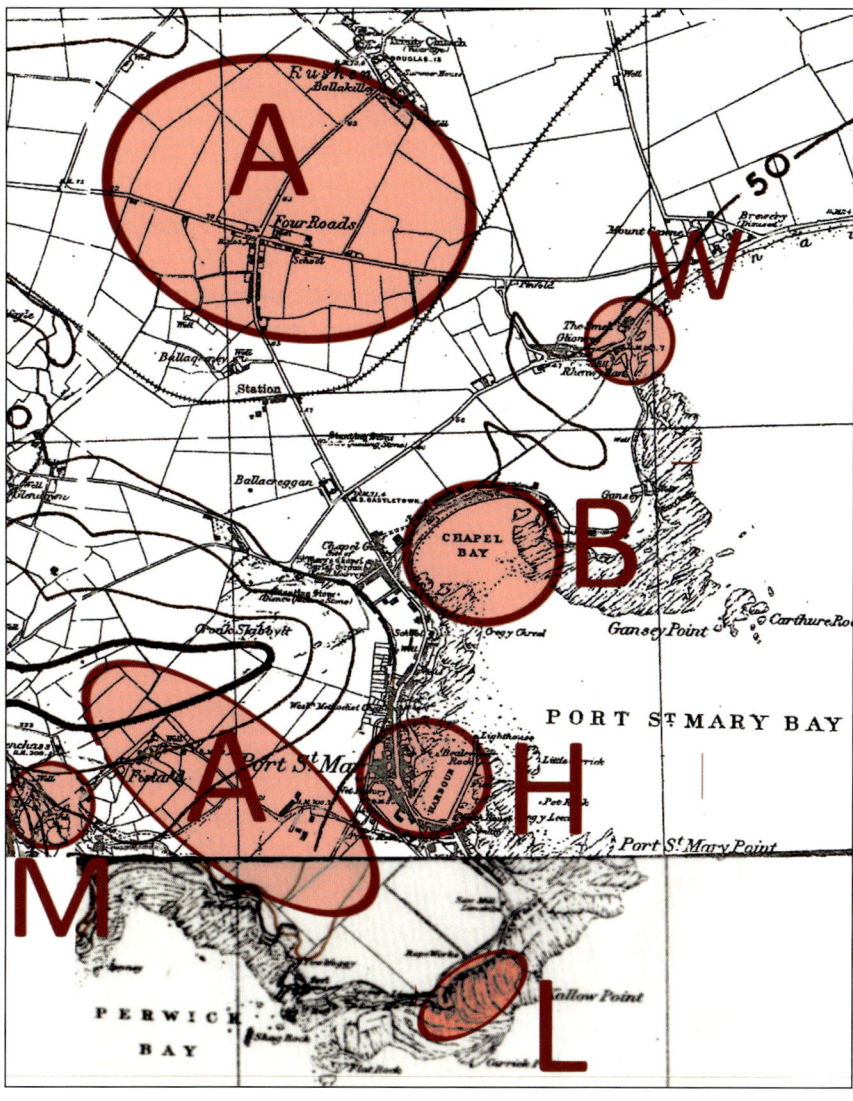

Figure 2:
Port St. Mary:
Natural Assets &
Resources in the
District.

A: Arable potential
B: Sandy beach
    sheltered and south
    facing
H: Natural harbour,
    herring & other
    fisheries
L: Limestone deposit
M: Metalliferous
    deposit
W: Potential for water
    power
C: Proximity to Calf
    and coastal features

to be dragged all the way or heaved off a boat at high tide on the Michael shoreline.

Few of today's main roads pre-date the mid-eighteenth century, before this there was quite a variety of route-ways. With little opportunity for personal leisure, most routes were needed for practical agricultural purposes, for subsistence, or enabled people to carry out their obligations as tenants and parishioners. Legal records often refer to the basic need for ways to "church, mill and market", these would usually have been travelled on foot, or with pack-animals, although the better-off could ride to church or the market towns. Moving livestock in numbers required drove-ways or drift-ways with protection for any crops alongside. An obvious location for ways of this type was the foreshore although once cliffs were encountered the route adopted had to swing inland. Unlike the position with land-ownership, no register was kept recording road and bridge-building activity, and the survival of relevant documentation is a matter of chance. The late Stuart Slack was great authority on the history of Manx roads and bridges but never wrote comprehensively on the topic. Nevertheless, his *Manx Milestones* (2003), *Streets of Douglas* (1996) and contribution to *Here is the News* (Ed. T. Cringle, 1992), contain much of his research.

Route A: The Castletown Road from The Mount towards Port Erin (header)

When Peter Fannín [1789] surveyed the interior of the Island for his map, none of the roads south west of Castletown and Ballasalla was classed as a *highway*. Even the lesser network of *cross-roads* did not serve Port St Mary. The present main road from Castletown southwards incorporates parts of an ancient drift-way which led along the

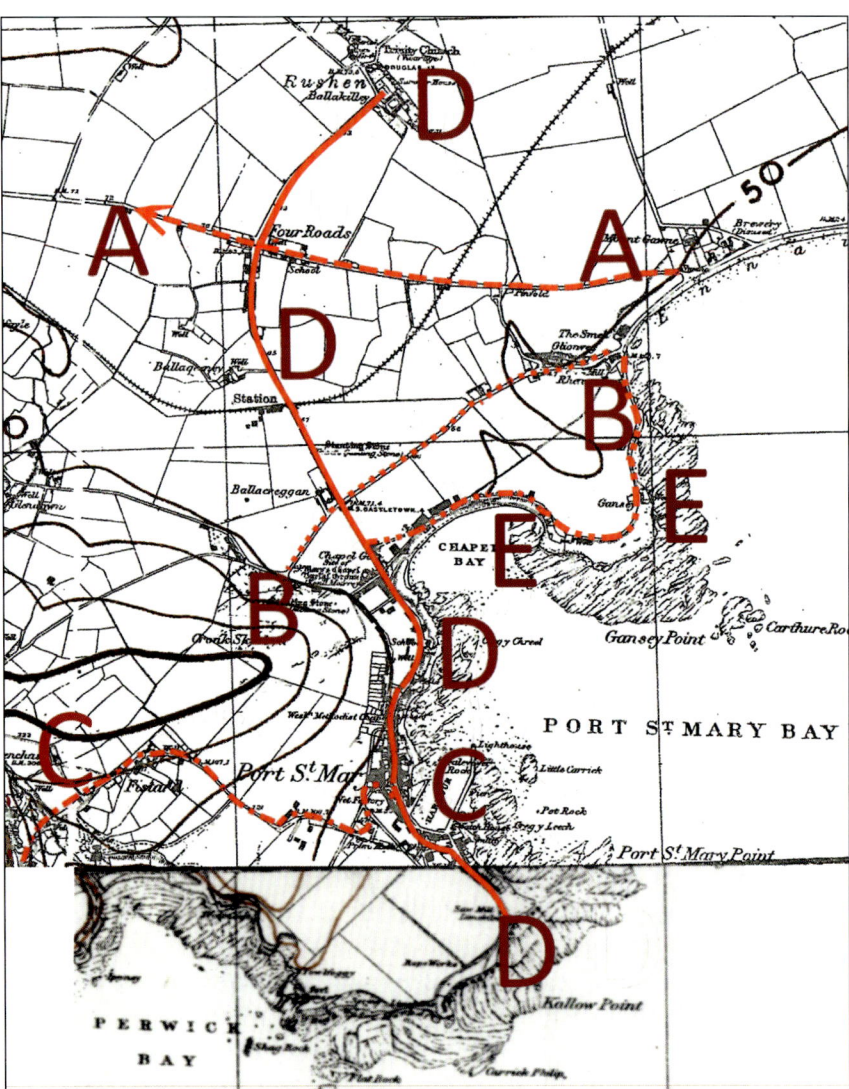

Figure 3:
Principal routes
discussed in this
chapter.

A: The Castletown
 Road from The
 Mount towards
 Port Erin

B: Beach Road from
 The Smelt through
 Ballacreggan

C: Fistard Road, from
 Glen Chass to the
 Port

D: The extended High
 Street from Kallow
 Point to Ballakilley

E: The (Upper)
 Promenade with
 continuation via
 Gansey to
 Rhenwyllan

coast from Queen Street in Castletown to Scarlett and then probably across the peninsula to continue through Pooil Vaish, then cutting across Kentraugh warren, crossing the Colby river and resuming its coastal identity all the way round Baie ny Carrickey; and the next headland of Gansey to enter Port St Mary at Chapel Gate. It was partly replaced by the main carriage route south from the capital, beginning with Arbory Street (Castletown Bypass being a very recent addition), passing *Balladoule* and emerging onto the coast to follow the ancient route for a while, skirting an anonymous Kentraugh. Stuart Slack wrote about the set of milestones which accompanied this route. Radiating from Castletown, the first milestone was at Ballakeighen; the second at Strand Hall; the third, since lost, appeared on the Ordnance Survey Map of 1957, sited at the bridge near the Shore Hotel, one of few in the parish of Rushen[1]. The presence of these milestones confirms the status of this highway as part of the strategic network of carriage roads. A looping routeway gave access to Cregneash, but no detail was shown of landward access to *Port le Marry*.

The carriage road (since widened) struck inland across relatively open land, heading for Port Erin and by-passing both Rushen parish church and Port St Mary itself. The layout of main roads still conspires to divert travellers away from the village!

The present road bears little resemblance to the narrow and more twisting way shown in the earliest maps of the area (Fig. 8). Widening could be carried out by the Highway Committee without taking ownership of land and such activities are rarely documented. The road is crossed by the railway line (1870s) and bridges a clearly re-routed watercourse which doubled as the boundary between the lands of Ballagawne and those of Ballakilley. It seems walls and hedges were also straightened and regularised

Figure 4: Extract from Peter Fannin's Map 1789. (Base mapping for this Figure together with Figs 6, 7, 11 & 16 taken from 25" County Series Sheets courtesy of DoI)

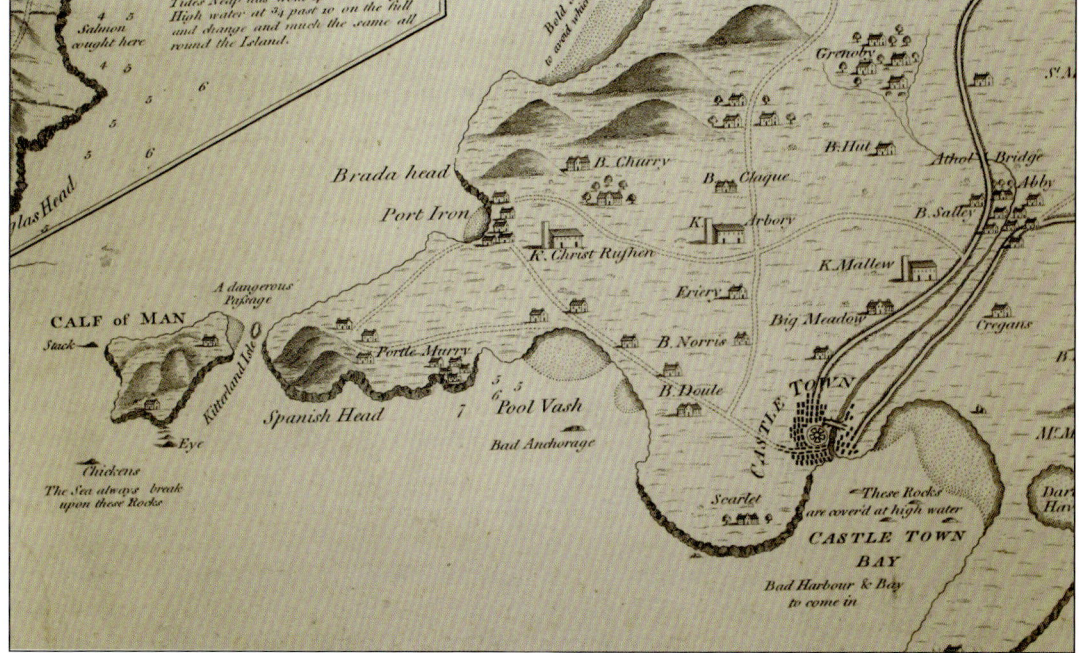

John Murray, 4th Duke of Atholl (1755-1830)

The head of the Scottish Murray clan, James, 2nd Duke of Atholl, of Blair Atholl, Perthshire, fell heir to the Lordship of Man in 1735/6, on the death of his cousin, the 10th Earl of Derby. This inheritance came about some eighty years after the marriage which had established the link between the families. The possibility of Murray succession had only recently emerged with the thinning-out of the senior branch of the family, descendants of Charles Stanley, 8th Earl of Derby. The Lordship of Man was permitted to pass down through the female line, in this case to the Murrays, whereas the Earldom and the Knowsley inheritance had to remain with the male line, and these devolved on a more remote Stanley relative[2]. With this example in the background, in October 1753 the marriage took place between Lady Charlotte, heir to the Lordship of Man, as only surviving child of the 2nd Duke of Atholl, and her first cousin John Murray who was the male heir. John became the third Duke of Atholl on his uncle's death in 1763, potentially reuniting the titles.

It was not long before the British Government implemented powers to acquire the lordship of Man in order to curtail what they looked upon as[3] an illicit trade in luxury commodities, alcohol and tobacco. The Duchess Charlotte and her husband found themselves with little choice but to negotiate the sale of their sovereignty, although many of their lesser interests in the Island were left intact. Their eldest surviving son, another John Murray, born in 1755, was educated at Eton. He succeeded to the Dukedom in 1763 and his mother passed over to him most of her remaining rights in the Isle of Man. He was to take a much closer interest in the Island than had any of its lords since the days of the English Civil Wars. The Fourth Duke conducted a long campaign to obtain additional compensation for the rights which his parents had been forced to sell. He eventually succeeded, although the effort occupied him for many years. One of his earliest successes in this direction was his appointment in 1793 as the Island's Governor-General. Although never a permanent resident, he established a home near Douglas, initially at Port-e-Chee. The Duke at first earned public popularity, however he was often opposed by the established landholders and native merchants, many of whom were members of the House of Keys[3] (constituent part of Tynwald, the Manx Parliament. He was more aware than the Manx of his status near the top of British society. He had a seat in the House of Lords; in 1794 he became the first ever Lord Lieutenant of Perthshire and, from 1797, a UK Privy-Councillor. In managing his Scottish Highland holdings, the Duke's policy was to move away from the traditional clan and feudal hierarchies towards the English model of a consolidated landed estate with mansion and grounds at its core, surrounded by an expanse of let farms with tenants dependant on him.[4] This was achieved by the purchase or sale of *feus* within the area of his *superiority*. On Man his position was rather similar. Although his rights as 'Lord of the Manor' extended to the whole Island, and (to the irritation of the Manx), he frequently referred to residents as his *tenants,* he personally possessed only a life interest, his annual rents were small and fixed, and he could not grant freeholds. The ancient castles where his forebears had maintained garrisons were now in British hands. In order to live on Man in the style to which he felt entitled, and considered appropriate and expected of his exalted rank, it was therefore necessary to establish a new family seat with a surrounding demesne, together with further lands contributing to an impressive rent roll. He also sought to increase his influence through "unblushing nepotism",[5] attempting to nominate first his younger brother, Lord Henry Murray, and later on his own son Lord James, as Lieutenant Governor; and appointing other brothers and his nephew to the Archdeaconry and Bishopric.

Soon after the Duke became Governor General he acquired Rhenwyllan Mill and lands, where he built a new facility for smelting ores from his mines in the south west of the Island. He spent almost £600 building a water-powered plant.[6] Though convenient for importing coal and shipping ore, the siting of the smelt meant the prevailing wind carried the noxious fumes over the nearby houses and farmlands. John Summers, the Duke's Mines Manager faced difficulties in maintaining neighbourly relations with the Gawne family. Before long though, mining was abandoned, and the problem disappeared.

The Fourth Duke of Atholl never lived in Port St Mary but long thought highly of the port's potential, with its convenience for his existing mineral rights and usefulness for access to the Calf of Man which he also owned. Eventually, in 1822 he took the opportunity of acquiring full ownership of most of the village, together with its hinterland.[7] His important purchases from the Nelson and Clucas families formed part of an even larger arrangement by which Rev. John Nelson, vicar of Santon, parted with all his lands in Rushen. Ballacreggan and Ballavrara were sold to the Duke to add to the adjacent Rhenwyllan.[8] The former Nelson home farm of Ballakilley along with land at Ballakneale was later sold to his cousin, John Clucas of Port St Mary.[9] It seems likely that Clucas would then have built the new Regency style farmhouse and model farm complex close to the parish church. He could afford this through selling the original Clucas holding to the Duke and granting a mortgage to Edward Gawne over his newly acquired property.[10] The Duke's acquisition of Port St Mary seems to have exhausted his appetite for Manx property and the following year having '…wearied of a long contest in which he had acquired nothing but unpopularity…' he intimated to the British Government his readiness to sell all his interests in the Island, and in 1825 Parliament passed an Act empowering the Treasury to buy them. The Duke had invested about £60,000 buying land in the Island.[11] Additionally, he had taken ten years, and claimed to have laid out a further £36,000 building Castle Mona, his seaside palace north of Douglas.[12] He, too, had resorted to mortgaging his Manx properties, raising £11,000 in this fashion.[13]

In order to account for the Duke's final disillusionment, we have to turn back some years. The obligation to pay annual tithes on farm produce was looked on with a sense of grievance by the majority of the Manx, especially the non-conformists. Tithes were not exclusively due to the parish clergy but could be demanded by up to three different owners. The bishop usually received a third of the tithes, and the Lord of the Isle as 'lay impropriator' claimed a further share of one or two thirds. The vicar of the parish was sometimes entitled to the last third or might only be paid a fixed salary by the tithe owners. The appointment of the 4th Duke's nephew as bishop in 1813 placed most of the tithe revenue in Murray hands. Unlike the lord's rent, most tithes had not been commuted to a fixed sum and represented the possibility of providing income growth for both the lord and bishop. Efforts to reinstate tithes on fishing, extend them to cover potatoes and other 'green crops', and achieve a composition for the payments triggered major unrest on the Island.[14] These new demands alienated many crofters and fishermen, driving this less prosperous group within the community to make common cause with the better-off farmers. Resentment over tithes was also among the factors which alienated many Manx families from the established church, sending them to the Methodist chapels or encouraging emigration to the Mormons' gathering places and elsewhere.

The British government took a while to process their deal with the Duke, but he left the Island early in 1825 and never returned. In the end he was left to find private buyers for Castle Mona, Port St. Mary and other purchased holdings. He ended up selling Port St Mary along with farms in Andreas and at St. John's to his banker, James Holmes. The Duke died at Dunkeld in 1830 before the disposal of all his purchased lands in Man had been finally completed.[15]

(Portrait of the Duke as a Masonic Grand Master, courtesy of the Museum of Freemasonry, London)

in the course of farm improvement and boundary simplification.[16] When the information contained in *Wood's Atlas & Gazetteer* (c. 1860) is added to the 1869 Ordnance Survey mapping (see Figs 5 and 6), the road has evidently been cut across the grain of the earlier holdings, some of which previously extended to both sides of the road.

We do not yet have an exact date when the Castletown Road was cut through, but it was probably just before 1726, when John Kelly and Richard Taylor, who held Ballaqueeney equally between them, reached agreement over what seem to be new arrangements for gaining access to 'the highway'.[17] Apparently there was already an older route 'the church way' running between Taylor's steading and the highway. At this distance in time, and lacking any map of Ballaqueeney older than 1840, we can only leave the matter for future research.

The village district of Port St Mary has its north eastern boundary at the junction of Castletown Road and Shore Road**.** Beyond this are several properties in Rushen parish which historically were closely associated with a Gawne family who continue to have links with the village although not resident there.[18] The original family home was Ballagawne on the Colby Road. Ballagawne land reached to the coast and included what is now known as Moorhouse Farm. On the coast, a brewery was established by Edward Gawne Senior and gave its name to Brewery Beach, the site later being occupied by the Shore Garage complex, and recently re-developed.[19]

In 1790 the brewery along with the tan yard[20] and other property down at the port was settled on Edward Gawne Jnr (1773–1837); the younger son of the family. The brewery prospered as did his other trading and lending enterprises, enabling him to build a handsome Regency style home commanding a sea view – now known as The Mount rather than Mount Gawne. His sloop *Amelia* traded out of the port, captained by Philip Shimmin.[21] We should nowadays call Edward a serial entrepreneur as all his enterprises appeared to thrive. Gawne's initiatives resulted in his appointment as a Harbour Commissioner in 1821.[22] So far, we have not been able to discover any of the detail behind the building of the older pier at Port St Mary but his contemporaries gave him the credit for organising its construction by private subscription in around 1810. The Gawne family was very well connected and Edward was the beneficiary of a property settlement made by his relative Miss Jane Qualtrough[23] (died 1810) from whom he inherited the estate of Kentraugh. He died in 1837 having created an English-style

Figure 5: Route A: A6: The Castletown Road from The Mount towards Port Erin. (Image courtesy of MNH)

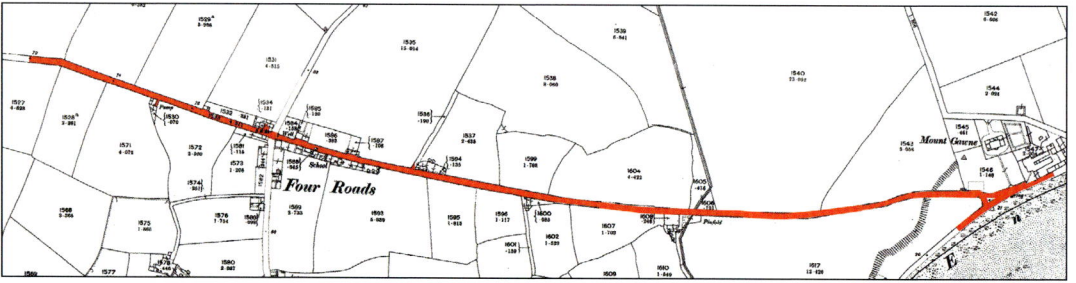

country house there and leaving enormous wealth (reputedly amounting to £200,000), certainly the biggest fortune accumulated on the Island up to that date.[24]

Thomas Gawne of Ballachurrry was apparently easier to deal with than his brother, Edward, of Mount Gawne and in 1795 the Duke was able to acquire substantial additional property and water rights from Thomas Gawne and his mother, Jane,[25] in order to improve the facilities at the smelt. In describing the boundaries of the land so acquired reference was made to a number of the routes which essentially turned the land into an island. One boundary followed the road leading from Castletown through Ballagawne to Port Erin. Another side fronted onto the road leading from Castletown along the seashore to the rivulet. Finally, there is reference to a road 'leading from the said rivulet between the lands of Thomas Kelly and John Taylor to the Port le Mary'.[26]

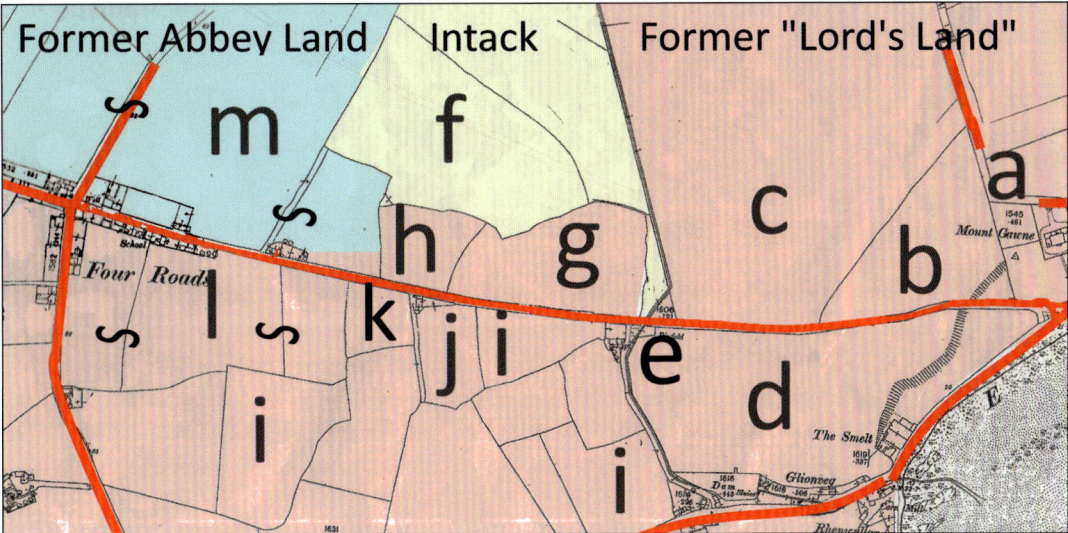

Figure 6.

a *The Mount* – formerly Mount Gawne, one of the most handsome and earliest dated houses in the area was under construction by Edward Gawne Jnr in 1798 alongside his brewery being on part of his family's lands of Ballagawne, (the seaward part of which is now known as Moorhouse Farm).

b Triangular parcel, called the "sheep field", sold in 1815 by Thomas Gawne to his brother, Edward Gawne Jnr and owned in 1860 by E M Gawne of Kentraugh

c Lands formerly belonging to Ballagawne and perhaps Ballachurry. The property of Edward Gawne in 1860. The bounding water course to the west was part of the system supplying Rhenwyllan Mill.

d Additional land, formerly part of Ballagawne and sold to the Duke of Atholl in 1793

e Parish Pound giving its name to a narrow winding lane running south and clearly one of the earliest features of the area.

f Parcel of intack called Rowany Curragh sold by John Gawne of the Rowany to J T Clucas, Ballakilley for £360 in 1874

g Two fields, part of Ballaqueeney, in 1840 when this land was held by Henry Kelly. Sold to J T Clucas of Ballakilley before 1860

h Another parcel of Ballaqueeney acquired by J T Clucas before 1874 and part of which was formerly laid out at an oblique angle indicating a field system of an earlier date.

i In this western area, Wood's Atlas makes the Castletown Road the boundary between the Abbey Lands (Ballakilley) and the Lords Land (Ballaqueeney). Given the oblique character of parts of the field system relative to the road, this seems to be a late development perhaps dating after land exchanges.

j/k/l Portions of Ballaqueeney; m Ballakilley.

Route B: Beach Road from The Smelt through Ballacreggan

Beach Road is another route which seems to divert traffic away from the port. In terms of geographical analysis, the road served to link together the old seaside route and another ancient way now partly incorporated into the line of Cronk Road and The Lhargan, described as the old road to Port Erin. Edward Woodworth (giving evidence in the Gansey court case in 1889)[27] recollected old people saying the coastal route was a high road 'before the present high road was cut up'. Being cross-examined he recalled it was a Jane Woodworth who said she remembered the 'present high road' being made – by this we imagine she meant Beach Road, which assumes an essentially bland aspect once it rises away from the coast, passing between what were once large rectangular fields belonging to Ballacreggan and clearly dating from the era of agricultural improvement. Most of the interest we will find centring around the eastern end. Rhenwyllan properly refers to a small farm classing as a half quarterland. As early as 1511 it was in the hands of the Waterson family[28] who paid the lord 2s 4d a year for their cottage and land. Descendants originally obtained permission to construct a "little mill" there. This had a status much secondary to that of the ancient manorial mill of Kentraugh to which were attached the tenants of all the large farms within the parish. The Watersons could only draw their customers from the ranks of intack holders and cottage dwellers.[29] A little mill[30] was a primitive affair descending from the earlier Norse mill type. Totally open to view, the milling was carried on out of doors using millstones located above a horizontally mounted paddle-wheel, towards which a stream would be diverted. Presumably planning to upgrade the facilities, William Waterson of Rhenwyllan with his wife, Margaret Cotteman, sold a half interest in the mill to the Gawnes of Ballagawne in 1753:[31] the buyers agreed that a mill race could be constructed on their land. Later the Wattersons (as they became) parted with the other share and almost all their land to the Duke of Atholl.[32] The last in the male line was Henry, whose daughter, Sarah, born in 1795 married the heir to Ballaqueeney. The present structure of the Mill is far from little, being one of the landmarks of the south. It was built for James Holmes, banker, reputedly in 1844.[33] When offered to let in 1862, the premises of 'Rhenwyllan Corn and Flour Water Mill' included a miller's house and additional cottage, while the mill itself was equipped with five pairs of stones.[34] An additional race had recently been provided. Once redundant as a corn mill, a woollen manufacturer named Hogarth operated it for a time then planned to have it converted into flats with a classical elevation onto the road. Instead, he built a mock Tudor house on the south side.[35]

Figure 7: Beach Road from The Smelt through Ballacreggan.

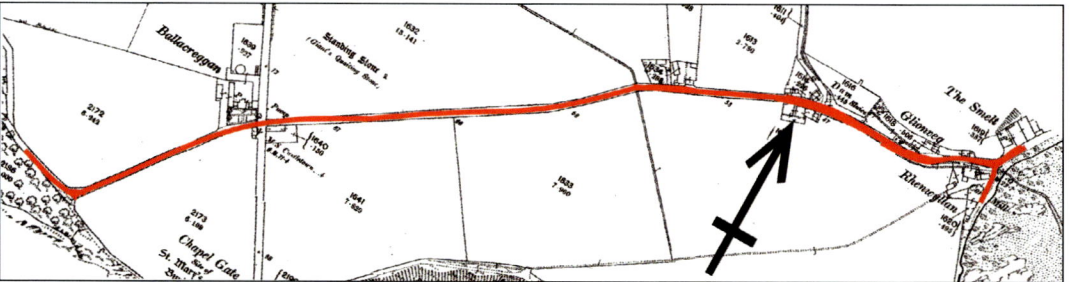

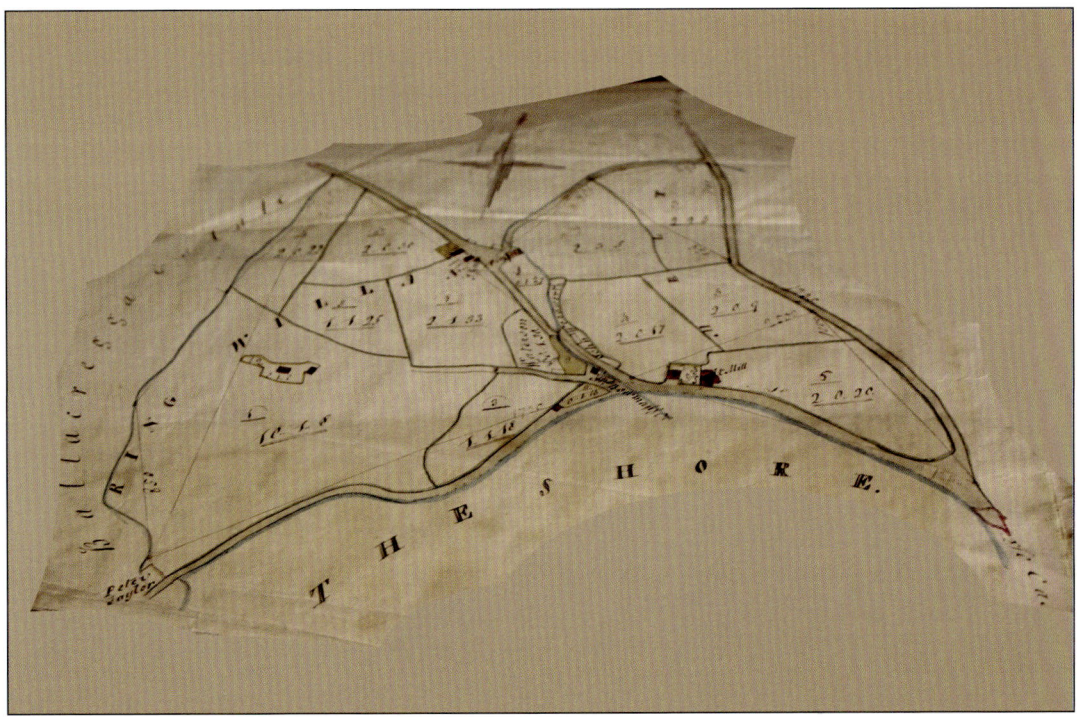

Figure 8: Earliest map of the Rhenwyllan area, lodged by James Holmes for the purposes of valuation under the Tithe Commutation Act. (Image – IOM PRO Rushen Tithe Plan – 109)

Cott-ny-Greiney

For centuries this remained the property of a single crofting family. A gravestone in the parish churchyard records the death of Thomas Woodworth's children (probably of smallpox) in 1765 He was described as being of "Glanbeg" when he followed them to the churchyard later that year, but occupation of the site by the Woodworths goes back to at least 1620. From the mid-18th century onwards, the parish clerks described them as resident at "The Smelt". In the following century the croft name "Grinea" or more formally "Cott-ny-Greiney" or "Sunny Cott" was preferred. The Woodworth family only parted with their last interests in the area in the mid-20th century.

Route C: Fistard Road from Glen Chass to The Port

The explanation of the origins of the Fistard Road must take into account both arable and pastoral issues. The *Treen* of *Fyshgarth* extended from Kallow Point almost as far as Cregneash and consisted of four quarterland farms of Port St Mary, Fistard, Corvalley and Glen Chass. Three of these farms lay side by side each probably extending across Glen Chass to give access to the arable core facing south in the area around and to the south of Fistard hamlet. These farms also ran south as far as Fyshgarth Mountain', a name applied to rough land lying upside of the Chasms. This must have been in communal use at an early period but eventually was partitioned between the holders of the quarterlands. Similarly, the arable lands would have been worked under the open field system in the Middle Ages hence the need for each farm to have its own access.

Figure 9: Rhenwyllan Mill along with detached house constructed by Mr Hogarth c. 1926. Not to be confused with the Smelt mill which was located further north on the site occupied by yellow brick houses. (Source: MNHL: PHN/pic/2125)

Port St Mary farm had grazing rights on Fistard Mountain which after enclosure crystallised as the largest individual parcel there extending to 35 acres in 1840 and including the chasms themselves. The chasms were sold with Port St Mary quarterland to the Duke of Atholl by John Clucas. The family apparently repented of this and J T Clucas bought them back at the auction sale in 1858.[36]

At a practical level while the grazing was communal, there must have been a drove-way to move livestock between the upland pasture and the main arable core. It is possible to identify a track on the 1869 OS Map running from the direction of the mountain down to the south west end of Fistard Road as it now exists. The same map also shows two narrow strip-like fields continuing down steeply on the same alignment to the Perwick shore and alongside the beach towards Fistard. The ownership boundaries there

Figure 10: Nestling out of sight opposite Rhenwyllan Mill, this property has been known by a number of names. (MNHL Collection: Cot ny Greinney PG 3343/2)

(recorded on Tithe plans and the O.S. Sheet) suggest there had been a change in the route of the drove-way, perhaps by invoking the 18th century legislation which provided for the closure of earlier roads and the awarding of the land thus released to landowners losing ground to new roads. Alternatively, more high-handed powers were available for mining entrepreneurs to mould the landscape according to their operational needs.

The most important development must have occurred when the steep vertical route was abandoned, and new routes laid out especially designed to allow the transport of extremely heavy loads. The new routes had to meet the needs of the miners who (following the discovery of mineral deposits in 1739) were active at Glen Chass from around 1745 onwards.[37] By working with both photographs and maps, it is possible to theorise as to which routes and settlement sites predated the mine workings, and which adhered to newer, 'engineered' lines.

The route begins outside the village district at the level of the former mine buildings and proceeds downhill by way of a graded incline to the Glen Chass bridge (Section A). At this point, a remarkable, straight boundary feature begins on the north west side of the route and extends the full length of the hamlet of Fistard, separating the old part from St Mary's Glebe. By referring to Woods's Atlas, a longer stretch of boundary, similarly straight, separated the farmland of Fistard quarterland from the other adjacent farms in the treen of Fyshgarth south of Glen Chass. Further research is required as to the status of the straight boundary which separates St Mary's Glebe (a relatively modern building development carried out by Mill Baldwin Limited actually not historically glebe land nor especially associated with St Mary) from the original hamlet.

The next, uphill section of Fistard Road (Section B) assumes a character which may have originated as a very wide droving/haulage way gradually encroached upon by cottages and gardens. A single storey cottage bears the date 1798, and while not recorded on an original date stone, this seems a plausible date for this phase of infilling. The hamlet of Fistard grew haphazardly without any form of planning or control. The Commissioners began to improve the road up in the late 1880s and ten years later the Highway Board was keen to restore a vehicular link through to the Howe Road.[38] A committee of Tynwald considering the possible extension of village boundaries in 1904 directed the commissioners to go further than planned and include the 28 houses in Fistard (of which 3 or 4 had been recently erected) in order that they could receive mains drainage.[39] The roadworks were eventually carried out in 1929/30 when the two authorities shared the

Figure 11: Fistard Road from Glen Chass to the Port.

A, B, C: Lengths of Fistard Road described in detail in the text
D: Port St Mary farm complex
E: Long narrow fields perhaps originating as driving way for farm stock
F: Area of metalliferous ore deposits
G: Notably straight boundary feature

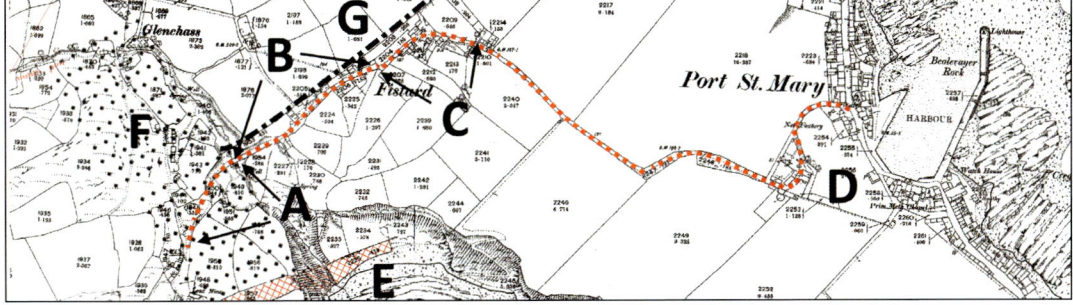

Figure 12: An interesting view of cottages at Glen Chass before the present heavy tree cover developed. On the map, the row of dwellings pictured in the centre mid-ground appear to be arranged randomly, only with the benefit of the third dimension can we understand that considerable engineering must have been involved to create a near level road line, to which they related. Much work to the infrastructure must have taken place to create the graded slope linking the Glen Chass bridge (actually appearing to be more like a culvert) to the mine site just off to the left. (MNH, Tom Pherick's cottage 1904, PG/11823)

Figure 13: View of the south west end of the Fistard Road showing the cutting (and possibly quarrying away of rock outcrop). A further view looking back from Glen Chass to Fistard suggests that considerable effort would likewise have been required to achieve the road grades leading up towards Fistard as it now stands, which facilitates the achievement of a steady graded rise from Glen Chass bridge into Fistard hamlet. At the top of the cutting the linear boundary feature appears. The chimneys in the foreground belong to the later, mid-19th century phase of mine working. (J W Qualtrough Collection)

cost of rebuilding "Fistard Bridge". The Commissioners laid 625 yards of concrete kerb, built 132 yards of dry-stone wall and created 16 gateways and 4 gulleys.[40]

Section C appears to have a rather different origin, threading its way perhaps between established settlement sites in the oldest part of the hamlet. Consideration of the field pattern and siting of the older properties flanking the road suggests that the enclosures there have early origins, perhaps being related to an arable field. The appearance and siting of one cottage in particular (below) seem to mark it out as among the oldest in the hamlet.

The next section of Fistard Road takes us through the settlement and ready to descend towards the Port. The onward road flanks a once favoured area of farmland which enjoys a southerly aspect, now part of the golf course. This may represent an original track across open fields; this length is notable for the gentle curvature of its alignment. There does seem to have been some ambiguity in its status. At the south east corner of the hamlet, it reaches the former lands of Port St Mary farm. Jumping to the very bottom of the road, where it joins the extended High Street, we encounter a distinctive feature which has so far attracted little attraction. A substantial pillar occupies the site of one of the traditional gate pillars marking the bottom end of a private road to Port St Mary farm.

It follows that residents of Fistard had to make use of a different route to Port St Mary. Considerable light is thrown on this issue by evidence given in connection with the Port St Mary right of way controversy 1895–1898. This dispute generated personal

Figure 14: Morphological analysis suggests that Maye Cottage stands on one of the oldest settlement sites in the hamlet of Fistard. The building itself must be of considerable age.

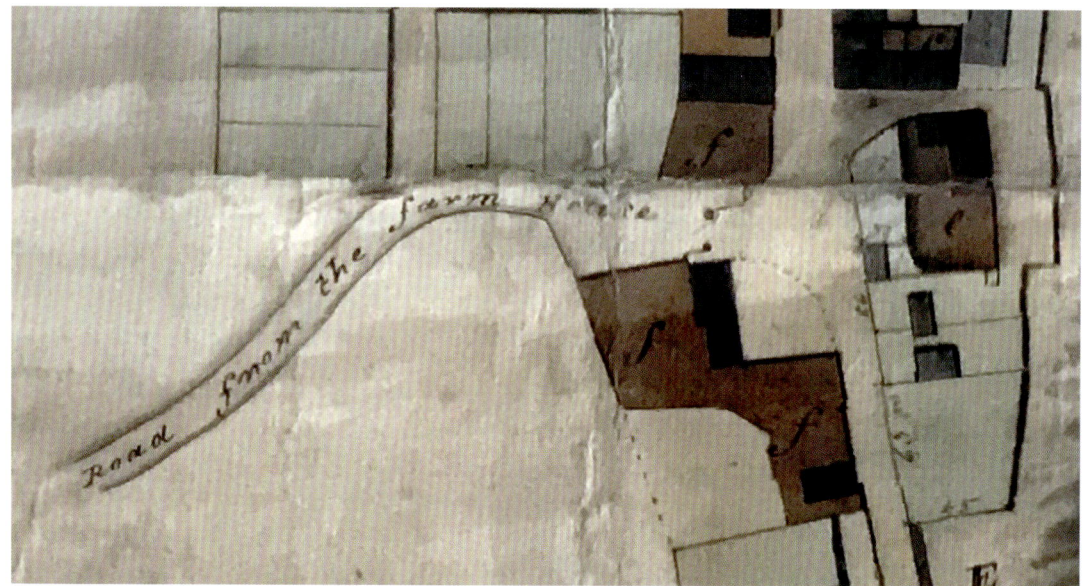

Figure 15a (left) – This substantial gate pillar stands on the site of one of the traditional farm gate pillars on which a gate would have hung securing what was apparently a private road, although now the public road to Fistard.

Figure 15b (above) – Extract from the Port St Mary plan of 1827 which shows two gateposts in position. (MNHL Reference P.6318)

depositions by knowledgeable residents of Port St Mary, Fistard and districts of that era.

The 'main drag' from Lime Street to the parish church
There are few aspects of the village scene which are more puzzling to the first-time visitor or long-time resident alike. What are we to make of the high street? Not just the relatively short section formally named as such, but an extended route beginning at Kallow Point and stretching as far as the parish church. To account satisfactorily for the character and extent of this, the village's backbone, must be a priority of its historians.

The bottom section is called Lime Street. The use of lime as an agricultural fertiliser was introduced to the Isle of Man as early as the 17th century, but it was still not in general use by 1780. The process of tanning leather also uses lime, and there is a record of a tannery at Port St Mary in around 1700.

By the late eighteenth century, the use of lime for agricultural purposes had caught on here, burning being first seriously carried on near Ballahot, Malew. The trade then moved to the coast where coal was more readily available (being continuously shipped from Whitehaven to Dublin) and was carried on 'to a prodigious extent' at Derbyhaven and already established at Port St. Mary by 1795, when artist Warwick Smith included a smoking kiln in the first illustration we have of the port [Fig. 14]. The farmers in the west of the Island petitioned for a new route south to allow access to the lime kilns.[41]

J.C. Curwen, writing in 1810,[42] named John Swinburn 'a speculator from Cumberland' as the person responsible for beginning lime burning at Derbyhaven. An 1825 account[43] suggests that this Swinburn was a brother to Curwen's steward and asserts that he also took a lease on "certain plots of land in Port St Mary containing quarries of limestone". In addition to leasing the ground from the farmer, Swinburn was said to have made overtures to the Duke of Atholl as owner of the minerals. He built 'spacious and complete' lime kilns and after his death his son William continued working them.

The Port St Mary main drag or extended high street was carefully engineered to optimise its use for the movement of heavily laden horse-drawn wagons from the harbour and lime quarry towards the interior of the Island. The regularly constructed parapet walls to the side of Athol Street (see Fig. 18) constitute our 'smoking guns' which combined with the graded approach to it leave little doubt as to the intentions of the original road builders. Although documentation has not yet been located to provide a date for the actual construction, the lower section was completed by 1810,[44] and must have been one of the routes Thomas Quayle was describing in 1812[45] when he wrote: 'From the beginning of April 'till the fall of the autumn rains impedes the carriage of lime, the kilns draw daily. Carts are in constant employ leading it away, even to the distance of eighteen miles, for the purpose of agriculture. At the kilns which adjoin the sea, boats are also constantly in requisition during the summer

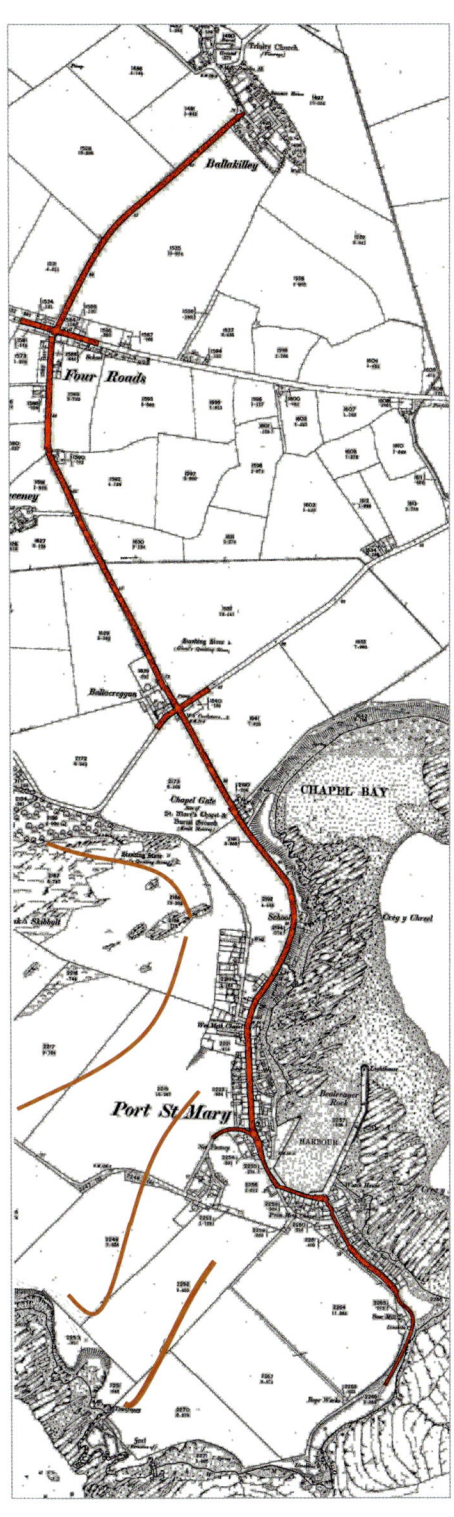

Figure 16 – The main drag starts with Lime Street, recalling the original purpose for which the route was constructed. It then turns and becomes The Quay. At the Albert Hotel, the name changes once more to Athol Street, continuing as the High Street proper. The next section is Bay View Road, which continues as Station Road and finally Four Roads. Outside the village district, the route continues to its termination as Church Road.

Figure 17: Detail from John 'Warwick' Smith's view of the port, commissioned by the 4th Duke of Athol in 1795. The Duke thought Port St Mary harbour had as much potential as Douglas, and as the owner of the mineral rights including copper, lead and limestone anticipated growing trade from mines and quarries. He already owned the Smelt, and in 1822 bought most of the village with its surrounding farmland taking his landholding in a single block to over 300 acres. (Painting in Museum Collection Reference No: 19954-7213. Official title 'Port le Mare')

Figure 18: Old Harbour, Port St Mary. This image reveals the 'smoking gun', the carefully graded 'inclined planes' which form part of the haul route *linking the lime kilns at Kallow Point with the agricultural hinterland. (J K Qualtrough, 2008)*

months, conveying cargoes to different creeks and ports of the Island'.[46] Farmers also took advantage of the new road to obtain sand from the beach close to the quarry, another resource used for improving soil quality.

Lime Street formed a functional link between the quarries at Kallow Point and the port area where coal was landed. Port St Mary lime was specified by Stephenson for the mortar used in the building of the twin Calf lighthouses. In 1823 the Duke (by now the owner of both land and minerals) leased the quarries to John Clucas of Port St Mary, who thought it worth erecting a crane on the pier in 1827 to load stone blocks for customers such as the harbour authority. They used them for the quay walls at Douglas and elsewhere. Burned lime was exported to Ramsey, which acted as a depot for the local distribution of lime.

It appears probable that Loch Road simply originated as a "bye-pass" to prevent the heavy traffic becoming disrupted by harbour-side activity. Physical evidence can be identified all along the route of the over-riding requirement to avoid unnecessary or

Figure 19a: Plan of Port St Mary and 'Ballacregga' dated 1834 showing the harbour section of the main drag. Very little has been constructed in the Port St Mary meadow at C and in particular there is no slipway or quayside in front of the new graded parapet wall. (W.J.C. Kelly)

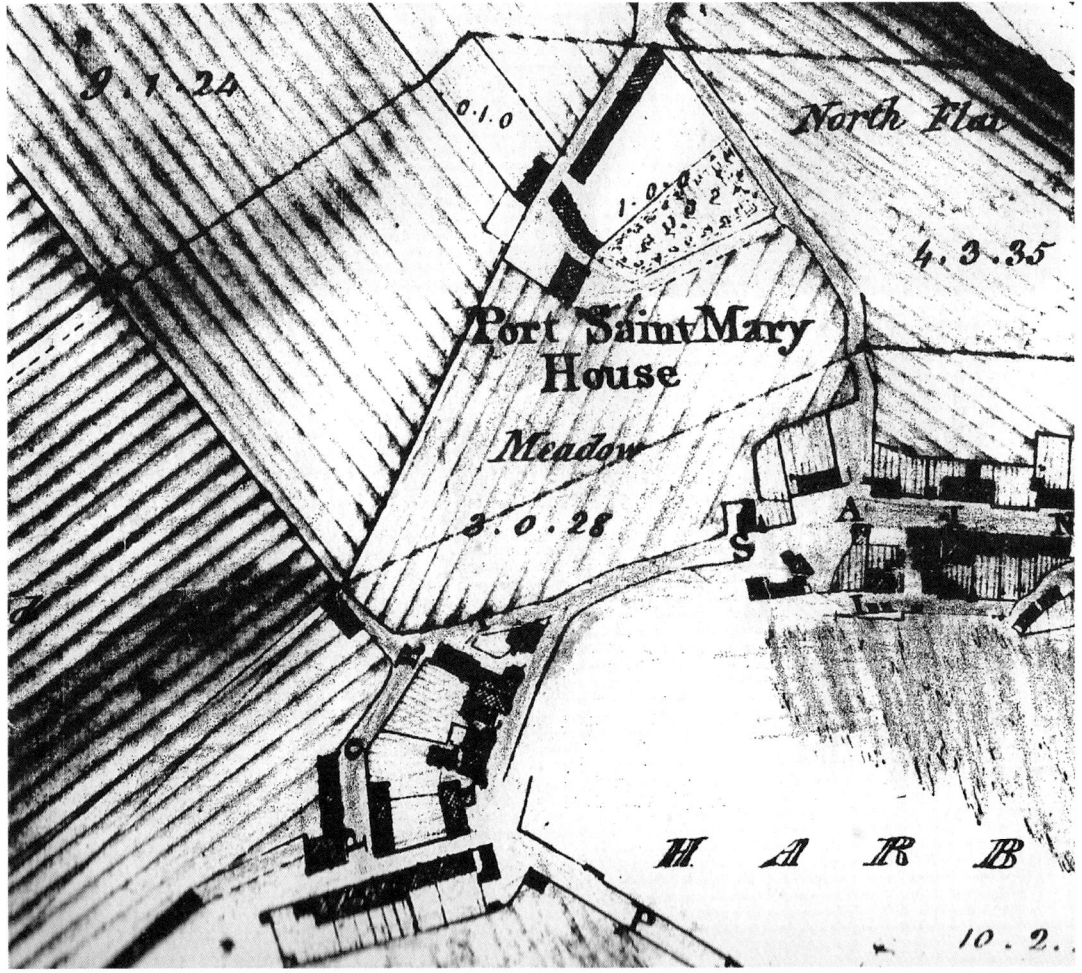

Figure 19b: Surviving pillar protecting the bottom end of the parapet wall which retains the main drag on its lower side.

Figure 19c: Corner detail of dwelling showing the construction indicating a sharp and constrained turn in the route which preceded the construction of both the main drag and also the quay and its access alongside the parapet wall.

minor changes of grade, and this led to the construction of retaining walls. In a prominent location between Ballacreggan crossroads and the railway station a cutting was formed for the roadway.

It is planned to account for major changes in direction rather than deal with every building along this route. The earliest properties developed in the village were concentrated around the old harbour. Based on its structure and orientation, one of the earliest surviving buildings is at the rear of No. 1 The Quay; in its appearance essentially a small farmhouse of the mid-18th century easily distinguished by the design of its chimney stack and the steepness of its roof pitch. Evidence remains of the original front door and accompanying windows looking to the south east.

The main drag partially superseded an earlier access from Port Erin to the harbour area and intersected the lowest part of its route which must have joined the south end of Queen's road to an unnamed slip which still emerges onto the Quay alongside Harbourside Apartments.

A detailed plan survives of the lower section of this route, commissioned by James McCrone, the Duke of Atholl's local agent, from John Taggart, architect of Douglas. He wrote to Carrington, the Duke's land agent at Blair Castle in 1827:

> *'I wish also for some directions as for fueing part of Port le Marie. There is some demand for houses there, and I have got a survey and building plan from Taggart, which I think may be acted on with success and profit.'*[47]

The layout of plots in relation to the new road can be compared with the layout of Athol Street, Douglas, by John Taggart at around the same time. The Douglas layout was designed for a single landowner and provided for full-sized plots on either side of the new street. Here the road was constructed under statutory powers using the compulsory highway labour and equipment which was mostly supplied by the farming community.

Below: Figure 20a: – Former miniature gable window opening and surviving 'front' first floor window in rear wing of No 1, The Quay.

Left: Figure 20b: Steep gable typical of mid-18th century Manx houses. There is a blocked gable window behind the big wheelie bin.

It took many decades before the original road started to develop sections which could be called streets. By comparing maps prepared at three dates, we can see this process taking place (See Fig 21).

The new route cut across the property of two landowners which then became concentrated in the Duke of Atholl's hands. However, the road had not been laid out in a manner which was especially beneficial to the landowners. On the east side, it kept close to the harbour and then skirted tightly behind existing properties before heading up along the cliff top to the lowest feasible point for rounding the projection of Cronk Skybbylt. Few usable full-sized residential plots could therefore be made available on the east side of the road. Aspects of the route became increasingly inconvenient, and a major series of roadworks was eventually carried out over several years by the Commissioners which involved shaving off gardens on the inland side, and jettying out

Figure 21: Athol Street/High Street as it developed between 1827 and 1869. The plots left white on the 1827 plan were available for sale by the Duke while the dark brown plots were already privately owned, and the tan ones already sold but still paying annual rent. The 1857 plan was prepared for auction purposes and plots with numbers were either available to be sold outright or yielded annual rent payments.
Sources for above: 1827 – 'Plan of Port St Mary belonging to his Grace the Duke of Atholl', J. Taggart, Douglas 1827, MNH Ref P. 6318; 1857 – 'Plan of Port St Mary (Holmes's Estate)', MNH Ref M.39310 & D.274/2xf (4); 1869 – Ordnance Survey County Series (1:2500) 1869, Sheet XVI/13.

with a cantilevered footpath on the seaward side. All this was insufficient to prevent the implementing of the one-way system in the lower Village in 1969. Unfortunate symptoms of the 200-year age of the route have been collapses where there are stone retaining walls on the lower side – a landslide was reported in 1990, and a major problem occurred at Happy Valley where there must have been a culvert.

The alignment of Station Road (as it now is) appears to be related to the site of The Pink Cottage (around which it bends) probably the site of an existing croft within the ownership of the family of Kelly (Curry) of Ballaqueeney. It is unfortunate that the location of the early church way cannot be definitely established, but it is likely that it would have followed a sinuous course originally threading its way between cultivation ridges in an area of open field lying between this point and the parish church. This would most likely be an unfenced *leading-way* or bridle way not available for the driving of livestock.

The 'Four Roads of Ballaqueeney' grew up after the extended High Street created a crossroads, the name first appearing in 1814,[48] and the change of direction by the road as it crosses over and heads towards the parish church seems to confirm the prior existence of Castletown Road. The Turnbulls were one of the earliest families to settle close to the crossroads, Thomas Turnbull, a blacksmith, buying a small piece of Ballakilley (once part of *Magher ny Crottey*) in 1813[49] which apparently had been severed from the farm by the earlier formation of the Castletown Road. The remaining houses near the crossroads were mostly built on former Ballaqueeney fields, but the plots were laid out on crofts already separated from Taylor's farm. In 1861 there were still two crofts, Thomas Turnbull's (some three acres) and Jane Watterson's (on the Beach Road) of four and a half acres.[50] Kelly's Ballaqueeney was then 46 acres in extent and Taylors retained 17 acres. By the time the little community became incorporated in the village district in 1905,[51] terraced housing was being constructed and occupied largely by fishermen; there were fifty-six houses, a lock up shop and girls' school, together with the nearby gas works and railway station.

One of the distinctive characteristics of the main route through the centre of Port St Mary is the presence of several substantial private houses, standing in their own enviable grounds on the seaward side of the road. Somewhat surprisingly, they began as holiday homes. The original hope was probably to tempt well-heeled visitors to establish a second home on the Island. To some extent, this aim initially succeeded but the properties have long since passed into permanent occupation. As residential locations go, the brooghs[52] here are still counted among the most desirable on the Isle of Man.

Originally forming part of Ballavrara, this coastal strip was severed from the bulk of that estate by the pushing through of the extended High Street. Very little development occurred on this coastal side for many years. At the time of the 1858 auction, it was lotted with the field opposite of some 4.5 acres as 'Lot 7'. The coastal land was described as:

> *"the brow at the opposite side of the public high road (save and except that portion thereof on which the school is erected, and that portion belonging to John Costain) together with the buildings thereon adjoining the seashore".*

The report of the results of the auction added that there were three cottages adjoining the seashore; the whole of Lot 7 being acquired by Robert Gelling for the sum £503. Mr Gelling patiently bided his time, his business as a timber merchant standing him in good stead when the land eventually became ripe for building development. The first disposal in the mid-1870s was a shallow plot on the landward side sold to the Commissioners for Northern Lights when they abandoned the Keepers' houses on the Calf and housed the families of the Chicken Rock men on the mainland.

Rocklands was the first of the big houses; James Martin Kissack (a Liverpool Manxman) took a coastal plot with a 70-yard frontage on a ground rent of £3 10s pa in the summer of 1877. Kissack held a senior administrative post with Liverpool police, so presumably built a holiday home there. Twelve years on, Rocklands became the permanent residence of his younger brother Captain Joseph Ashton Kissack (retired from a career in the Pacific merchant marine). The Captain became heavily involved with lifeboat and Commissioners' affairs. He died aged just fifty-five in 1902, and his widow Harriet remained in residence until 1919, when Henry P. Kelly acquired the property for £1,000,[53] his family's connection lasting over sixty years.[54]

Figure 22a: the three large houses and the hotel – far left is the Cliff Hotel, then Ballamona; Ballamaria in the middle (formerly Beach Villa) and Rocklands on the right. The Port St Mary National School can be seen between Ballamona and Cliff Hotel.

Ballamona was the holiday home of one of the port's best-known part-time residents of the turn of the century, Judge Edwin Jones, and his family. Their main residence was in Longsight, near Manchester. They bought their vacant plot with 45ft frontage from Robert Gelling in 1888 for £32 10s. When residing in the port, they involved themselves in community activities including the Regatta. The Judge was the motivating force behind the proposal to build a public hall for the village. He and his sons were the largest subscribers to the enterprise and Judge Jones was the first Company Secretary.[55] The name of the Jones's house, Ballamona, has caused some puzzlement. No connection with any of the farms of that name or the families associated with them has yet come to light and it may purely be an invented, composite name mixing up the Manx 'Balla' and the Latin 'Mona', meaning Isle of Man-farm! Ballamona was sold by the Jones Trustees in 1914 for £3,700.

Mr Gelling seems to have identified an Onchan man, Frederick Callow, who had married a local girl as the right man to get involved with the development of his seaside land. He was certainly responsible for the erection of the Golf Links Hotel, now Carrick Bay Apartments.[56] There is some uncertainty as to the builder responsible for the three

People of Port St Mary

GEORGE DRINKWATER LUCIUS CARY 1845–1901
Owner of Ballacreggan and developer of the Promenade

When Eleanor Drinkwater left Old Kirk Braddan on the arm of her Irish bridegroom Lieutenant Clarence Horatio Cary in 1844, she was not the first Manx heiress to yield to the addresses of a military officer of gentry status.[62] The Woods family succeeded to Balladoole, the Goldies to the Nunnery and the Cuninghames of Lorne House to a significant portion of the Taubmans' wealth in the same way.[63]

Eleanor's late father, William Leece Drinkwater belonged to a merchant family which traded between Liverpool and Man for several generations. After retiring to this side of the water, he became an MHK, and invested in farms spread across the Island. His most notable purchase, perhaps, was the Calf of Man, bought from the Crown in 1832 for a little over £3,000. Eleanor received a settlement of her late father's property in the year of her marriage. She had expectations from her mother's side of the family too, including a house which her grandfather, Deemster Crellin, had built on the seafront in Castletown.[64]

The young couple began their married life at the original Drinkwater home, Leece Lodge, near The Strang, Braddan. Here their elder son George Drinkwater Lúcíús Cary[65] was born in June 1845. The young George was soon joined by a brother and sister, but around 1850 the family moved to Castletown to live in Deemster Crellin's 'Beach House'. George attended King William's College from the age of 9 as a day-boy, his brother, William joining him the next year, both leaving for Cheltenham College in 1859[66]. George proceeded to Emmanuel College, Cambridge in 1864, where he secured a First in the Science Tripos in 1868. Called to the Chancery Bar in 1873, he began practising in the Middle Temple. Meanwhile the Calf

had been let by his parents to a succession of tenants. In the summer of 1878, George retired from his Chambers and moved to the Calf of Man of which he was the heir apparent. This seemingly triggered the following from his cousin John Drinkwater in Valparaiso, Chile;[67]

> *Dear Old Farmer George, I hear by last mail you have thrown up all your briefs and intend to farm on the Calf, you are a wise man and will have a glorious time of it , should you want a ploughboy or any other officer send for me. I would be only too happy to be there with you. Do you think there is any trade to be done between the Calf and Chili in exports? What is your address now? King George the 1st. The Palace, Calf of Man, via the Sound and Port Erin harbour …*

The first member of an owning family to reside on the Calf, he was responsible for considerable improvements both to the farmland and the main dwelling house.[68]

Eight years later still residing on the Calf, George Cary had apparently come into capital – it seems unlikely that he would be in a position to save out of his income while living and investing in the Calf. A sale by auction of Ballacreggan, Rhenwyllan and the Smelt was advertised to take place at Port St Mary:

> *"… there was an immense gathering of capitalists and others, including several English gentlemen who came across with the intention of investing their capital".*

George DL Carey was ultimately the successful purchaser of all three properties with a final bid of £11,800, then regarded as an immense sum.[69]

Figure 22b (above) Part of former coastal brooghs included with Lot 7 in the auction of 1858. In the foreground are the three large houses. Other landmarks include the Northern Lighthouse Commissioners lighthouse keepers' accommodation. (1:500 Map prepared by Kay Architectural Practice on a base photographically enlarged from the 1869 1:2500 sheet. Courtesy of Port St Mary Commissioners)

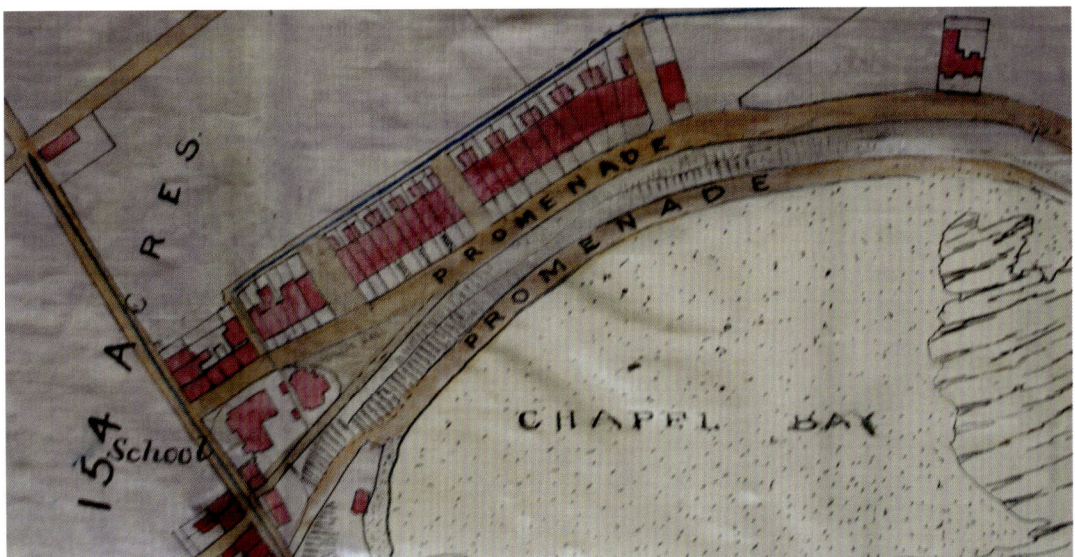

large houses; the late J. K. Qualtrough suggested that one of the McArd family was the builder of Rocklands.[57] Whoever the builder, he was fairly fearless in his approach to the exploitation of the plots which were carved out and secured by the use of extensive retaining walls and underbuilding all executed in Manx stonework. The four structures all shared a certain similarity with multiple floors and numerous bay windows enjoying the wonderful views across the bay towards Scarlett.

Beach Villa, described as 'a well-built and commodious lodging house, situate on the brooghs and of a modern character',[58] was built as an investment for Robert Gelling

Figure 23: The Upper and Lower Promenades at Chapel Bay at the time of the boundary extension in 1904/5. (IOM PRO Third Div SOG 1905 #13)

Laying the foundation stone of the first house on P.S.M. Prom. Endfield.

Figure 24: Stone laying ceremony at Port St Mary Promenade 14th June 1888. (J.W. Qualtrough Collection)

himself and let on a five-year lease from 1894 to a Mr Lynn. It formed part of Gelling's estate the next year and was bought at auction by Walter James Cannell, banker of Peel[59]. Cannell's widow, Sarah, was residing there from at least 1908[60] until her death in 1927.[61]

Although outside the village district, the inland termination of the extended High Street deserves a mention. As originally constructed, it seemed to finish nowhere in particular. Whether it linked with another route which has since been abandoned, or perhaps was planned but never constructed remains to be seen.

E: The Promenade and its continuation via Gansey to Rhenwyllan

This semi-circular route has been subject to partial redundancy by the construction of more modern carriageways, damage due to coastal erosion, and partial replacement by purpose-built promenades at high and low level.

Before the railway was constructed between Douglas and the south in the 1870s, Port St. Mary was not recognised as a holiday resort, although the attractions of the locality were recognised, and adventurous visitors staying in Douglas could 'make a day's excursion to Port St. Mary, Bradda and the Calf'. This was done by taking the Castletown coach, and catching a connecting service to the port. It was thought enough to provide a 'station' for the village at a wayside halt the best part of a mile away from the fishing port. Ultimately, public taste evolved and leisure expanded to generate demand for weeks' or fortnight-long holidays. At the same time, the district began to gain a reputation as a healthy and scenic location where the well-to-do could maintain a second home, or even spend their retirement, anticipating the policy which the whole Island pursued from the early 1960s.

Interesting proceedings took place on 14th June 1888 on top of the brooghs at Chapel Bay. These were but part of the well documented process by which this field was transformed by the building of a terrace of properties devoted to catering for tourists. A holiday atmosphere prevailed, and the worthies of the village were in attendance to witness the landowner's wife tap the foundation stone of the first terraced house with her silver trowel. Sadly, Thomas Qualtrough's ownership of his newly built Sky Bright House, appears to have lasted only until 1899 when he met with a financial reverse. They had chosen one of the most desirable spots for such a development. Most of the grossly optimistic scheme (which would have seen development in-depth, possibly on the lines seen in Blackpool) was never implemented. Although relatively few of the hundreds of potential plots were taken up, enough had been sold to generate excitement on that June morning. It seemed that Mother Nature had been kind to Port St Mary when Chapel Bay was formed – more accurately the local capitalists of the 1880s chose to dwell on the 'excellent shore … very attractive to bathers' and the height above where a 'magnificent promenade about half a mile long' had been laid out and construction begun. The site seemed destined for 'handsome houses meeting every modern requirement, ornamental and commanding the finest marine and mountain view'. It was said only partly in jest that all the members of the new commissioners board invested in the promenade and by the next year, it was reported that £14,000 had been spent in building there.

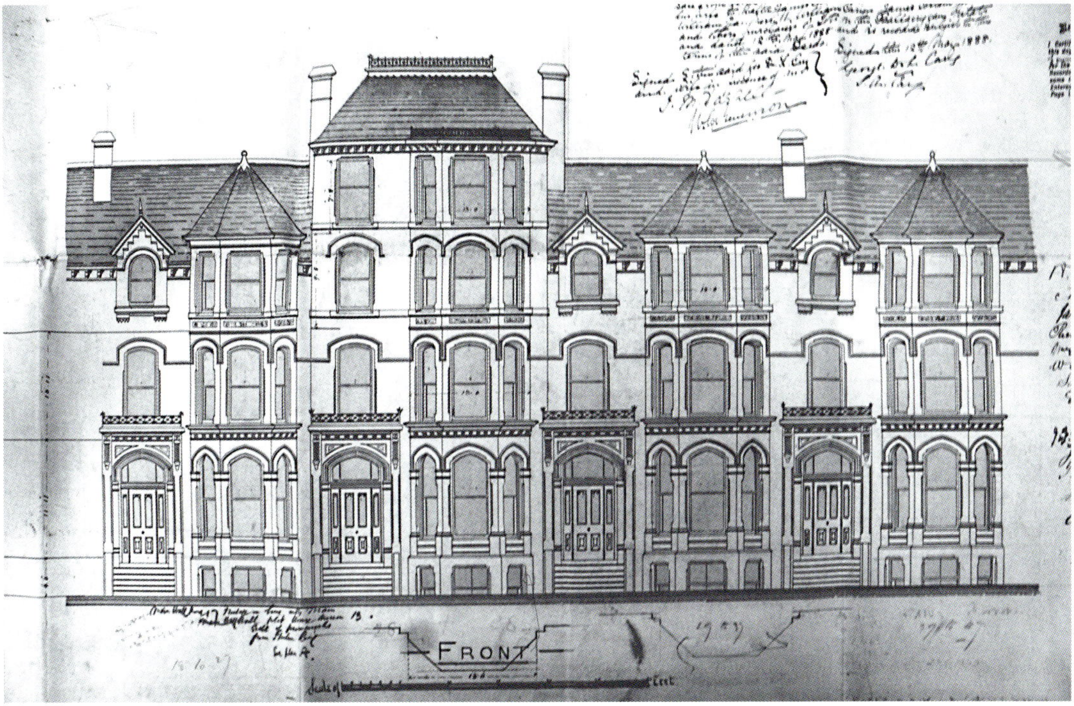

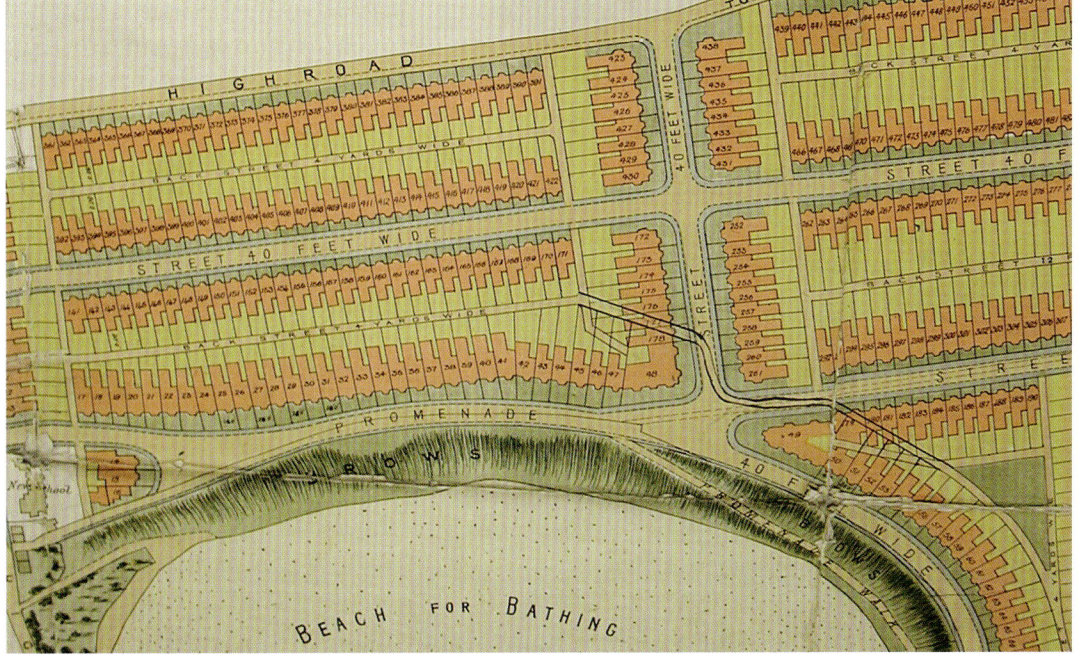

Figure 25a – Approved elevations for the Promenade. (MNHL Registered Deeds June 1888 114)

Figure 25b – Original layout plan for the Promenade and backland (MNHL Registered Deeds June 1888 115)
Additional reference for standard printed conveyance. (MNHL Registered Deeds November 1888, 165)

By 1888 there were plenty of Manx precedents for the development of seafront terraces to cater for visitors. The earliest, at Strathallan Crescent at the north end of Douglas Bay was built by the 4th Duke of Atholl in the early 1820s; single family houses intended for occupation by middle or upper-class visitors who were expected to take them for a whole season. The *sine qua non* of Manx Victorian tourist development, Loch Parade, came fifty years later at the initiative of Governor Loch and under the hands of the Douglas New Street Board. Requiring reclamation of land from the seashore and tied into an improved street network by means of an extensive programme of compulsory purchase and reconstruction, the Douglas scheme was by no means straightforward.

Ramsey Commissioners also had also been through a long campaign of legislation and land acquisition before the designation of numerous plots on the Mooragh Estate.[70] These had been put up for auction the year before following the formal opening of the Promenade by Governor Walpole. Practical and legal problems still lay ahead, mostly owing to the difficulty of bridging Ramsey harbour. Neither Loch Parade nor the North Promenade at Ramsey enjoyed the benevolent southern exposure nor sheltered archetypical seaside cove ambience which was readily available at Port St Mary. The take up might up have been limited but it was sufficient to ensure a respectable show on the seafront and the houses have remained in strong demand down to the present.

Not only was the site naturally favoured, and ready to build without the immediate need for retaining walls and reclamation works, the other aspects of servicing which were by the 1880s requirements, had been taken care of by other individuals or organisations which had sprung up in the recent past. These included the Rushen Waterworks Company and the relatively new board of village commissioners. The development itself was professionally designed and laid out; conveyances were ready printed and only needed the identity of the purchaser to be added. The house fronts along the terrace had to be constructed in line with the approved design.

Figure 26: Houses at Gansey one of which shows the characteristic profile of an 18th century dwelling. The Taylor family lived here for many years and became involved in litigation with George Cary who had attempted to prevent them making use of the new promenade roadway. (Postcard courtesy of MNH Ref MS 8348)

One drawback which the developer, George Cary, encountered stemmed from the continued presence of a scatter of modest homes between his building development and Rhenwyllan. Clearly the residents there needed access to their houses. While in the18th century, supplies could probably arrive on the back of a packhorse, lifestyles were becoming more sophisticated and by the late 19th century, deliveries of coal and bread were being made by tradesmen's carts. At the time of the auction in 1858, a right of way from the vicinity of Chapel Gate round Gansey Point to Rhenwyllan was flagged up in the presence of all bidders. In the late 1860s, however, high tides in two successive years rendered the road in the direction of the Smelt effectively impassable. The sometimes disagreeable Mr Cary instigated litigation in 1888 against a well-known resident, Peter Taylor, claiming damages for breaking down his gate and smashing the lock.[71] The defendant made no objection to the action being tried by Deemster Sir William Drinkwater despite his family connection to the plaintiff. Various members of the Taylor family and their neighbours turned out to give evidence. Peter Taylor, who had spent most of his life at the point, explained that there were five houses at Gansey, four of them being in one group. His brother, Thomas, whose memory of the area stretched back fifty years had heard the old people saying that it was once the road from Castletown to Port St Mary. Henry Kelly of Ballaqueeney referred to his use of the road for fetching sea wrack over a period of thirty-three to thirty-five years. His mother, (who would have been ninety-five years of age had she still been living) was brought up at Rhenwyllan and in fact owned that property. He had heard her say "it was the old public road from Castletown to Port St Mary and it was always an open road". Peter Taylor had heard reference to the old road as a route to St Mary's Chapel.

The jury found the road to be a public one for carts, horses and foot passengers and the Deemster awarded costs against his relation.

Around 1860 when Woods's Atlas was prepared, a Peter Taylor Snr (died 1877)[72] owned a very small parcel of Ballavrara. His name also appeared earlier (c. 1840) as an adjoining owner on the tithe map of Rhenwyllan (See Fig 8). Peter Taylor Jnr (died 1911) also owned a plot on Rhenwyllan in 1860. Peter S. Taylor (died 1966), born in the former family home, retired from Liverpool around 1960 to live in Gansey Point Cottage. Mr Taylor remembered the days before piped water was supplied to the area when there was a well outside the sea wall. This had to be cleaned out after high tides. Meanwhile in around 1918, the former family home and adjoining buildings had been converted into Gansey Point House by the late Jonathan Royston, later passing through the hands of Dr Henry Cubbon, and Anthony and Belle Hyde.

This chapter has to be concluded without dealing in detail with each road and street, let alone every building of interest, although more information is provided in Chapter 8, which looks at the names of the streets and roads of Port St Mary. It is hoped, though, that enough has been written to demonstrate the range of circumstances surrounding the origins of the roadways in and around Port St Mary. Achieving an understanding of such roads or routes is a useful first step in more wide-ranging analysis of both townscapes or rural landscapes which will continue to be topics of interest and the subject of further research and writing.

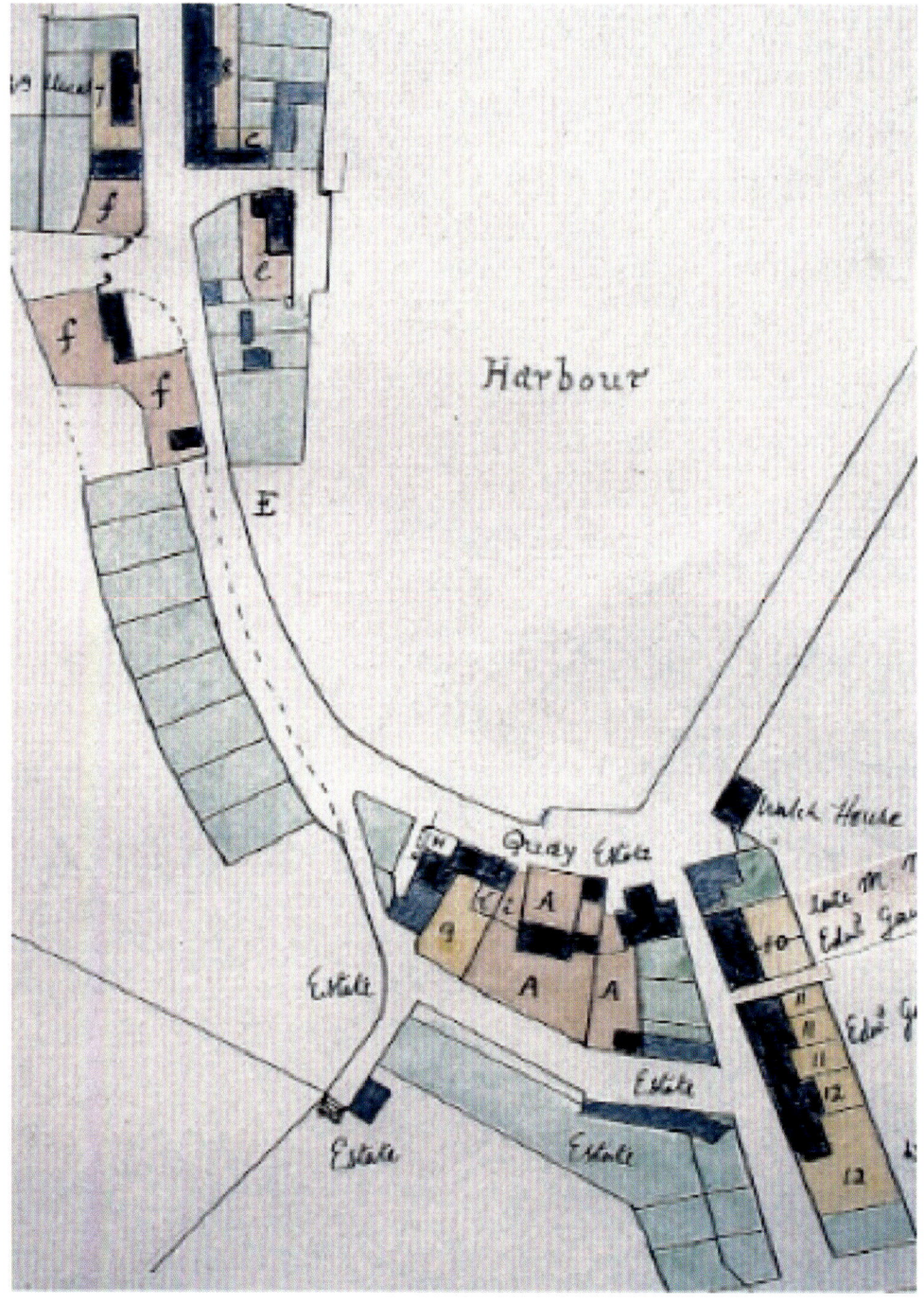

Figure 1: Part of plan of Port St Mary belonging to his Grace, the Duke of Atholl, by J. Taggart Douglas, June 1827.

Farming Purt Le Moirrey Style

CHAPTER 3

CATHERINE CLUCAS

At one time, Port St Mary was a combination of wide-open expanses and smaller enclosures on the surrounding uplands, within this landscape farm sites developed where conditions were suitable. Smaller dwellings sprouted along the sheltered natural cliff and shore lines on the edge of the arable land of the Port. The position of the Port, buildings and farms reflects the symbiotic interrelationship between the sea, the land and the people over thousands of years.

The boundaries of the village have changed, not just physically on the ground, but have expanded and adapted to the Port's changing functions, these are: as a rateable commodity for its services, amenities, electoral, civic, ecclesiastical and postal boundaries. All the farms within the Port St Mary area have had their location, size and layout determined by factors such as contour, access to fresh water, sunlight, shore, roads and rights of way, soils and drainage.

The farms around the Port can be roughly categorised into two main types, upland and lowland; the upland smaller farms being Fistard, Glen Chass, Corvalley (the Howe), Glendown; and the lowland farms being Port St Mary, Ballacreggan, Ballaqueeney, Gansey and Ballakilley. Over time each farm developed its own distinct individual character, and the farming methods used evolved to make the best use of the land they sat on and thus through time the farms have changed, keeping in step with those within farming and society.

The Island's landholdings has its own unique pattern of scattered settlements rather than a village focus, mixed farming was employed with a preference for cattle rearing.[1] There are suggestions that the narrower land divisions indicate there were earlier commonly farmed strips[2] by tenants suggesting similar to the runrig system found in Scotland. The earliest documented records of landholding are commonly known as the Manorial Rolls. They are made up of *Libri Assedationis* (Setting books) dating from 1507–1911 they show the rents paid by tenants to the Lord of Mann; *Libri Vastarum* (Wast books) dating 1511–1916 they show changes of tenancy.[3] Rents and changes were witnessed and noted down at half yearly courts, over time the system changed, due to the impact of changes from acts and legislation relating to landholding, for example the Act of Settlement 1703 often referred to as the Manx Magna Carta.[4] Barony records are also important historical land records; a fifth of the Island was administered differently and these lands were under the ownership of various religious houses. Any land changes were recorded by Baronial Courts and noted in *Libri Monasteriorum* (Abbey books).[5] Deeds prior to 1690 were deposited or noted in the *Libri Cancellarii* (Chancery Court book) and occasionally within other Manorial Rolls.

Taxes known as tithes were collected from tenants and owners by the Lord of Mann and the Church, a percentage was taken from any, crops, fish, stock, wool or anything produced by the people. There were also expectations to contribute a work tithe for the Lord and the Church, providing agricultural labour and other duties. There were areas that were part of the Lord's Forest known as common lands animals were grazed on these usually upland areas in the summer months whilst crops grew in the lower fields. Much of the marginal land was known as intack land, waste land that had been granted permission by the Lord of Mann to be enclosed and cultivated. Intacks have usually smaller fields often found on the slopes of hills, near rivers and marshy areas, many smaller farms or crofts were to be found in such areas. A Croft being a smallholding not entirely dependant on the land but also on fishing and other trades, such as weaving, spinning, cobbler etc. Often people living on crofts could get seasonal work labouring on larger farms at busier times such as harvest. There were also landless itinerant workers that moved from farm to farm, usually sleeping in the barns where they were working at the time as casual labour. Fish was a major source of protein over the scarce winter months, many of the men on the smaller landholdings and crofts were away at sea for long periods of time. This left the women and those either too old to too young to work away at sea to manage the land, animals, prepare for the winter and cope with any emergencies.

Many of the developments within agricultural on the Island are reflected within the history and people connected to the farms of the Port within this chapter. For example, in the late 18th to early 19th centuries cheaper farms tempted many English and Scottish farmers to the Island. Some were also tempted by the business opportunities for the increased demand to supply goods for rapidly developing major ports such as Liverpool and in the industrial towns of North West England. Improved sea links to export livestock and crops in conjunction with better links via canals and rail to inland towns made it possible to supply these markets. Many retired military officers and their families settled and farmed on the Island, many officers were on half pensions, on the Island their pensions stretched a lot further.[6] Many were interested in farming employing the very latest in agricultural methods and technology. Occasionally due to over investment in their farms, their money did not stretch far enough and as a result some of the gentlemen farmers ended up in debt and lost their farms. The development of agriculture and tourism are often intertwined throughout the Island on many levels which can be seen in the rapid expansion of the Port in the late 19th century.

Port St Mary Farm

Port St Mary was regarded by many of its older natives as only referring to the lower part of the Port, that is up to an old land boundary around the area where the Garden of Remembrance is today. Port St Mary was a quarterland[7] farm originally of around 100 acres within the treen of Fyshgarth.[8] Bounded on the west by the upland hamlet of Fistard and to the north boundary with the abbeyland known as Ballavrara,[9] an area of land in the past that belonged to the Cistercian Church of Rushen Abbey in the parish of Malew.

There has been documented evidence of farmland in Port St Mary since the early 1500s.[10] The family linked to the land was named as McLucas, through land deeds and family history records there is evidence that suggests the Clucas family were continuously associated with Port St Mary Farm up until the 19th century.

In 1822 John Clucas[11] sold 'Port le Mary Mansion House, houses, offices and buildings' and other houses clustered around the harbour and easterly seashore[12] to John Murray, 4th Duke of Atholl.[13] In 1827 the Duke had a map drawn up of his recently acquired estate of Port St Mary by the surveyor John Taggart.[14] The plan shows some proposed building plots and roads over some of the estate. Three years later the Duke and his wife[15] had to sell the farm and other estates to James Holmes the banker. The Duke had borrowed money from Holmes Bank to finance his property speculations on the Island.[16] Figure 1 shows Taggart's 1827 plan.

By 1836 it was noted, during a tour of the Island by John Welch, that 'the whole of Port le Mary with the exception of one house, belongs to James Holmes, Esq. banker'.[17] Whilst under the ownership of Holmes, Thomas Clucas had the tenancy for the farm during the 1820s till mid 1830s while Thomas and John Clucas were also involved in the burning and exporting of lime from the nearby quarry.[18]

By 1835 the tenancy of the farm had changed hands to newlyweds William and Isabella Jefferson[19] from Ballahott Farm, Malew. William was a son of the farmer and limeburner Thomas Jefferson,[20] whose father's business prowess had caused a bit of a stir in 1827 by having a suit issued against him by the 4th Duke of Atholl for extracting and quarrying lime from under his land at Ballahott without a licence. The Jeffersons ran the farm, extracting and burning limestone as well as maintaining close involvement with the church, charities in the Port and the Island's agricultural societies. Judging by the media of the day Port St Mary Farm had a good reputation for modern farming methods with newsworthy results – '20lb swedes' and 'carcass of sheep fed by Mr Jefferson 33 lbs per quarter'.[21] William had ceased working the lime kilns by 1850 and not long after returned to Ballahott Farm.[22] It was said that most of the houses along Lime Street were lived in by the men and the families of those employed by Jefferson on the quarry and limekilns.[23]

Every autumn the Manx newspapers ran numerous adverts for farm and fields for letting, end of tenancy sales of stock, crops, and implements. Farm tenancies seem to have been an almost nomadic life for the tenant farmers and their families, having to sell 'your hard work' and move on and start again on a new farm. It was the custom on the Island that farm tenancies changed on the 12th November, known as a quarter day, there were also hiring fairs for male servants and markets, often associated with Hollantide, which also falls on the day after the Old Hop Tu Naa.[24]

John Kermode from Ballagale, Rushen[25] had not long started his tenancy at Port St Mary Farm in 1852 when disaster hit the Port. On the morning of 29th December, thirty men from Port St Mary and its surrounds were salvaging cargo from a brig wrecked on the small islet of Kitterland. Twenty-nine of the men were killed instantly when the wreck exploded.[26] John Kermode was remembered for many long years later in the Port for his kindness and the practical support he gave the widows and orphans in the early days after the disaster, providing food and acting as a champion for their fundraising campaign. During Kermode's tenancy Port St Mary estate's owner James Holmes died in the following October,[27] Holmes's death marked the beginning of a lengthy and complex liquidation of his assets[28] and changes to the estate. Port St Mary Farm was 'lot 1' at a public auction held at the 'Port-Le-Murray Hotel' at midday on Thursday 16th February 1858 – figure 2 shows details of the lot, and figure 3 the accompanying plan (with additional field names and other details). Many of the other lots of the Port were advertised as prime building plots of interest to capitalists.

The farm was bought by Captain Peter Petrie,[29] a retired naval officer, with the sale administered by Samuel Harris on behalf of the estate of the late James Holmes in March 1858.[30] In the following months Captain Petrie purchased other lands, dwellings and

Figure 2 (right): Lot 1 as advertised in the Manx Sun November 07 1857.

Figure 3 (below): Plan A. Plan of Port St Mary Farm, Rushen 1857 with later super-imposed field names and other features.

LOT 1.—All and Singular, that capital ESTATE and those LANDS and PREMISES, situate in the parish of Rushen called PORT LE MURRAY FARM, including the Mansion House, Out-offices, and Buildings, and twelve COTTAGES, together with Lace's Rope-walk, House, and Premises, containing 96 Acres or thereabouts, the whole being now under lease to JOHN KERMODE, at the clear yearly rent of £200, payable on the 12th November in each and every year; nine years of the said lease, from the 12th Nov. instant, being unexpired.

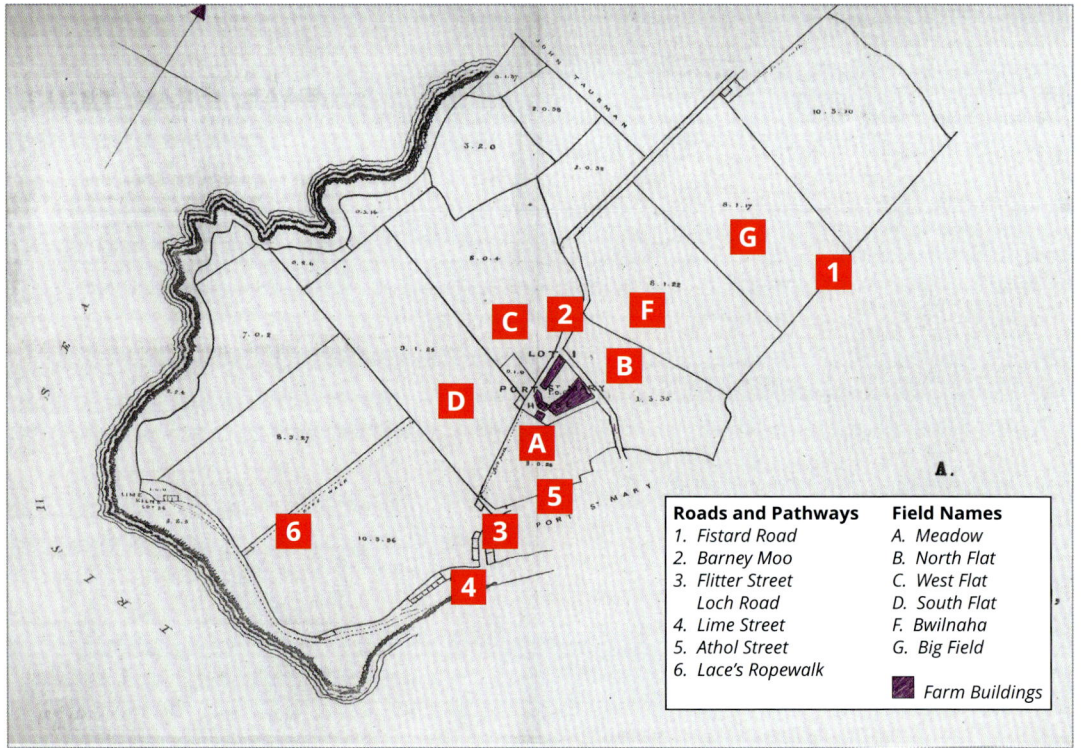

Roads and Pathways	Field Names
1. Fistard Road	A. Meadow
2. Barney Moo	B. North Flat
3. Flitter Street	C. West Flat
Loch Road	D. South Flat
4. Lime Street	F. Bwilnaha
5. Athol Street	G. Big Field
6. Lace's Ropewalk	
	▨ Farm Buildings

estates near the Port[31] – 'Ballacreggan Farm, Rhen Wyllan and the Smelt'.[32] Under his ownership, plots of land and estate dwellings were sold on and crumbs of the estates built on, re-sold or mortgaged. Parts of Port St Mary Farm and the adjoining Ballacreggan and Ballavrara estates started to look how they are today, reflecting the complex relationships of land use and ownership and mixed with the occasional oases of freehold within and next to the estates.

November 1866 saw the end of John Kermode's fourteen-year tenancy during which time nine children had been born and reared,[33] two wives buried – Catherine in 1857,[34] Caroline in 1860,[35] and a third marriage in 1865.[36] His stock and implements were advertised for sale as he was giving up farming and moving to Ballagale, Rushen. Thirty years later he was called upon to give evidence over a rights of way dispute on Port St Mary Farm in July 1896[37] due to his personal knowledge of the farm and of having a reputed good memory.

Kermode recalled that he thought David Petrie (Captain Petrie's son) had run Port St Mary Farm for a few years after Captain Petrie had bought the estate.[38] David had also run Ballacreggan Farm since late 1862 after his older brother, Walter, who had farmed Ballacreggan since 1858, died unexpectedly.[39] Captain Petrie and his remaining family moved to Port St Mary during the 1860s and the Captain died at Port St Mary House in October 1870. His widow, married daughters and grandchildren were still living there during the 1871 census.[40] In the same census David had moved from Port St Mary to Peel with his wife and young family, having the year before his father's death sold all the crops for both farms, that being '60 acres of wheat, 30 acres of barley and 10 acres of beans'.[41] In June 1864 Captain Petrie and wife had made a deed of bond and security with John Blyth of all their lands in Rushen, and in January 1871[43] the will of Captain Petrie named both sons-in-law John and James Blyth[42] as the trustees. In the Chancery and Exchequer Courts at Castletown on 7th December 1871 John Blyth was the petitioner of 'an execution against David Petrie for £400 who had refused to pay it and had since left the Island',[44] with the Coroner granted permission to proceed.[45] Figure 4 shows an advert that appeared in all the Manx newspapers from November 1872 until May 1873 for a Coroners sale of David Petrie's right, title and interest in all the lands owned by his father in Rushen.

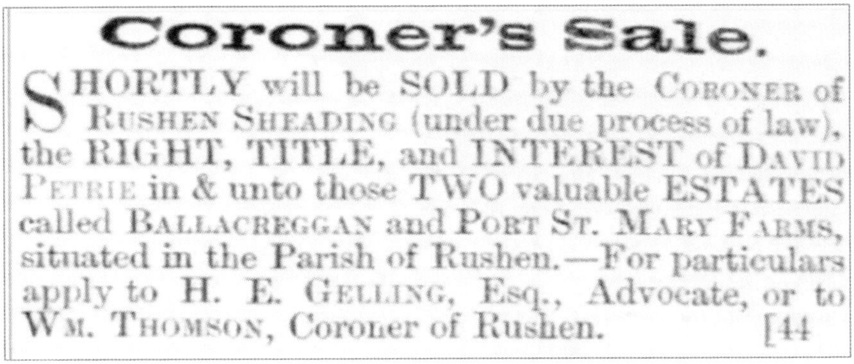

Coroner's Sale.

SHORTLY will be SOLD by the CORONER of RUSHEN SHEADING (under due process of law), the RIGHT, TITLE, and INTEREST of DAVID PETRIE in & unto those TWO valuable ESTATES called BALLACREGGAN and PORT ST. MARY FARMS, situated in the Parish of Rushen.—For particulars apply to H. E. GELLING, Esq., Advocate, or to WM. THOMSON, Coroner of Rushen. [44

Figure 4: Advert that appeared in the Manx Press in 1872 to 1873.

Ballacreggan exchanged hands many times over a short period, all the sellers and buyers were interrelated as illustrated below in a short timeline.

1864 Captain Petrie and wife made a deed of bond and security with John Blyth[46] of all their lands in Rushen.

1866 James Blyth signed as a witness on the will of Sir James Young Simpson (Alexander M.R. Simpson's father[47]). Sir James Young Simpson was also the uncle of David Petrie and Mrs John Blyth (Margaret Petrie), James Blyth's sister-in-law and Mrs James Blyth (Elizabeth Petrie) James Blyth's wife.

Nov 1874 Alexander M.R. Simpson buys Ballacreggan and Port St Mary farm (he is a 1st cousin to David Petrie, Mrs John Blyth and Mrs James Blyth).[48]

Jan 1875 Alexander sells to John Blyth (married to David Petrie's sister Margaret).[49]

Within this unsettled period a new tenant, David Patterson, was shipped in to Ballacreggan Farm from Scotland. He farmed for just one year and by October 1873 the Manx papers were reporting that his stock and equipment were up for sale as he was leaving the Island.[50]

By 1874 John Blyth was the new owner of Port St Mary Farm, Ballacreggan, Renwyllan and the Smelt. He and James Blyth were the sons of John Blyth,[51] a Scottish farmer who had come to the Island in the late 1830s, settling at Ronaldsway House, Malew. John Junior took over the 400-acre family farm in 1839 after his father died. John married Margaret Grindley Petrie at Patrick Church in 1850,[52] while James bought and farmed Glentraugh, Santon in 1857, a few years later he too married into the Petrie family, Elizabeth Robertson Petrie in 1860 at Braddan.[53] John increased his monopoly on the land around Port St Mary by purchasing parts of Fistard in 1876, in that same year William Kneen commenced his twenty-year plus tenancy of Ballacreggan Farm. By the mid-1870s Edmund Carine commenced his tenancy of Port St Mary Farm, with regular morsels of news appearing in the newspapers about the farm, such as dates of threshing corn, cutting hay and the like. There were some snippets of information that help give a slight sense of who the Carine's were, in 1880, two of Edmund Carine's children marry,[54] details of their shares in the local banks, public duties and Edmund's death in May 1887.[55]

On his father's death, William, the eldest son, had the intention to continue the tenancy until it expired in November 1890.[56]

By 1887 Port St Mary Farm and estate was up for sale again, following the death of James Blyth in 1886, his brother John having died eight years earlier. Adverts in the local press started to appear from August 1887: 'Mr Thomson is instructed by R. Nimmo and W.F. Dickinson Esqs, executors and trustees of the estate of the late James Blythe to sell by auction on Thursday 25th August'.[57] The advert was pitched at speculators, builders and captalists focusing on the Port's potential as a holiday resort with easy access by sea and rail. The pitch worked – in an exciting auction, Port St Mary Farm Estate was bought by a Mr. Sparrow of Manchester, a member of a syndicate of businessmen, for £8,010.[58] There was plenty of local speculation as to who the business syndicate were. The *Mona's*

Herald appeared to have insider information on the synicate's intention: 'The estate will immediately be laid out in building plots, and we have no hesitation in saying that a more eligible property for the purpose is not to be found on the Island'.[59] The Port St Mary Estate Company Limited, was formed in 1887, the company began the laying out of roads, building plots, tennis courts and other leisure amenities from late 1887. During the works there were some antiquarian surprises found near the farmhouse; arrowheads, flint scatters and stone coffins, in close proximity to an earlier discovery in 1882 of an 'ancient' coffin.[60] Later in 1889 Park Road was created through the North Flat field to join with the Old Fistard Road, Queens and Clifton roads, a house[61] had been demolished to cut through the back of the High Street. This is between where the Old Bank (Capital House) and number 33 the High Street currently are.[62]

November 1888 saw the commencement of Thomas Clague Junior's 'tenancy' of the farm. According to a newspaper article in 1937 Thomas said he only actually lived in the farmhouse for three years because of 'the ghost and supernatural happenings', which, Thomas said, made it 'unliveable to live in'.[63] Thomas and his young family were living there at the time of 1901 Census, with farm workers living in two adjacent cottagers – yardman Henry Nelson and horseman Joseph Crellin, with their families.[64] By November 1902, Thomas was giving up the farm, with a sale of 'live and dead stock, crop and farming effects' advertised in the local press. Mr and Mrs Clague Senior lived in Athol Street, a short walk away from the farmyard, their house backed onto Paddock Lane, the ex-holding area for stock and an abattoir, can still be seen in 2019.[65] Both Thomas Clague Junior and Senior wore many hats: farmers, butchers, hoteliers, village commissioners, members of numerous boards and committees, and enthusiastic entrepreneurs.[66] The Clague family had interests in hotels, farms and lands in Port Erin, Port St Mary, Fistard and the Calf of Man. Thomas Clague senior had also been a chairman and director of the Port St Mary Estate Company Limited.[67]

From the late 1800s up to WWI many Manx farmers were also hoteliers, or their close relatives- they had the land on which to build hotels and supply food to the hordes of holidaymakers that came to the Isle of Man during wake weeks from the industrial north western English mill towns.[68]

From Hollantide 1903, William and Catherine Taylor[69] took up the tenancy and quickly settled into the social fabric of the Port, Mrs Taylor putting on 'a good spread' at a Primitive Methodist church social at Mount Tabor.[70] During their nine years running the farm they had five[71] daughters, and that number seemed to have been a theme for the Taylor family, in April 1909 it was reported in the Manx newspapers that one of their ewes had given birth to five lambs. Later in the same year, it was noted in the local press that the owner of the farm, E.F. Qualtrough, had plans approved for the construction of a new shed. At harvest time of the same year, tragedy struck; while William and two farm labourers were building a barley stack, a labourer fell from the top. Thomas Cannell was conveyed to Noble's Hospital by train with a broken spine and died from his injuries.[72] The Taylors' tenancy expired in 1912, they moved on to Church Farm, Malew, where they farmed up until their retirement in 1930.

At the start of the Taylors' tenancy the farm was still under the ownership of the Port St Mary Estate Company, sales had been slower than expected on the building plots, with various schemes introduced to encourage more sales and visitors. The company had asked Dr Alfred Haviland to produce a pamphlet exalting the virtues of Port St Mary as a health resort and place of great natural beauty and interest,[73] and to hopefully encourage the sale of the remaining plots. Possibly due to the climate of economic uncertainty at that time on the Island, the decision was made by the directors in June 1904 to liquidate the company. The estate was sold to Edward Clague on 23rd November 1904, who then sold it to Edward Qualtrough in December of the same year.[74]

William Faragher was the next tenant from November 1912, having moved down to Port St Mary Farm from the hill farm of Balnahowe, Rushen where he had farmed since 1900. While in his twenties and thirties, William had worked as a fisherman, living in the Ballafessson and Surby area of Rushen.[75] By 1912 he had an eighteen-strong dairy shorthorn herd, as well as growing wheat, barley, oats, potatoes and turnip. Farms still needed a good-sized workforce in those days, as much work was labour intensive and most machinery used was still horse powered. When WWI broke out in August 1914 soon after a few of his agricultural labourers joined up to do their duty, by 1916 he was in the exemption tribunals to argue the case for his grandson, aged nineteen, to stay and work the farm with him.

William gave evidence and told the tribunal the only workforce he had to help him was 'his 71-year-old wife, son, grandson and youngest daughter', the tribunal ruled that his grandson could stay.[76] His appeal had caused much amusement at the tribunal when it was suggested he should get more women to help him instead. Four Faragher sons were in the Isle of Man Constabulary, with William Faragher Junior stationed at Port St Mary Police Station during WWI. Edward, the son working the farm, had served in the Liverpool Police force prior to WWI. By 1922 William was 'declining from farming' according to adverts for a crop, stock and implement sale. Edward appeared to have been still working on the farm until 1924, Edward latterly farmed at Southampton Farm, Santon until his death in 1947.[77]

Edward Fleming Qualtrough was the son of Edwin Qualtrough and Mary Ann Fleming of Point House, Port St Mary. An ex-King William's College pupil and banking assistant, from 1915 Edward was commissioned as a 2nd Lieutenant in the Princess Victoria's Royal Irish Fusiliers, returning home to the Port in the 1920s to run the farm estate.[78] Edward had a dairy herd as there was an advert for milk for sale from the farm.[79] Edward was also a member of Port St Mary Commissioners from 1923 until his retirement from the board in 1931, when he commenced training as a barrister, by 1940 he had been appointed a high-ranking position in the legislator and magistrate of Gambia. On his return to the Island in the 1940s he farmed Ballagick, Santon.[80]

The field previously known as the North Flatt had been cut through in 1889 to create Park Road, and c1920 the commissioners decided this was a good location for working families to live.[81] Land was bought from the executors and trustees of the farm estate, who in addition gave the land at the rear of the plot for free for a lane and side pathway (where the post-box on Park Road is now). The social housing was built by

Figure 5 – Three photographs of the fields around Port St Mary Farm taken in the early 1920s, when the Faraghers were farming. (Source: Taylor Family Private Collection)

local builder Henry Collister and designed by architect Mr. Du Kay. The first phase were numbers 11 to 16 Park Road and the second phase in 1929 saw a further ten houses added. 1929 seems to have been a time of significant change to Port St Mary Farm, with an advert appearing for 'an unreserved sale of valuable farm stock' on the 14th November, stating 'Mr. E. F. Qualtrough is declining farming and letting the estate'. The advert included a comprehensive list of stock, crops and implements, and other adverts followed for the letting of fields for cutting and grazing.[82] Two years later saw the complete urbanisation of the farmyard site, when Edward submitted plans for the conversion of a stable into a dwelling, followed in 1932 by the erection of a garage, construction of two new dwellings and a bungalow,[83] by 1934 a freehold building on Port St Mary Farm was offered for sale.[84]

The 1930s saw a serious depression within Manx agriculture, a time when many farms went under or were amalgamated into bigger farms. It was during this depression that the Manx Government bought land as it came up for sale as investment for the future.[85] In 1934 the nine-hole golf course on the Ballacreggan Farm Estate closed. However, the Commissioners felt that a golf course was an asset to the village[86] and Port St Mary Farm Estate was suggested as the new venue, with ratepayers asked to vote on the proposal – 90% of the residents voted, with 299 in favour.[87] An application was made to the Local Government Board for £5,500 to buy the 68-acre estate and additional expenses to create the course.[88] In 1936 a special bill was passed through Tynwald so the Commissioners could run the golf course to create income for the Port, the new nine-hole course was opened on June 3rd.[89]

When the Commissioners had bought the farm estate they had a proviso that they could sell building plots and increase public sector housing also. During the 1940s there was a housing shortage on the Island, in response to local demand, the Commissioners felt more housing needed to be built. Queens Road housing scheme was officially opened on 13th April 1948 and the first tenants moved into Seafield Avenue, by 1950 St Mary's Avenue was also built. Prior to the building of the avenues, the field had been subdivided into garden allotments. During WWII the golf course, out of necessity, was put under the plough again, with as much land as possible needed to be cultivated to meet the demand for food created by the increased population of the Port, that being internees and military personnel.

Figure 6: Port St Mary Farmhouse, Queens Road. (photo source: Costain-Richards private collection)

The 1930s is the point the farmhouse became 'The Old Farmhouse' and passed from being a functioning farmstead to a house. On 15th October 1935 Willie and Rhoda Clucas's daughter, Edna, married Thomas Collister – Figure 6 shows their marriage party outside the farmhouse, the photograph provided by Maureen Costain-Richards, Willie and Rhoda Clucas were her maternal grandparents. Willie Clucas had been a sailmaker in the Port, son of John Clucas, sailmaker, and Eliza Coffey.[90] The Clucases had lived at the Old Farmhouse from sometime prior to 1935 to the early 1960s.

The next residents were Bob Faulkner and family – Bob ran the popular Port St Mary café Smokey Joe's, later his daughter Maureen, with husband Jacques Gueudre and family, lived there through to the end of this small snapshot of the history of the farm.[91]

Ballacreggan and Ballavrara
The southern boundary of the abbeyland Ballavrara was in the region of the current Garden of Remembrance, on the east by the sea and brows, the west by the slope of Cronk Skibblyt and to the north bounded by Ballacreggan quarterland farm and treen boundary of Gleton.[92] Within the area known as Ballavrara there had been remains of a keeill and burial ground; nowadays on some modern maps the area is known as Chapel Gate and is almost entirely built over today. Sometime in the 1800s Ballavrara became integrated into the Ballacreggan Estate but was still distinguished as different, referred to as Ballavrara orally, on documentation, and on plans. Part of the treen of Gleton includes a narrow strip of land that leads to a past area of common pasture on the slopes of Meayll Hill.[93]

Ballacreggan, in documentary evidence from the early 18th century, within Rushen burial records in 1732 names a Daniel Callister of Ballacreggan.[94] It is not clear if the Callisters lived on the current location of Ballacreggan Farm or possibly within the earlier farm buildings as shown in photographs figure 9. It is believed from various sources that earlier farm buildings were changed when the farm buildings were 'modernised' in the early 1800s, some of the buildings belonging to the farm were knocked down to widen the road. The 4th Duke of Atholl owned the estate and he sold Ballacreggan along with Port St Mary Farm to James Holmes (mentioned earlier in this chapter). Whilst Holmes owned the farm, his steward was John Kelly, reputed to have fed the 'largest ox ever reared on the Island, weighing 1,888lbs'.[95] Ballacreggan was a model farm highly esteemed on the Island for its 'superior system of cultivation'. The farm was often exalted: 'There is now to be seen upon Ballacreggan a field of fine barley in ear being the earliest we have heard of so forward in the Island'.[96] The cattle reared on Ballacreggan by John Kelly were exported to the Liverpool markets for reportedly good prices, the Kelly family had left the farm by the late 1850s and went to new pastures in New Zealand. Ballacreggan went through a time of frequent change from 1858, farmed by Walter Petrie till his death in 1862, taken over by his younger brother, David, until 1870, and Scottish tenant farmer David Patterson 1872–1873.

William Kneen Senior had worked on Ballacreggan years earlier for Walter Petrie as his farm steward, he taken over the tenancy by 1874 while under the ownership of John Blyth of Ronaldsway Farm.[97] William had a good reputation as a stockman; his

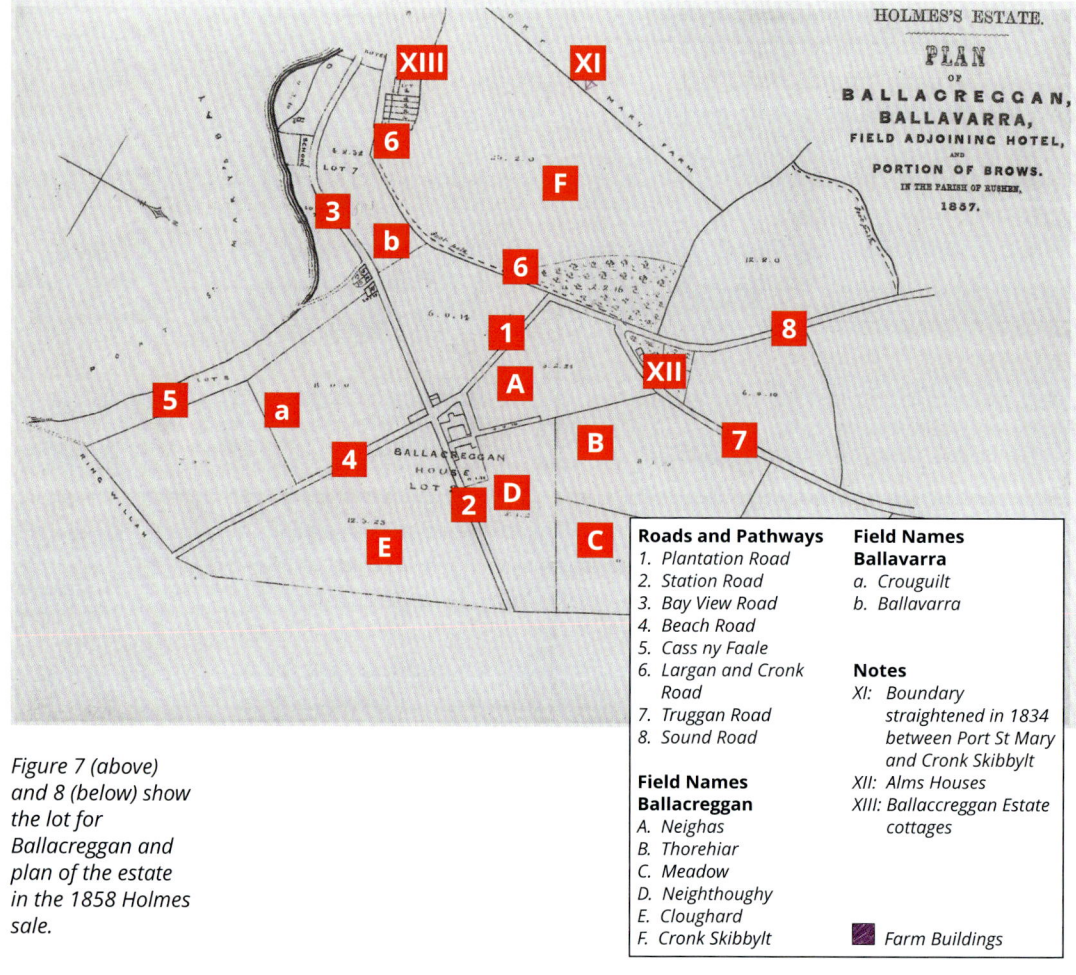

*Figure 7 (above)
and 8 (below) show
the lot for
Ballacreggan and
plan of the estate
in the 1858 Holmes
sale.*

Roads and Pathways
1. Plantation Road
2. Station Road
3. Bay View Road
4. Beach Road
5. Cass ny Faale
6. Largan and Cronk
   Road
7. Truggan Road
8. Sound Road

**Field Names
Ballacreggan**
A. Neighas
B. Thorehiar
C. Meadow
D. Neighthoughy
E. Cloughard
F. Cronk Skibbylt

**Field Names
Ballavarra**
a. Crouguilt
b. Ballavarra

Notes
XI: Boundary
    straightened in 1834
    between Port St Mary
    and Cronk Skibbylt
XII: Alms Houses
XIII: Ballaccreggan Estate
     cottages

Farm Buildings

reserving Footpath along the upper Fence of Field called "Cronk Skibbatt," also a Footpath from the public Road leading from Port St. Mary Farm-house to the Rope-walk, as marked on Plan A.

LOT 2.—PLAN B.

All and singular, the Estate of Ballacreggan and part of the Estate of Ballavarra,

Situate in the said parish, and adjoining the Estate of Port-le-Murray, and containing 120 acres or thereabouts, with Mansion House, Stables, Coach-houses, Cow-houses, Cart-sheds, Thrashing Mill, Barn, Farm-yard, Out-offices, and Premises thereto belonging, including two Labourers' Cottages, situate near the said dwelling house, one Dwelling House and Premises on the opposite side of the public road, a large Cattle-shed with Loft above, in front of the said last mentioned dwelling house, and five small Thatched Cottages, and the ruins of a Cottage, Gardens, and Premises, erected on the road above the hotel, subject to the life estate of William Kegg and Margaret his wife, both aged 74 or thereabouts, Elizabeth Collister, aged 70 or thereabouts, Thomas Collister and Ann his wife, aged 74 or thereabouts, and also a Ground Rent of 10s. each per year, payable out of three of the said cottages during the respective lives of the said tenants, together with the Plantations on the said Estate, and that portion of the Brows (subject to right of Cart road on the top of Brows, from main highroad to and from Ring Willan) lying between Cronguilt and the sea, to the road leading from the Chapel gate to the Sea Shore, reserving Footpaths as marked upon Plan B. Possession of Lands and Farm Houses on payment of Purchase Money.

name appeared frequently in Isle of Man Agricultural Society shows for winning prizes and highly commended.[98] 'Ballacraggan, Ring Willan and the Smelt estates' were taken over by James Blyth,[99] on James's death the estate and other lands were put up for auction by his trustees on the 26th August 1886. A description of the auction appears a few days later: 'At the sale on Thursday, there was an immense gathering of capitalists and others, including several English gentlemen who came across with the intention of investing their capital. Lot 4 comprised of lot 1 and 2 as a whole, and brought out a few good competitors. Mr. Kneen the tenant offered £9,000, he was quickly followed by Mr Cary with £9,250, Mr E. Qualtrough then bid £9,500.' The bidding continued between Qualtrough and Cary to a final total of £11,800, being sold to Mr. George Cary of the Calf of Man.[100]

George Drinkwater Lucius Cary had returned to the Island with his wife Sarah Ann to farm on the Calf of Man after a short time working as a barrister in London.[101] The year after the auction, Cary had plans drawn up by George Kay, architect and surveyor, for the Ballacreggan Estate that showed a promenade, roads and building plots marked out. Some plots were purchased at an auction in 1887, with Cary giving a complimentary dinner for the buyers who were mainly from the Port, it was during after dinner speeches he complimented the locals for 'showing an amazing amount of pluck in this little village'.[102] Edward Qualtrough (who had been his main rival at the auction in 1886) said about Cary's development was 'an enterprise such as his was wanted for many years past, and now they had obtained the land to build on. He hopes they would try and push the place as much as possible'.[103]

Cary was well-known and liked for his kindness, he gave a complimentary dinner for all the twenty workmen building the houses. He owned large tracts of land throughout the Island and was one of the first landlords to reduce the rents during the agricultural depression, and provided 'proper' farmsteads for his tenants.[104] At some point before his sudden death in June 1900 Cary had given the Brows on Port St Mary Promenade and Gansey Point for free enjoyment of the public, it was common knowledge he had intended when the lease was up on Ballacreggan Farm to hand over the Cronk for the purpose of a park.[105] Cary's sudden death must have been quite a blow for the Port, closely followed by the death of his father Colonel Cary. This left the Cary estate in an unusual position as the heir had predeceased the father. George's brother, William Leece Drinkwater Cary, as the now heir-in-law, inherited his father's and brother's combined estates, Sarah Anne Cary became a devisee. At the time of their deaths William lived in America and the press sensationalised his windfall.[106] Sarah Anne continued to sell plots on the estate after her husband's death,[107] she remained on the Island during the 1901 census living near William and his eldest daughter, Eva.[108]

William Kneen, of Ballacreggan, had available capital for offering sizable bids at the auction for the estate in 1886; previously in 1879 he had purchased a dwelling in Arbory Road, Castletown, plus he had shares in banks and other companies. William and two of his sons had also purchased and sold various plots of land in the Port to and from other directors, companies and societies located there. From exploring the registered deeds, the interrelationships between William Kneen senior and other entrepreneurs of the Port are tightly interwoven, here are two examples his eldest daughter, Annie, married Samuel Watterson in 1881 (commissioner, baker and flour dealer),[109] a younger daughter Elizabeth marrying John Clague in 1880, the brother of Thomas Clague Senior, mentioned earlier in this chapter.[110] William Kneen was a member of the first board of Port St Mary Commissioners as was Samuel Watterson his son-in-law. His tenancy for Ballacreggan ended in November 1887, his eldest son William took over the tenancy until 1900. Before his retirement, William had invested in building plots on the Promenade and became one of the directors of the Port St Mary Estate Company Limited in addition he had become an investor and member of other companies and boards.[111] William Kneen Junior from 1900 became a corn merchant until his death in 1925, his brother John James Kneen sold and bought land and houses, and ran a drapery business from one of the newly built premises on Station Road.[112]

12th November 1900 marked the start of a new phase in Henry Alfred Cooil's life; a tenancy for Ballacreggan Farm within a fortnight of marrying Isalen Jane Corrin, followed by the births of three sons over the the next decade.[113] Ballacreggan Farm corner appeared regularly within the local press as a location for collisions between old and new worlds: cars, lorries and motorbikes versus horses and carts. The corner remained a problem until the roads were widened just after 1957; it was considered by many to be one of the most dangerous corners on the Island.[114] The road widening scheme required removal of a stone barn that had been part of an earlier farm complex, the commissioners purchasing the land and demolishing the barn.[115]

In July 1919 Ballacreggan was put up for sale by auction on the instructions of Mrs. Cary as a 'freehold farm, containing 142 acres, 2 rods, 2 perches with dwelling house and farm buildings'. The Ballacreggan farm estate was bought by Henry A. Cooil, July 2019 marked the centenary of the farm being under the ownership of the Cooil family, spanning over four generations.[116] Ballacreggan through the years has had a continuously good reputation for its well-draining fields and excellent stock, winning a 'good scrutch' of prizes at agricultural shows for cattle, horses and sheep. Manx farms and all the people that have worked the land have played their part in the Island's continuous farming heritage. They have helped form the landscape we see today which directly links us all to the Island's past, present and future.

Ballacreggan Farm is still very much part of the present-day Port's identity and many residents have their own reminiscences about the farm, those that worked on it, the characters they knew and events that happened there. To conclude this section about Ballacreggan and bring it up 1979, a time within living memory, I feel it is essential to move into the personal and first person. Two interviews with Johnny Corkish[117] were the main source for this information.

Johnny Corkish said how Ballacreggan was one of the 'first farms to get modern era', they had a Fergusson tractor. Johnny offered to tell Rushen Heritage about his working life and experiences as part of these interviews, Johnny talked about when he worked at Ballacreggan farm. Johnny worked there from 1953 to 1966 (aged 18 to 31)

Figure 9 shows photographs of Ballacreggan before the corner was widened. (Source John Qualtrough Collection)

as an agricultural labourer 'John, Robbie's father, was advertising for a man, so I applied, and, of course, I got it'.

In 1953 'the farm hours were still a 56 hour week' 'farm workers did not get full wages until they were 21'. Johnny luckily got a full man's wages which was '£5 and a few coppers', when he got married his wages went up to £5 6 shillings, the rent for his cottage was 6 shillings. Included with wages were vegetables and a pint of milk and a few eggs were easy to come by, 'wages were small, but food was cheap an' all'. By the mid-1960s farm worker wages had increased to around £9 for a 48-hour week.

From my own personal memory as a child I remember the smell of drying seaweed in the winter on the Ballacreggan fields,[118] Seaweed is a good free fertiliser available on the shore at Port st Mary, there are photographs from the 19th century showing farmers' horse and carts filled with seaweed on the shore. Cooil's at Ballacreggan had a milk round and they delivered milk round the Port and to my home, if we were ever short of milk I was sent up to the farm to get extra. Cooil's earlier milk cart that was in a downstairs gallery of the Manx Museum, my mother recalled how she sometimes used to get a lift to school on it. Qualtroughs Glendown, Truggan Road also had milk rounds as did Walkers Belle Abbey, Colby. I remember sheep been driven through the Port past where I lived by the Examiner Shop. Sheep, cattle and crops were in the field where Scoill Phurt le Moirrey is now built, farm life was still very much part of the Port.

Short summary of other farms in or close to the current village district of Port St Mary:

Year	Fistard Farm	Glen Chass Farm	Corvalley Farm	Glendown Farm	Ballaqueeney Farm	Ballakilley Farm
1823					William Kelly Esq.	John Nelson
1837	John Maddrell	William Gawne			John Taylor	
1843	John Maddrell	William Gawne	William Watterson	William Gawne William Qualtrough	John Taylor	John Clucas
1846		William Maddrell	William Watterson	William Gawne William Qualtrough	John Taylor	John Clucas
1863		William Maddrell	William Watterson	William Gawne	John Taylor	John Clucas
1881	Edward Corrin Thomas Gale	Patrick Crebbin		William Gawne	Henry Kelly	
1883		Patrick Crebbin			Henry Kelly	
1889	William Nixon	Thomas Keggan Nicolas Kermode Henry Maddrell Thomas Nelson	William Watterson Edward Collister John Collister William Keggan John Qualtrough	William Gawne		Thomas Taylor
1894	Ann Kinley William Nixon	Thomas Keggan Nicolas Kermode Henry Maddrell	William Watterson Edward Collister William Keggan James Maddrell	William Gawne	Henry Kelly John Kelly John Taylor William Taylor	Thomas Taylor

LIST OF FARM TENANTS/OWNERS FROM BUSINESS DIRECTORIES NEAR PORT ST MARY, RUSHEN

Treen of Fyshgarth

Port St Mary quarterland makes up the coastal part of the treen of Fyshgarth the other three quarterlands are on the hill land above the Port.

Glen Chass (known earlier as Glensast)

The farm was located by the road between the Glen Chiass turning area and the Howe Road, the road connects to older cart tracks to Cregneash. It was advertised by the 1938 'as a 26 acres farm' with farmhouse, buildings and electricity. The fields are all on a gradient with large stone walled fields one boundary being a cliff. The farm was sold by auction in 1899 at that time for sale there were 'two horses, four milch cattle, two bullocks, two pigs, twenty ewes, one ram and a number of young barn-door fowls'. Crops for sale were swede turnips, potatoes, rye grass, hay and barley, plus various farming implements. In 1890s it appears to have been tenanted or owned by a family named Kinley. There is a chasm of no information within the Manx newspapers until a for sale advertisement appears in 1938 from Mrs E.S. Ruse (she was a granddaughter to William Shepherd who had previously farmed on the Calf). By the 1940s it appears to have been farmed by Joseph Preston and family.

Corvalley Farm, The Howe

This quarterland bounds on part of the Truggan Road to just before Glendown Farm in width. It is a narrow quarterland that covers the area that the Howe Road goes through up to the treen boundary with Cregneash. Within the quarterland there are remains of a few smallholdings. Corvalley Farm was at the bottom of the Howe Hill on the left side towards Port St Mary. John Watterson gave up his tenancy in 1899. The farm appears to have been taken over by William Arthur and Margaret Keggin and family. The Keggin's farmed Corvalley up to 1957, implements and stock were auctioned, and the farm was sold in 1961 by William Arthur Keggin junior (1885–1962). One of William Keggin junior's two daughters Isabel wrote an account of some her memories of growing up on Corvalley Farm in the early 1930s: 'As a child we used oil lamps and candles and we thought it was marvellous when my father bought a two-wick brass lamp'. The farm no longer exists where it was situated there now stands a house and garden.[119]

Fistard earlier known as Fyshgarth

This is the area that includes Perwick Bay area and small hamlet of Fistard there are several remains of smallholdings and agricultural type buildings. There are many small fields with sod hedges with a network of connecting footpaths. Fistard requires further research, a place that potentially has evidence of earlier farmsteads.

Treen of Gleton

Other than Ballacreggan Farm, Glendown Farm is in the same quarterland the only other quarterland in this treen is Ballahane.

Glendown Farm, Truggan Road

According to Woods Atlas Gleton was listed as part of the quareterlands of Ballacreggan and Ballahane. There are numerous track ways heading uphill from the farm and where there are abandoned farmsteads close to the track within a small glen by a stream. One track leads to the boundary with Corvalley quarterland in the treen of Fyshgarth another on the upper boundary of Corvalley, halfway up the Howe Hill. The farm and landholdings are very complex, the Qualtrough family have been associated with the farm for many generations. Other families living in the Howe area with land holdings are Watterson, Kelly, Maddrell and Karran. The Lower boundary goes along part of the railway line between Port St Mary and Port Erin, possibly does not follow older boundaries as the railway line cut through fields the boundaries.

Treen of Edremony

Part of the village district of Port St Mary now includes farms from other treens that are more associated with Port Erin nowadays, Edremony is a small housing estate originally the name of the treen. Edremony is thought to have meant in the Manx Language *eddyr* (between) *daa* (two) *moaney* (turburies). Edremony also includes the quarterlands of Ballakneale, Rowany Heese (lower) Rowany Heose (upper) and Ballaqueeney which is now part of the village district of Port St Mary.

Ballaqueeney, Edremony

Ballaqueeney did not become part of the village district until 1905 when the village boundaries were extended. Henry Kelly the farmer and owner, objected strongly, among others, to being included within the village boundary. Ballaqueeney lies between the edge of Ballacreggan and the Four Roads and the lands of Ballakilley, Rushen. There is documentary evidence for the quarterland since the early 1500s and associated mainly with the Kelly family over numerous generations. There have been many historical finds close to this farm, keeill and graveyard site, ogham stones, coin hoards, Viking age sculptured stone monuments. The railway cuts through some of the lower fields of the quarterland which has resulted in some of the quarterland been lost from an earlier lay out.

The Kellys were also involved in the hotel business and this is discussed in more detail within other chapters, there were sports facilities (tennis, cricket) and a small café on a field on the railway station side next to the road by the railway line, Port St Mary Bowling Club still has a green there at the far end.

In 1934 Johnny Corkish was born at Ballaqueeney, Rushen the youngest of eight,[120] his parents and older siblings had moved to Ballaqueeney in the early 1920s from Ballaglonney, Malew. His father worked for Kellys supplying the Ballaqueeney Hydro and the farm with milk, vegetables and fruit[121] (the walled orchard can still be seen by the entrance to the farm). After his father had recovered from pneumonia the family moved to the Ballaqueeney Gardens House, which is at the bottom of the path by the present allotments. Before WWII the gardens had been a Market garden and become overgrown, Johnny's father used horses to remove young sycamore trees 'got it all ship shape again'.[122] During WWII 'the garden was split into smaller allotments with shelter fences and he let them out for half-a-crown a year and has carried on as allotments ever since'.[123] After the war the land was left to a Mr Taylor from Birkenhead he could not afford to do the repairs so the land was sold to Ballaqueeney Farm.[124]

Ballakilley, Rushen but Port St Mary?
In most internet search results for Ballakilley Farm it will be placed in the postal district of Port St Mary but is actually in the district of the Parish of Rushen. The farm was once part of abbeylands connected to Rushen Abbey, the name Ballakilley translates as farm of the church in the Manx language. The farm came under the ownership of the Nelson family, past vicars of Rushen parish. Ballakilley was later owned by the Clucas family of Port st Mary Farm from 1846 the adjacent farms of Ballakneale, part of Ballaqueeney and Scard were also under their ownership. Past tenants on Ballakilley were the Taylors in the late 19th century, they were connected to the Taylors who had been tenants on Port st Mary Farm in the early 1900s. By the 1940s Johnny Corkish recalls spending a lot of time with the Comish family at Ballakilley, 'thinning and weeding turnips for a bit of pocket money' as he got older he helped with the harvest too. Johnny preferred to be working on Ballakilley then going to school 'I think from the age of thirteen, I was counted as a man at Ballakilley and at harvest time I was carting corn home on the horse and cart'.[125] The Comish family were farming Ballakilley into the 1960s possibly into the early 1970s. The Clucas family still owned Ballakilley as well as other lands throughout the Island, John Donald Clucas lived on the Ballakilley estate at a bungalow named 'Thornhill' on the Castletown Road, up to his death in 1939, his home still exists next to the Southern Group Practice health centre near the Four Roads.[126]

Gansey, Farland
Gansey appears to be partly marginal land which has been suggested as a place cattle are driven for grazing.[127] According to J.J. Kneen's place name map of Rushen, Gansey had been included within abbeyland, based on information from the Manorial Roll of 1511. If correct it could suggest part of the block of land known as Ballavrara. There was evidence of a small farm, on older maps the area was also known as Farland. According to John Watterson's reminiscences there was an old royal way that went past the farm from the area of the Smelt (at the bottom of Beach Road) and was the main way to Ballavrara and Port St Mary from other parts of the Island. The current Beach Road was constructed as an alternative to the earlier routeway, often parts of it were reputedly regularly washed away by the sea. On maps c1850s Peter Taylor was listed as the farmer, it would appear the farm was on freehold land.[128]

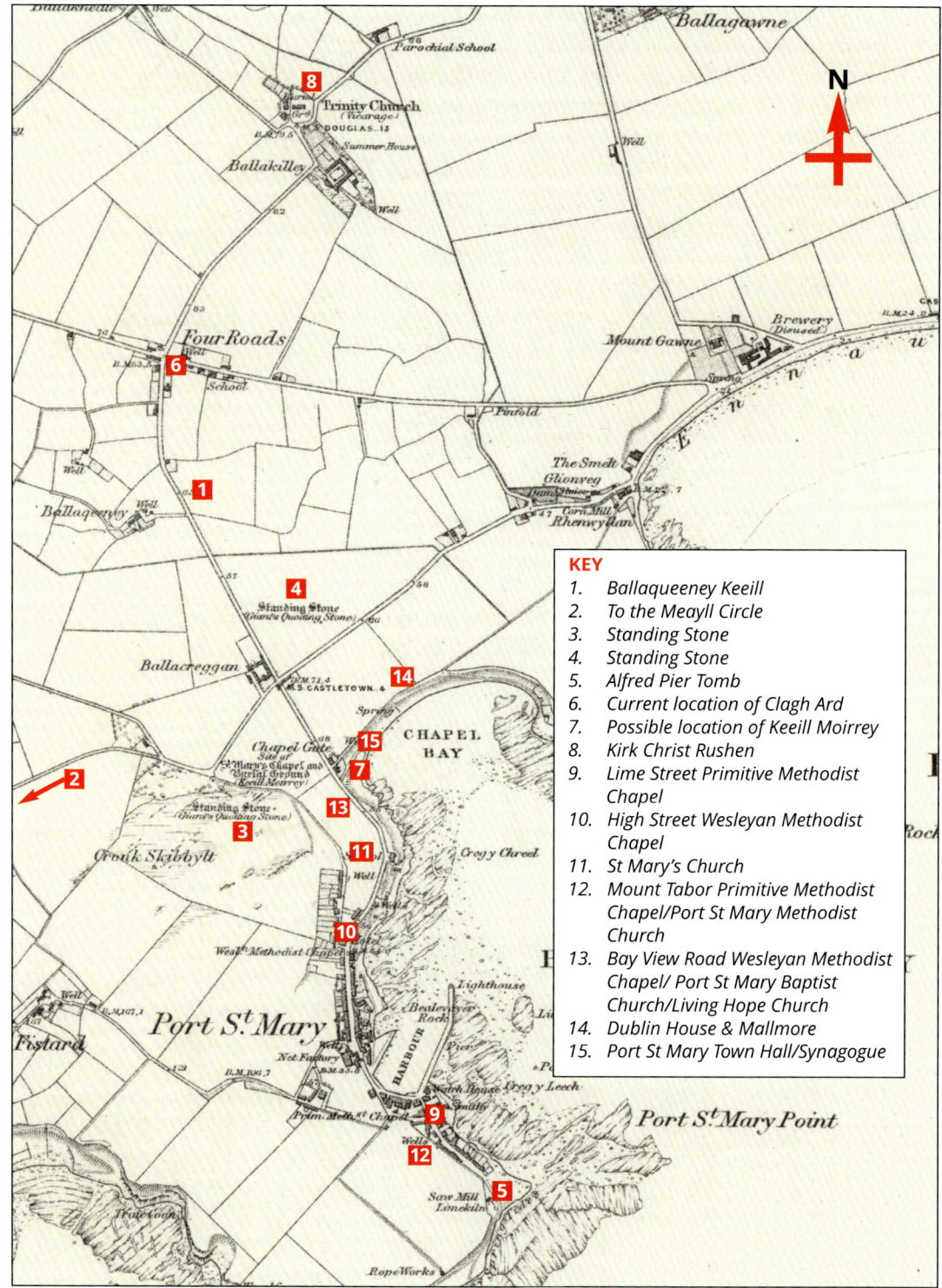

KEY

1. Ballaqueeney Keeill
2. To the Meayll Circle
3. Standing Stone
4. Standing Stone
5. Alfred Pier Tomb
6. Current location of Clagh Ard
7. Possible location of Keeill Moirrey
8. Kirk Christ Rushen
9. Lime Street Primitive Methodist Chapel
10. High Street Wesleyan Methodist Chapel
11. St Mary's Church
12. Mount Tabor Primitive Methodist Chapel/Port St Mary Methodist Church
13. Bay View Road Wesleyan Methodist Chapel/ Port St Mary Baptist Church/Living Hope Church
14. Dublin House & Mallmore
15. Port St Mary Town Hall/Synagogue

Places of worship in the Port St Mary area: ancient and modern. (Map 1868)

Places of Worship

CHAPTER 4

ANDREW D. FOXON

W hen we think of 'places of worship' we tend to visualise buildings within which people gather to share acts of religious worship. For Christian denominations in the Isle of Man these would usually be called churches or chapels and for most of the period explored here these buildings and ancillary rooms and halls formed a focus for worship and for community activities.

Drawing of the Clagh Ard stone from Ballaqueeney by P.M.C. Kermode. (Image courtesy of Manx National Heritage)

There are, however, other places of gathering both indoors and outdoors where worship took place. Any general reading of 19th and 20th century newspapers tells of a variety of associated activities which played a full part in the broader life of the churches and chapels (educational, social, missioning, campaigning, fundraising) or for specific groups (fishermen, young persons, ladies, bachelors). Small acts of worship usually formed part of those ancillary social activities wherever they happened. During this period there were also discoveries of prehistoric and early Christian sites which must have led to discussion, speculation and reflection about how the familiar landscape of daily life also held sites of spiritual significance for forebears and ancestors.

As a result, 'worship' was not confined to the single physical building designed for services but extended into the likes of church and chapel halls, the Rushen Hall and, from 1898, the Public Hall (later renamed the Town Hall), Sunday School picnics, the harbourside for Fishermen's Farewells and temperance meetings. For many Port St Mary residents, as for people in other parts of the Island, church and chapel were significant influences throughout the year. Port St Mary's growth as a visitor destination also resulted in a summer growth in attendance which needed additional space and facilities.

Churches and chapels provide a place of gathering for believers and adherents, with internal features to enable acts of worship according to their particular traditions. In their external physical presence, they also make statements in the community landscape; the location, size and external features of the building and the invitation on the noticeboards are daily reminders to those living in the village, passing through or visiting of the roles the church and chapel have.

The Prehistoric background
Evidence for settlers dates back more than 9,000 years and traces of this Mesolithic period have been found at Perwick Bay and around the village.

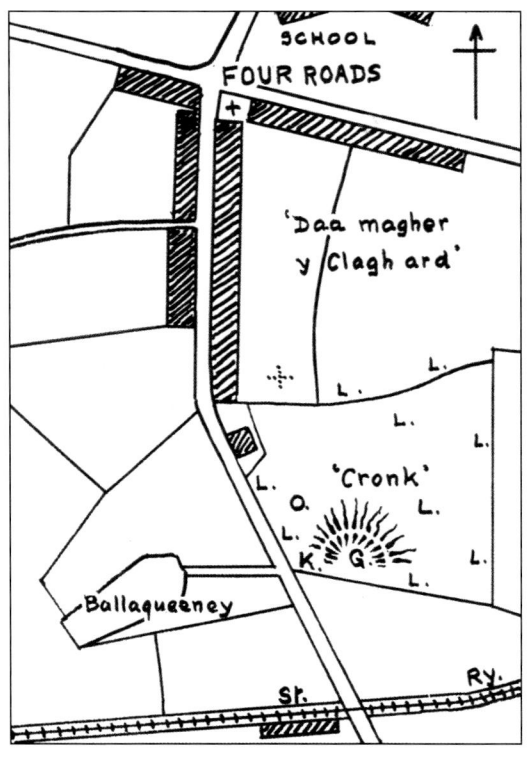

K. Keeill site ?
⊹ Original site of Cross.
+ Present site of do.
O. Ogam stones site
L. Lintel-graves
G. Gravel-pit

[Material removed for railway works (1871-4) mainly from W.side of 'Cronk'].

SCALE _ ft.

Location of Ballaqueeney keeill, graves and grave markers from a line drawing in the Manx Archaeological Survey.

Domesticated animals, crops and pottery skills were brought to the Island by new peoples of the Neolithic period. Some of their dead are buried in the graves of the Meayll Circle and others in a Neolithic/Bronze Age burial mound near the head of the Alfred Pier which was investigated between 1885–88 and destroyed in roadworks in 1889.[1]

At the time of discovery, this burial mound had been long forgotten, and drawings made by Frederick Swinnerton are an essential record of that unexpected find. Such tombs were not simply burial places for the elite but have evidence for being gathering places for other ceremonies.

More obvious in the landscape are the single standing stones on Cronk Skybbylt and in the 'stone field' diagonally opposite Scoill Phurt le Moirrey. These are standing stones of the late Neolithic/Early Bronze Age. Contemporary with Stonehenge, they are believed to be ceremonial and possibly also burial sites. The significance of the sites was forgotten over time and when later people tried to name and explain them, they turned to their own stories and called them the 'Giant's Quoiting Stones'.

In a sense the Alfred Pier tomb, which was discovered during our period of interest, and the standing stones are the earliest evidence for places of worship in Port St Mary.

The Early Church

Christianity is believed to have been brought to the Isle of Man around the 5th and 6th centuries. Its arrival and spread are strongly associated with names like St German, St Patrick, St Maughold and other priests, saints and missionaries from Ireland and from the west and north of Britain. There were certainly cemeteries established in which the dead were buried in graves lined with stone slabs (lintel graves) and oriented east-west, with inscribed grave markers. During the 9th and 10th centuries, the Isle of Man came under the influence of Viking raiders, traders and settlers who arrived as a pagan people but are believed to have adopted Christianity during the 10th century. Small chapels (*keeills*) or shrines were built throughout the Island often on the site of burial or ceremonial sites of the Bronze Age, already some 2,000 years old. The Norse Christians took on and developed the Christian traditions of the Isle of Man and brought the use of inscribed and decorated grave markers to a new high point.

We know of thirteen of these chapels in Rushen parish and two in particular are important for Port St Mary.[2]

The Ballaqueeney burials and keeill

In the early 1870s ballast was being dug for the development of the railways and just north of where the railway line now crosses Station Road was discovered a cemetery with large numbers of early Christian burials. Two of the graves were marked with stones which have early Gaelic inscriptions in the Ogham alphabet, possibly 6th or 7th century. A keeill (field chapel) site had been known about in this location and was also excavated.

Within the cemetery once stood the Ballaqueeney cross (Crosh Ballaqueeney or Clagh Ard), the tallest of the Island's 10th century Norse Christian cross slabs. In the early 19th century it was moved to the Four Roads on the route to the burial ground at the Parish Church, only to be built a few years later into a cowshed. It was again moved to the Four Roads and in 1951 mounted on a plinth on the south-east corner of the Four Roads crossing on which it still stands. Heavily eroded, this grave marker depicts a ring-headed cross with traces of ring chain pattern below and other interlace to the sides.[3]

Ogham-inscribed grave marker from Ballaqueeney keeill now on display in the Manx Museum.

Keeill Moirrey

The chapel dedicated to St Mary is said to have stood at the edge of the tide at Chapel Bay but there is considerable doubt about the precise location. Speed's map of 1610 (based on a survey of 1595) shows a 'Chappell' on the shore at 'Portell Morrey'. In Feltham's 1798 *Tour through the Island of Mann*, 247, he says that the 'ruins of an old chapel' are visible near 'Port le Mary', but this may be better seen as a reference to the Ballaqueeney keeill. There are records in the late 19th century that graves from the burial ground were still visible on the slopes below Chapel Gate in the area that is now 'Happy Valley' and near Chibbyr Moirrey and graves were found at the bottom of Victoria Road and along Bay View Road.

Chapel Beach and Chapel Gate in the 19th century.

Modern view of the supposed 'burial ground' looking towards Chapel Gate.

Dedications to St Mary were probably re-dedications during the 12th and especially the 13th century with the establishment of Rushen Abbey as a Savignac and later a Cistercian Abbey, where it was traditional to dedicate the church at the abbey to St Mary. The land around Chapel Bay was part of the Abbeylands owned by Rushen Abbey so a dedication to St Mary would be appropriate. In addition to Chapel Gate (meaning 'the road to the chapel') there is Chapel Bay and the variously named Chibbyr Moirrey, Lady's Well, and Chapel Spout, which now forms the wishing well on the Lower Promenade.[4]

Perhaps the most important aspect for this book is that the 'Mary' of Keeill Moirrey and Chibbyr Moirrey gave her name to the port – Port St Mary/Purt le Moirrey.

The Parish Church – Kirk Christ, Rushen

It is believed that a major reorganisation of the church in the Isle of Man took place in the late 12th century and led to the selection of significant keeill sites to be developed as places for communal worship for the new parishes. Kirk Christ is located at virtually the central point of the parish as is the case with some of the other parish churches.

Kirk Christ, Rushen, was the parish church within which congregational worship, the sacraments and the major ceremonies of life took place. Around the church grew the parish cemetery. It was the focus for Christian worship from the 12th century, through the medieval period, and emerged from the Reformation as the Church of England parish church for Rushen, and effectively had an exclusive call on the religious life until various forms of dissent appeared in the Island during the 17th and 18th centuries. In 1773 Kirk Christ was described as ruinous, and extensions to the building were made in 1774-5 and again between 1775-90, providing the core of the building we see today.[5]

People from throughout the parish, including those from Port St Mary, would have been expected to attend church and at times the use of horses, traps or carts would have been frowned upon, so that up until the early 19th century we can imagine that those who saw themselves as good churchgoers would have walked from the Port to Kirk Christ.

The Coming of Methodism to the Isle of Man and Methodist places of worship in Port St Mary

Charles Wesley (1703–1791) was an English cleric and theologian whose revival preaching struck a strong chord with ordinary people. Throughout his life he remained within the Church of England and he saw 'Methodism' as a strand within that church, but at times was prevented from preaching on Church of England premises. The first Methodist preacher came to the Island, diverted by a storm, in 1758, but it was John Crook's arrival in 1775 that saw a significant impact on the Isle of Man population and visiting fisherman. When John Wesley himself visited the Island in 1777 and 1781 to preach and meet people, there were already some groups following his teaching. Wesley would preach in a church or meeting room if allowed, or else in the open air. On both visits he preached in Castletown: once indoors and once in Castletown Square.[6]

Following Wesley's death, the revival movement which followed his teaching formed its own church and ordained its own ministers. In the Isle of Man, Wesley's hymns were translated into Manx in 1795 and, in the early 19th century at least, preaching took place in both English and Manx.[7] For some members of the church this was a complete break; others might attend both Methodist chapel and the Anglican church. As with many religious movements there was dissent among the members on how best to go forward and the Primitive Methodist Church (among others) developed

A view of Port St Mary in 1895 with High Street Wesleyan Chapel on the middle left.

The former Lime Street Primitive Methodist Chapel redeveloped as a store.

and separated from the Wesleyan Methodist Church. Primitive Minister John Butcher was sent to the Island from Bolton in 1822 to mission for the cause and within twelve months he had established at least fourteen societies, the Castletown area being first to be missioned.[8] As Chapman[9] says about Primitive Methodism:

'Its simplicity and its emphasis on lay responsibility appealed greatly to the farmers, miners and fishermen of the island.'

In the 1830s, although there were voices of dissent and expulsions within Wesleyan Methodism[10] both strands flourished at a time of missioning and revival. Expulsion for drunkenness and smuggling reduced membership and some emigrated, though the outbreaks of cholera in 1832 and smallpox in 1837 had brought many to challenge their views about personal and religious values and come to faith.[11] Concern about the impact of drunkenness on the Island saw the formation of the first temperance societies, and Oddfellows, Foresters and Rechabite lodges appeared offering affiliate societies additional to those of the churches.[12]

A pattern of two Methodist chapels (one Wesleyan and one Primitive) in a village was a common sight in the 19th and early 20th centuries.[13] In Port St Mary this resulted in the first place of worship built in modern times being opened in May 1832: the Primitive Methodist Chapel on the corner of Lime Street and Loch Road (Flitter Street), on land purchased from the Duke of Atholl and where there are now garages.[14] The date stone, however, is reputed to have read MDCCCXLI – 1841.[15]

A Wesleyan Methodist Chapel had had its foundation stone laid a year earlier in August 1831[16] and opened in 1835 in a prominent position on High Street at what was

The location where High Street Methodist Chapel stood is now the British Legion Garden of Remembrance.

then the entrance to the town (where the Garden of Remembrance is now) on land belonging to a Mr Gelling on the understanding that the chapel would be built with four corner spires (finials) and generally similar in design to one he had seen in Scotland and following temperance principles: no alcohol or gambling.[17] It was erected by Mr Harry Moore who also built the Bay View Hotel and Rhenwyllin Mill.

In 1836 the Methodist Church finally seceded from the Anglican Church,[18] though members in the Isle of Man often maintained contact with both strands of Christianity.

St Mary's Church, Bay View Road

There was a feeling in Port St Mary and other places that the Parish Church was too far a distance to travel, especially in winter, and seating for 400 was considered too small to hold the total potential congregation in the middle of the 19th century – 3,200 people.[19] The presence of Methodist places of worship within Port St Mary from the 1830s may also have acted as a stimulus for the decision in 1847 to create a 'Chapel of Ease' for the village: a building consecrated for all Church of England purposes which would provide a place of worship more local to the developing community. From 1848 a room in now demolished Port St Mary schoolhouse was used for services and the congregation attending increased.[20]

The intention had been to build a new Chapel of Ease and £300 was raised for this in the 1840s, with additional monies at other times.[21] But it was following a meeting in 1880 that Messrs Barry & Son of Liverpool were commissioned to design what would become St Mary's, on land given by Mrs Emily Maria Gawne of Kentraugh.[22] By this time the local population was regularly increased by summer visitors. The estimated

View from behind St Mary's Church taken before the tower was built in 1904.

cost for the building was £1,200 and did not at that stage have a porch or a tower nor did the initial fundraising cover the costs of an organ, lighting or heating.

Following acceptance of the plans and site clearance, the foundation stone was laid in May 1882 and almost twenty months later, on 25th January 1884, St Mary's Church of England was consecrated by Bishop Rowley Hill.[23] Gifts of communion rails, communion plate, the font and the mosaic floor in the sanctuary were given by ladies of the Gawne family.

In 1896 the porch was added and that year saw the first marriage in the church. 1904 saw many additions, with the tower and its clock and bell, the stained-glass windows, the eagle lectern, the gas fittings to light the church and other items, paid for by local benefactors and through gifts from UK residents who had associations with Port St Mary: the positive response of those holidaying in the Port.

The church developed an active religious and social life in the village. By the beginning of the 20th century the annual Christmas tree, entertainment and meal was a winter highlight. The church had no hall of its own until it purchased the former Oddfellows' Hall in 1922. The Ladies Working Party acted as a fundraising and social committee and when electricity came to Port St Mary in the 1930s, the church acquired the modern lighting.

The New Methodist Buildings

In the late 1800s and early 1900s.with Port St Mary developing as a harbour and as a holiday resort, the resident population was greatly increased in holiday time, especially after visitor accommodation was built during the 1880s along Chapel Bay. The Methodist chapels from the first half of the 19th century looked small and old-fashioned in their style and facilities. Church-going was a major Sunday activity for most of the holidaymakers and the social activities organised were also popular. From 1884, St Mary's Church formed a new focus for Anglican worship in the village. As a result, schemes were developed to build larger chapel buildings on new sites. The move to renovate or to build new facilities and premises was happening across the Island, not just in Port St Mary.

In May 1892 the decision was made to build a new Wesleyan Methodist Chapel, with a spire, to seat 390 people and replace High Street as the main chapel, at a cost of £1,500–£2,000.[24] The impact of tourism had meant that in the summer there were not enough seats in the old chapel for all who wanted to attend.[25] The land was bought from Thomas Clague in February 1894 on behalf of Robert Gelling and the other Trustees of Port St Mary Methodist Church[26] and the foundation stone laid in July that year. The building was designed by Thomas William Cubbon of Birkenhead (who was also involved in a range of civic projects on the Island) and built by John McArd & John Moore. It opened in 1895 on Bay View Road, with a new organ installed in 1899.

There are records of all the fundraising activities – collections, sewing meetings, and all sorts of events – in the church, in homes and in Rushen Hall. The old chapel became the Sunday School (the Wesleyan School Room) when the new Bay View Road Chapel

Opposite:
St Mary's Church.

opened and was used for other meetings,[27] providing a base for the Band of Hope, Bright Hour, the Wesley Guild, the Wesley Fellowship, concerts, Manx Teas and jumble sales.

Growth also meant that the Lime Street Primitive Methodist Chapel was considered too small. An ambitious plan was devised to build on a new site near the harbour and include a dedicated school room and other rooms in addition to the main worship space. The grand scheme came to fruition through the efforts of the Trustees and the Rev W Harris, who had served for many years in the Isle of Man and retired as a supernumary to Port St Mary in 1901.[28]

Mount Tabor Primitive Methodist Chapel opened in 1903 on Athol Street, fronting onto Loch Road and above the old chapel. It was designed by Todd & Morris of Southport to seat a congregation of 320 people and incorporated a school room and other buildings. Costing £2,100, it completely replaced the old Lime Street chapel which was sold off and later used as a coal store, having had a wide sliding door inserted. The old chapel was demolished, and the road widened, with garages built for new houses.

During the 1890s and 1900s the Church of England and the Methodist Churches worked separately, sometimes challenging each other, but occasionally working together.

In 1893 the Fishermen's Farewell service was revived:[29] a farewell service on the quay to wish 'godspeed' to fishermen departing for the Irish fishing season. It was said that the men were very busy but '200 of them' sacrificed a little time to show appreciation and in 1894 the ceremony involved both Wesleyan and Primitive ministers.

Temperance was a major issue for church and chapel communities in terms of practice, preaching and activity. In 1898 the ministers of the Wesleyan and Primitive Methodist Chapels and the Anglican vicar all opposed a licence for the newly built Station Hotel at Port St Mary[30] which was, however, eventually granted to some consternation the following year.[31]

The two Methodist Churches joined together for their Sunday School picnics which

Port St Mary Methodist Church originally built as Mount Tabor Primitive Methodist Church 1903.

were big social events for the village children, adults and visitors. In 1896 as many as 300 adults sat down to tea (locals and visitors) at Laxey Glen Pavilion.

Port St Mary Beach Mission
Beginnings (1901–1914)

1901 saw Port St Mary become the site for a new branch of the CSSM (Children's Special Service Mission) with regular meetings in a corner of Port St Mary Promenade. The annual beach mission had previously been held in Port Erin, with occasional visits to Port St Mary by Robert Matheson, later known as Mr Matt, and Will Rhodes (Mr T.W. Rhodes), known as T.W. The Matheson family were to be involved in the Beach Mission for four generations, creating continuity of Mr Matt's work.

Plaque commemorating the centenary of Port St Mary Beach Mission 1901-2000AD.

Mr Matt's health prevented him from going overseas to do missionary work, but T.W. went to Spain, so his brother, Ernest, took over his role, playing the harmonium as accompaniment for the singing for many years. By 1911, other men from around the British Isles and some ladies, including Mr Matt's two sisters and Mr Rhodes' sister, had become actively involved in the growing mission.

Before WWI, a permanent base for the mission was created when Dublin House, on the Upper Promenade, was rented from Mr R. Kneen, becoming the focus for many CSSM activities, despite there being no electricity installed.

WWI (1914–1918)

War was declared during the 1914 beach mission, so it was suspended until hostilities ceased. One reason being that many of the Isle of Man Steam Packet Company ships were commandeered by the Admiralty for war service.

The inter-war years (1918–1939)

The pattern of the Beach Mission changed very little during this period and many missionaries, whose commitment had begun in Port St Mary, went far and wide across the world.

The mission team stayed in Dublin House, but many participating families stayed next door at Mallmore Hotel, which gradually expanded when the Qualtrough family took charge. The Balqueen Hydro, in the care of the Kelly family, was the venue for other participants.

CHILDREN'S SPECIAL SERVICE MISSION.
FOUNDED 1867.

PORT ST. MARY BRANCH
OPENED 1901.

AUGUST 7th to 23rd, 1928.

HOLIDAY SERVICES

For Boys and Girls visiting Port St. Mary, will, D.V., be conducted by the undermentioned and others, on the Shore at 10.30 each week day morning (Saturdays excepted), and on Sunday Afternoon on the Rocks at Gansey. (If wet all Services will be held in Town Hall).

A PRAYER MEETING will be held each morning at 7.45 in the TOWN HALL.

Robert N. Matheson	- -	Dublin
Ernest Rhodes	- - -	Dublin
A. Lindsey Glegg	- - -	London
Roy T. Green	- -	London
Arthur T. Watts	- -	Hoylake
Jack Nelstrop	- -	Disley, Cheshire
Cyril Park	- -	Southport
Robert Fleming	- -	Devonport
Donald Orr	- -	Dublin
F. Darling	- -	Dublin

ASSISTED BY A NUMBER OF LADY WORKERS.

CRICKET, PODEX, BATHING, PICNICS, ATHLETIC SPORTS, ETC., ETC. WILL BE ANNOUNCED AT THE SERVICES

The 1928 team

World War II (1939–1945)

As Port St Mary became part of the women's internment camp in 1940, the beach mission was once again suspended. During the war Dublin House came on the market. The owner told his daughter that if Mr Matheson wanted to buy it, she was to sell it to him. In wartime, Mr Matheson was unable to travel to the Island, but he did put in a successful bid.

After the War (1946–1960)

Mr & Mrs Matt and family – Cherry, Will, Noel, Bob & Phyll. (1946)

1946 saw the re-starting of the mission with new assistant leaders William Matheson (Mr Matt's son, Will) and Leith Samuel. Mrs Matt had been in charge of housekeeping since the beginning, assisted by a cook and two cleaners who came with her from Dublin. Family members Phyll and Helen succeeded Mrs Matt in 1950 and 1976 respectively, but all were responsible for forging strong links with local shopkeepers and suppliers and recognised by the Commissioners and Churches in 1975 with a plaque, positioned on the Lower Promenade, in celebration of seventy-five years of the mission. A further plaque was placed in 2000 to celebrate the centenary.

Coming through the war unscathed, Dublin House had become a useful permanent base for the mission and was also used during the year by missionaries on leave. Ownership, from a distance, of an empty house in the winter can be a cause of concern, so the mission was grateful to Walter Moore and Bobby Bridson for 'caretaking' and organising any repairs.

In March 1950, Mr Matt died. He entrusted the joint leadership to Will Matheson and Leith Samuel, who went on to be supported by their wives and families, while the mission continued in its pattern of tried and tested activities.

Inevitable Change (1960–1979)

The basis of the mission had, until this point, been an unbroken consistency of people and activities. However, things were changing – holidays abroad, hotels closing, reduced train services. The tourist industry in Port St Mary was in decline.

The mission had been designed initially for families visiting the Island, with some local children joining in, but now the numbers of local children increased annually. 1960 saw the formation of an independent group for teenagers with an appropriate schedule of activities. Subsequent years saw additional groups created to cater for different ages and the enlisting of team members with proficiency in supporting these groups.

Further changes continued to happen – the harmonium, carried up and down from Dublin House, finally succumbed to guitars; individual song sheets replaced large sheets displayed by team members, and drama became an activity. However, the mid-morning services were still the focus, with 'sand seats' dug out and canvas mats to cover them.

The Beach Mission, under the banner of Scripture Union, continues to go from strength to strength, encompassing aspects of both stability and change, which, so far, have safeguarded its future.

Methodist unification

The Wesleyan and Primitive Methodist communities in Port St Mary had worked together on issues of abstinence, in joint Sunday School outings and other matters of mutual interest, though their own strong separate traditions ran deep. Through the 19th and early 20th centuries there had been reform and unification movements within the British Methodist Connexion and in the Isle of Man. Talks about unity came to fruition when, in September 1932, the Island Methodists took part in the Union of the Wesleyan Methodist Church, the Primitive Methodist Church and the United Methodist Church and Port St Mary continued with two places of Methodist worship, which also acted as a focus for social life.

World War II

The impact of World War II on the Isle of Man and Port St Mary was significant. The combination of local people continuing to try to earn a living while young men were at war, internees in the hotels and guest houses, and the military from, especially, the RADAR station on the top of the Meayll Hill (RAF Cregneish), must have made an interesting and challenging mix in the village. For the RAF men, St Mary's Church established a canteen in the church hall.[32]

Port St Mary Town Hall. A room was used during the period of internment as a synagogue.

Worship in St Mary's and the Methodist Churches continued during the war and provided support to both local people and 'new residents'. The pastoral work of the Rev Harry Johnson is perhaps best known, but there was an additional need for those of other faiths and Christian denominations who were interned. In her description of life as a Jewish internee in the Port St Mary camp, Rosemarie Dalheim recalls that the Jewish community all lived in the Ballaqueeny (sic) in order to keep their diet kosher, and for their Synagogue they were able to use Port St Mary Town Hall. Lutheran and Catholic internees had services in Cowley's Café on Bay View Road (now the Manxonia building) or Newlyn and were led by visiting preachers.[33]

More recent times

In the 1960s Port St Mary Commissioners wanted to widen Bay View Road to improve the flow of increasing traffic in the village and this impacted on two sets of premises. The garden in front of St Mary's was reduced in size and its wall moved back several feet.[34] Further towards the harbour there was a pinch point between the Bay View Hotel and the old Wesleyan Chapel which was being used as the Sunday School and Hall. This was a period when the unification of the two Methodist congregations in Port St Mary was being discussed. For some years shared services were held in Bay View Road in the summer and Mount Tabor in the winter. In 1968 Mount Tabor became the home of the united congregation and the re-named Port St Mary Methodist Church had an inaugural service on Easter Sunday 6th April 1969. This provided the opportunity to sell the old Wesleyan Chapel on High Street to the Commissioners in 1970 for demolition and to widen the road, and to sell Bay View Road Chapel as a home for what became Port St Mary Baptist Church, who made the alterations necessary for Baptist use. In 1975 the British Legion Memorial Garden of remembrance was opened on part of the footprint of the old Wesleyan Methodist Chapel.[35]

Less physical change had happened to St Mary's as viewed from the exterior, but

View along Athol Street towards Mount Tabor Primitive Methodist Church.

those who came to worship saw that memorial windows had been given in the 1970s along with many other gifts and bequests.

Conclusion

The legacy of worship over the centuries has left traces in physical remains as well as place names. In 1979 there were three principal places for congregational Christian worship in Port St Mary – St Mary's Anglican Church (within the parish of Rushen and the Diocese of Sodor and Man), Port St Mary Methodist Church (within the Castletown Circuit of

View from the Cronk with Bay View Road Methodist Chapel in the right foreground.

the Isle of Man District of the Methodist Church – Mount Tabor) and Port St Mary Baptist Church (the former Bay View Road (Wesleyan) Methodist Church). Later in the century the structure of the last of these was to deteriorate and a new church building replaced it in 2000, now the Living Hope Community Church. Even now the landscape of places of worship is not confined to the indoors alone: the Beach Mission continues each year with a fortnight of events and activities in the churches, Town Hall and, of course, in the open air and on the beach.

Living Hope Community Church built on the site of Bay View Road Wesleyan Chapel.

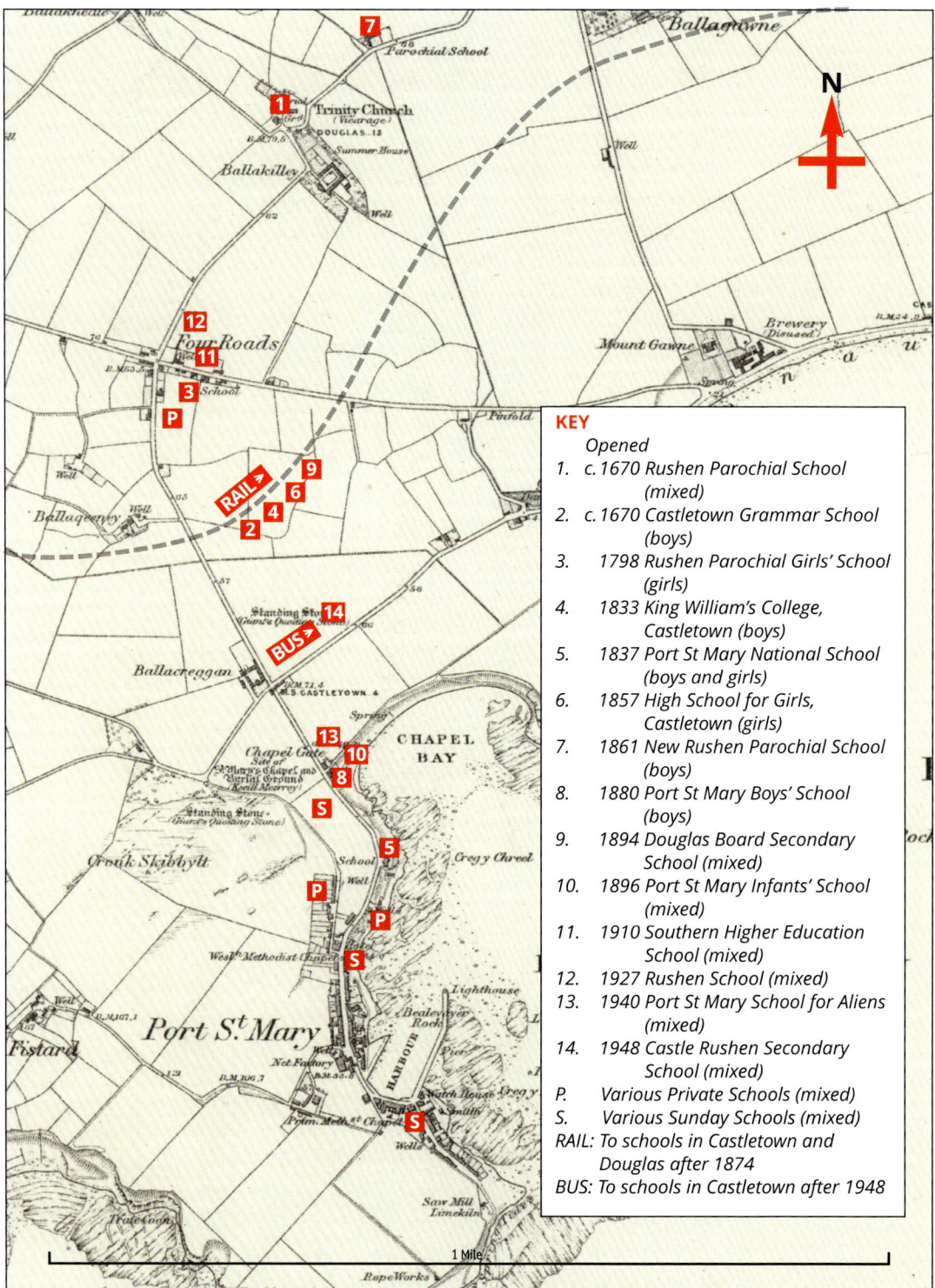

KEY
Opened
1.   *c.1670 Rushen Parochial School (mixed)*
2.   *c.1670 Castletown Grammar School (boys)*
3.   *1798 Rushen Parochial Girls' School (girls)*
4.   *1833 King William's College, Castletown (boys)*
5.   *1837 Port St Mary National School (boys and girls)*
6.   *1857 High School for Girls, Castletown (girls)*
7.   *1861 New Rushen Parochial School (boys)*
8.   *1880 Port St Mary Boys' School (boys)*
9.   *1894 Douglas Board Secondary School (mixed)*
10. *1896 Port St Mary Infants' School (mixed)*
11. *1910 Southern Higher Education School (mixed)*
12. *1927 Rushen School (mixed)*
13. *1940 Port St Mary School for Aliens (mixed)*
14. *1948 Castle Rushen Secondary School (mixed)*
P.   *Various Private Schools (mixed)*
S.   *Various Sunday Schools (mixed)*
RAIL: *To schools in Castletown and Douglas after 1874*
BUS: *To schools in Castletown after 1948*

Figure 1: Schools serving Port St Mary, 1670–1979. (Map 1868)

Education for All... and for the Few

CHAPTER 5

ANGELA W. LITTLE

It is September 1927. Edythe is eager to put on her coat and begin her daily walk – and run and skip – to the Rushen School situated at the 'Four Roads' Port St Mary. The fine purpose-built building is brand new and opened a few months earlier. The school is an amalgamation of six smaller schools and serves the children residing in the Parish of Rushen. In this chapter we explore the development of 'education for all' and 'education for the few' for the young people of Port St Mary. The map (Figure 1) shows the village and its environs, the location of schools and the dates they were established.

Rushen School, established 1927.

A step back in time

We can trace the history of the schools that became the Rushen School back to the 1660s. Most historians of education in the Isle of Man attribute the establishment of 'education for all' to the vision and determination of Bishop Barrow.[1] On his arrival in the Island from New College, Oxford, in 1663, Bishop Barrow was somewhat scathing about the Manx people he encountered:

> *I found the people for the most part loose and vicious in their lives, rude and barbarous in their behaviour; and – which I suppose the cause of this disorder – without any true sense of religion, and indeed, in a condition almost incapable of being bettered; for they had no means of instruction, or of being acquainted with the very principles of Christianity.*[2]

Barrow's main objective was the civilisation of the rude and barbarous people of Man through the principles of Christianity. Although a common prayer book had been translated to Manx in 1610 by Bishop Phillips, this was available in manuscript form only. Barrow reasoned that 'the best way of Cure' was to establish schooling through the medium of the English language, despite the fact that the mother tongue of most was Manx Gaelic. By 1672 English-medium schools had been established in each of the seventeen parishes as well as in its small towns of Douglas, Castletown, Ramsey and Peel.

The Rushen Parochial School was established at the site of the current Parish Church on a date between 1666 and 1672 [1]. The children – we believe girls as well as boys – were taught by a clergyman who held a teaching licence issued by the Bishop.

Parents paid a modest fee towards the clergyman's salary and could be fined for not sending their children to school. The clergyman was expected to admit to the school the children of the very poorest parents, without the payment of fees. Thus, in one of the earliest examples of its kind worldwide, the principle of access to *education for all* was established on the Isle of Man.

During Bishop Wilson's time (1697-1755) on the Isle of Man, school buildings were separated from the church itself. The Rushen Parochial School moved into a building erected close to where the Lych gate now stands, in 1734.

A second school in the parish, for girls only, was established at the Four Roads, Port St Mary [3] through a donation from Miss Jane Qualtrough of Kentraugh in 1798.[3] Managed by the vicar and wardens of the Rushen Parish Church it became known as the Rushen Parochial Girls' School, or simply the Girls' School. In 1809 a Parish Sunday Schools with 80 scholars was established.

As with any education policy, implementation usually falls short of ambition. Barrow's scheme for 'education for all' was no exception and its successful implementation faced many obstacles during the seventeenth and eighteenth centuries. Enrolments waxed and waned. So too did teachers' performance. In answer to the question 'how often do you visit your Parish school', the Revd. Joseph Qualtrough, Vicar of Rushen wrote 'The Master being incompetent and incapable there is scarcely any Parochial School'. After a further exchange of letters, the Governor of Sodor and Mann saw fit 'to withdraw the licence of the incumbent parochial schoolmaster from 12th October 1822', with a further order to collect the key of the school house from him on the 12th day of November 1822.[4] Nonetheless, by the first quarter of the 19th century the principle that the children from ordinary families should have access to basic education, and that it should be fee-free for the very poorest, was becoming well established.

Secondary and Higher Education – education of the Manx elite

Those destined for elite roles in society – in the church and the law – enjoyed a separate and superior education. Already by the mid-17th century there were 'Free Schooles' for secondary education in Castletown, Peel, Douglas and Ramsey, though it is unclear how many of these were still in operation by the time of Bishop Barrow's arrival.[5] In the seventeenth century a 'Free' school meant 'free from the jurisdiction of the ordinary' rather than fee-free.[6] In 1666 Bishop Barrow established funds for a new Free school, the Castletown Grammar School [2], for young men to follow a superior education in preparation for roles as clergy in his Island-wide diocese. Among the male children of the 'gentry' in the Rushen parish, of whom there would have been only a few, some may have attended the parochial schools before transferring to the Castletown Grammar School, boarding in Douglas, or travelling 'across' to schools in England. Or they may have attended a school run privately by the incumbent Vicar of Rushen. The Revd. John Clague (Vicar 1782-1816):

> *Allowed his pupils diet, washing, and lodging, and taught himself the*
> *English, French, Greek, and Latin languages, also Euclid, algebra,*

navigation, geography the use of the globes, arithmetic, book keeping, writing and spelling, all for £12 (British)... His fame, it seems, extended very far, for he had many pupils from Liverpool and the North of England and a few even from the West Indies.[7]

Clague's successor, the Revd. Joseph Qualtrough (1816-1824) opened an Academy for instructing 'young Gentlemen' in the various branches of a liberal education and offered two places to boarders.[8]

During the seventeenth and eighteenth century the daughters of the gentry would probably have been tutored at home; in the early 19th century they may have attended the private venture Castletown Green School for Young Ladies or the Young Ladies Country Boarding School at Rushen Abbey in Ballasalla.

Figure 2. Isle of Man Education Legislation and developments in Port St Mary and the Rushen Parish	
Isle of Man Education Legislation and Milestones	Education developments in Port St Mary and Rushen Parish
c.1665 Bishop Barrow establishes scheme for basic education in parochial schools, fee-free for the poorest and compulsory. New type of Grammar school established	1666 Castletown Grammar School established c.1667 Rushen Parochial School established in the Parish church
1704 Ecclesiastical Ordinance reinforces compulsory education, including the imposition of fines on parents for not sending children to school	1782 Revd. John Clague runs private school in Parish church annex 1798 Rushen Parochial School for Girls established
1802 Sunday School movement begins	1809 Parish Sunday School established, followed by the Wesleyan and Primitive Methodists 1817 Revd. Joseph Qualtrough runs private academy in Parish church annex 1831 Foundation stone laid for King Williams College (opened 1833) 1837 Port St Mary National School established (1st National school estd. Douglas 1810) 1840s Private schools for young children
1851 Act. Parish committees empowered to raise local rates to increase teacher salaries, erect dwelling houses for schoolmasters/mistresses, buy books and apparatus, provide teacher pensions. School inspections from England in return for financial grants	1855 Rushen Parochial School for Girls extended 1861 New Parochial School for Boys established on Church Road, plus dwelling for school master
1872 Education Act School Committees established in 17 parishes and 4 towns; gradual handover of control of schools from church to state. These schools became known as Board schools	1875 High School for Girls (later The Buchan School) established in Castletown 1876 Rushen Parochial Girls' school building (now a Board School) replaced on same site
1878 Education Act Compulsory education for those aged 5-13 years	1880 Port St Mary National School closed and Port St Mary Boys' (Board) School opened, infants' section opened 1896
1892 Education Act Abolition of fees in state-supported elementary education	
1896 Commission of Enquiry of Secondary Education	
1906 Report on Secondary Education (the Jackson Report)	

1907 Higher Education Act, four Higher Education Boards created, including one for the South	**1911** Southern Higher Grade school/classes established opposite Girls school at Four Roads. Known as the 'Tin Tab' school
1915 Education Act Provision of free school meals for children in need	
1918 Education Aid Grant Act. Teacher salaries raised	
1920 Act Abolition of twenty-one school committees and four higher education boards. Replaced by the Central Council of Education and the Isle of Man Education Authority	**1927** Six elementary and infants schools in the Rushen Parish merged. New Rushen School established at the Four Roads **1931** Castletown Grammar School closes
1939-1945 War time measures and establishment of Camps for 'alien' internees	**c. 1940** Kindergarten for internee children (up to six years) established in former Port St Mary Boys' SchoolSchool for internee children aged six to sixteen established in the Cornaa boarding house. Adult education classes
1949 Education Act. Free compulsory education five to fifteen-year-olds. Primary (5-11) and comprehensive secondary (11-15) schools become separate institutions. Subsidised milk and school meals, free dental and medical inspections and treatment. College of Further Education to be established. Scholarship scheme to support UK university entrants	**1948** Castle Rushen Secondary School established in Castletown. Children aged 11-15 years transfer to CRHS from Rushen School which becomes the Rushen Primary School
1987 Raising of school leaving age to sixteen	**1974** Rushen School separated into an Infants school and Junior school **1993/4** New primary school for Port St Mary - Scoill Phurt le Moirrey. Rushen Infants' and Junior schools recombine

So already by the start of our period of main historical interest, 1829–1979, there were at least two tracks of schooling, one for the children of the 'common folk' and the other for those of the gentry. The Manx saying '*Ta ynsagh coamrey stoamey yn dooinney berchagh, as t'eh berchys yn dooinney boght*' translates as 'learning is the fine raiment of the rich man, and it is the riches of the poor'. It conveys the readiness with which the mass of the population accepted the idea that a superior education was, 'if not wholly unattainable, at least a luxury, while for the wealthy it was their natural right and privilege'.[9] It followed that children of the ordinary classes were content with their position in the inferior route of a dual track system in which one track served the few and one served the rest.

But how did these two tracks of schooling develop between 1829 and 1979? Figure 2 summarises they key milestones in Isle of Man legislation alongside the dates of establishment of education of varying kinds available in Port St Mary.

1829–1878

We do not know how many children were attending schools in 1829. However, the population census indicates that in 1851 out of 153 children aged five to fourteen living in the census district of Port St Mary village about half (50.3%) attended school, with more boys attending than girls (56% vs. 45%).

The Rushen Boys' and Girls' Parochial Schools

By 1843, the Parochial School, now enrolling mostly boys, was located next to the church. Land for a new Parochial Boys' School, complete with a dwelling house and garden for the schoolmaster, was purchased by the church from Thomas Gawne, owner of the Ballachurry Estate. The new school was built on Church Road and opened in 1861 [7]. The Parochial Girls' School was extended in 1855 with funds donated by Mrs Emily Maria Gawne, wife of Edward Moore Gawne, the landowner, Member of the House of Keys and Captain of the Parish. In 1876, following the 1872 Act of Education, the school was demolished and a new school built on the same site by the Rushen School Committee.

The Port St Mary National School [5]

In 1837, the children of Port St Mary gained a new school, the National School. 'National' in this context did not refer to the Isle of Man nation. Rather it referred to the National Society for Promoting the Education of the Poor in the Principles of the Established Church throughout England and Wales. This society and a parallel one with an equally long name – The Institution for Promoting the British System for the Education of the Labouring and Manufacturing Classes of Society of Every Religious Persuasion[10] – competed with each other to open schools in the industrialising areas of England with rapidly growing populations of the 'working classes'. Both societies promoted the 'monitorial system' of teaching, in which a single schoolteacher was responsible for large numbers of children in one large classroom, assisted by a team of monitors. Little older than the children they taught, these monitors were tutored by the schoolmaster/mistress in reading, writing and some arithmetic skills before transmitting their skills to their 'row' or 'class' of children.[11]

The titles of both societies also made clear that the schemes were intended for the children of the labouring and manufacturing classes. The first monitorial school was founded in Douglas in 1810 under the non-denominational scheme. In Douglas the better classes saw the monitorial school as a cure for the 'rude, insolent and savagely unmannered' creatures plaguing the town.[12] From 1815 the Anglican Diocese aligned itself with the National Society's monitorial scheme, and it was under this scheme that Port St Mary's National School was established on land purchased from James Holmes Esq. There are no records that indicate whether the school was seen as a way of curing the 'rude, insolent and savagely unmannered' behaviour of the youth of Port St. Mary in the same way as in Douglas.

In 1847 Mr Robert Quayle was the master and thirty boys and twelve girls were enrolled. He taught reading, writing, arithmetic, geography and history, supported by monitors. Mr Quayle 'was a cripple and he was named the Little Master, being a short man walking on two crutches. He taught the boys very well and learned them for seafaring'.[13] In 1851 Legislation was passed that enabled local rates to be raised to pay for school improvements, required teachers to have training and schools to be open for inspections from England. Mr Quayle was succeeded by a Mr Binns and Mr Stibbings, both from England and graduates from the National Society's Training College in

People of Port St Mary

EMILY MARIA GAWNE

The great granddaughter of John 3rd Duke of Atholl, Emily Gawne, was born in 1814 and died in 1889. Married to Edward Moore Gawne in 1835, she lived on the Kentraugh Estate from 1837. She is one of only four women to appear in A W Moore's Manx Worthies published in 1901. Moore credits her with having inaugurated 'a systematic plan of almsgiving which she carried out during the rest of her life', describing her as 'a true lady bountiful… regarded with affection, mingled with profound admiration and respect for her pious and amiable life'. Her influence extended across the parish of Rushen and beyond. In 1843 she established the Rushen Female Benefit Society, one of only two such societies on the Island during the first half of the nineteenth century created to support the welfare of working women. The Irish famine affected many Manx families very badly and she started a shop that sold tea, groceries, and other necessaries at cost price. She supported the Rushen Girls' Parochial School in many ways and funded its extension in 1855. She funded the building of St Mary's church in Port St Mary in 1884.

Her husband was Edward Moore Gawne, with whom she had five sons and five daughters. Edward Moore Gawne was an MHK from 1829 and Speaker of the House of Keys from 1854 until its dissolution in 1867 when a democratically elected body replaced the self-appointed members of the House.

After her husband's death in 1872 Emily Maria continued her good works. In an 1880 debate in the House of Keys she was cited by Robert Sherwood, MHK for Glenfaba, as a woman who deserved to have the right to vote in general elections. Sherwood contended that 'as a principle of justice, taxation and representation should go together', arguing that many well known ladies were far more deserving of enfranchisement than many male householders. By January 1881 property owning widows and spinsters had gained the right to vote through legislation believed to be the first of its kind in the world.

An ardent supporter of girls' education, it was an education that prepared girls and young women for their station in life. One of the girls who attended the Rushen Parochial Girls' School shared a memory with her daughter:

> *my mother…. said when she went to school they were taught sewing and everything at school, you see, and this particular teacher, she used to show them how to embroider little things and all. But when she (Mrs Gawne) came to see them, the children all had to put those away and just do ordinary little bits of plain work because the Gawnes thought …. that the children were getting ideas above their station …if they were taught embroidery and things like that. So there was that and there was class distinction, wasn't there?[14]*

Whether the Gawnes would have been impressed by and pleased to see the embroidery that was 'put away' we do not know. We simply know that girls who attended the school at this time were aware that they were being socialised for their 'station in life'. A stained-glass window is dedicated to Emily Maria's memory in the Rushen Parish Church.

The Port St. Mary National School, opened in 1837, situated between the Cliff Hotel and Ballamona.

Battersea, London and Mr Robert Watson. Mr Cornelius Squires arrived in 1877 and was remembered by John B Gawne as 'a sea captain, a native of Nottingham … (who) taught navigation at nights'.[15] Perhaps it was this and similar memories that led some Port St Mary residents to refer, even today, to the National School as the Port St Mary *Navigational* School. Figure 3 lists the names of all schoolmasters of the National School, and all other schools serving the children of Port St Mary, 1829-1979.

The school was also used for Anglican religious worship on Sundays and for many community activities – concerts, tea meetings, public meetings and meetings organised by the Harbour of Peace Lodge of the Oddfellows.[16]

Private Schools in Port St Mary

While Port St Mary did not see a growth in private education at the rate seen in Douglas, a government committee recorded at least two private schools in 1847.[17] A Mrs Cregeen taught reading to twenty-four children in one and a Miss Carran taught eighteen children reading and writing in the other. There appear to have been others. Edward (Ned Beg Hun Roy) Faragher, the Manx author, translator and folklorist, is recorded as having attended an Infants' School in Port St Mary around the age of six, run by an old lady…who taught 'writing and ciphering'.[18] Ned Maddrell, the last surviving native Manx speaker, recalled in 1958 that Edward Faragher had attended Margaret Bredgeon's school in Cregneash. John Gawne recalls in 1950 that a Jane Watterson's mother kept a school in Fistard in the 1880s. John Watterson recalls a school c. 1850 on the Lhargee (probably the Largan) run by the 'little schoolmistress and her sister Magead'. He also recalls the school run by Miss Jane Harley in a house on the seaside of Primrose Terrace. Miss Jane Harley appears in the 1851 census, aged twenty-seven, as an unmarried schoolmistress. Her school was often referred to as Harley's College:

> *One day a ship's captain was travelling home by train and chatted to some visitors in the coach. When approaching Castletown, he was asked what was the imposing building on the left (sic). When he said that this was King William's College, he was asked whether he had gone there as a boy. He replied 'No, I went to Harley's College'.*[19]

Most of these private schools probably catered to the needs of the younger children, some of whom may have moved on to the Parochial schools or the National school in later years.

Figure 3. Master/Mistress/Headmaster/Headmistress of schools attended by children of Port St Mary 1829-1979
(Sources: School Log Books, Lists of Charities, Directories (Porters, Thwaites, Slaters), Newspaper Obituaries. Excludes schools in Douglas and Castletown)

Rushen Parochial Boys	Rushen Parochial Girls	Port St Mary National	Port St Mary Infants	Southern Higher Education
1837–1846 Mr Thomas	1831 Mrs Pollard	1837?–1851 Mr Robert Quayle	1896 Mr M J Quilliam	1910?
1846–c.1863? Mr Thomas Qualtrough	1837 Miss Anne Corrin	1851-1853 Mr Binns	1896 Miss Mary Cowley	1924–1927 Mr J Fletcher
c.1863–1888 Mr Edgar Allan	1846–? Miss Margaret Cubbon	1853–? Mr Stibbings	1897 Miss Elizabeth Harris	
1888–1896 Mr J Quilliam	1860–1863 Miss Warburton	1863?–1873 Mr Robert Watson	1905–1927 Miss H Sansbury	
1896–1927 Mr William Cubbon	1863–1890 Miss EC Kewley	1873–1876 Mr Grindley		
	1890–1898 Miss H Hodgkinson	1877– Mr Cornelius Squires		
	1898–1905 Miss Rose A Mully	**Port St Mary Boys' School**		
	1905–1913 Miss Essie Cain	1881–1898 Mr Cornelius Squires		
	C 1913-? Miss E O Marshall	1899–1918 Mr James Place		
	1926–1927 Miss E Kellett	1919–1925 Mr R J Wilkinson		
		1925–1927 Mr FW Wilcock		
Rushen School (Rushen Primary from 1948)				
1927–1943 Mr Wilfred E Kelly				
1943–1953 Mr Percy Cubbin			**Castle Rushen High School**	
1953–1974 Mr William Furth Little			1948–1955 Mr Godfrey Cretney	
Rushen Infants'	**Rushen Junior**		1955–1976 Mr John R Smith	
1974– Miss Audrey Barker	1974– Mr Denis Lewin		1976– Mr Harry Taverner	

Sunday schools

In this period not all children attended the day schools described above. Their only opportunity for learning was afforded by the Sunday schools. In October 1831 eleven guineas were collected at a sermon preached to raise money for the Sunday schools of the Rushen Parish which offered instruction to 300-400 children.[20] In 1847, the Port St Mary Wesleyan Sunday School was run by four male teachers and one female teacher for twenty boys and eighteen girls. The Primitive Methodists also ran a Sunday School. Many of these boys and girls would also have been attending day schools. The 1851 census indicates that of the 76 Port St Mary children *not* attending day schools, nine attended a Sunday School.

King William's College, opened 1833.

Secondary and Higher Education

Until the late 19th century education for the children from ordinary families finished at around the age of thirteen or fourteen. Parents who aspired for a superior education for their sons had options. As noted already the Castletown Grammar School was established in the mid seventeenth century. But in 1830 the foundation stone was laid for the new King William's College [4] and by the late eighteenth and early nineteenth century private secondary education was offered by the Vicars of the Rushen Parish. Some 160 years earlier, Bishop Barrow had created an endowment for a university level college for the training of Island clergy. This vision was never fulfilled. Instead, King William's College offered a secondary level traditional liberal curriculum of English, mathematics, geography, history and writing. This was not unlike the offering of the Castletown Grammar School located nearby, the main difference being that the College charged higher fees and had boarding facilities. Though more expensive than the nearby Grammar School the fee level attracted many 'from across'.[21] In 1834 the College's roll of boys was seventy English, fifty Irish, thirty Manx, ten Scotch (sic) and a few missionaries' children from India.[22]

The sons of a small number of well to do families and clergy living in or near to Port St. Mary attended King William's College. The names of those admitted between 1834 and 1904 are recorded in a remarkable register (see box overleaf).[23]

This register suggests that over a period of seventy years Port St Mary boys enrolled in this elite fee paying school averaged just 0.14 of a boy annually (10/70). For boys from Port Erin it was 0.07. The rest of the Rushen Parish topped the league with 0.16 of a boy enrolled annually over seventy years! Enrolment in this elite school was highly exclusive, socially selective and, except for the sons of the clergy who paid no fees, expensive.

The High School for Girls, Castletown [6]

The main development in schooling for the daughters of the 'better classes' during this period was the establishment in 1875 of the High School for Girls in Castletown with funds donated by Laura, Lady Buchan and Mrs Newton, in a large private house in Castletown. It became known subsequently as the Buchan School. We do not know whether any Port St Mary girls attended this school in its early years.

BOYS FROM THE PARISH OF RUSHEN ATTENDING KING WILLIAM'S COLLEGE 1834-1904

The first boy to enrol at King William's College from the parish of Rushen, in March 1834, was William Corrin, son of the Rev. William Corrin, the Vicar of Rushen. Over the period to 1904 there were just ten boys listed as being from Port St Mary.

Henry, son of William Kelly

Henry Percy, son of Henry Kelly

Edwin and Henry, sons of E Qualtrough the net manufacturer

Thomas, son of J. Qualtrough, the Harbour Master

John and Thomas, sons of J. Lace

Frank, son of T. Lace

Miles son of Mrs Kissack

Francis, son of F. Kitto

From Port Erin there were five boys.

George and Walter, sons of G. Trustrum

James, son of J. B. Thorpe

Henry, son of E. Maddrell

James, son of H. Dalgleish

The remaining eleven boys were from the Parish of Rushen.

William (mentioned above), John, Thomas, George and James, the sons of the Rev William Corrin

Hugh, the son of the Rev H. S. Gill

Charles and Herbert, the sons of the Rev. F. F. Tracey

The other three Rushen Parish boys were the sons of landowners.

Henry, son of E. M. Gawne (Kentraugh Estate)

Edward Murray, son of E. B. Gawne (Kentraugh Estate)

John, son of W. Watterson (Strandhall Farm)

The Isle of Man 1872 Education Act

The Isle of Man Education Act of 1872 is a significant milestone in the Island's education history. A central Board of Education was established and twenty-one School Board Districts constituted in the Island's seventeen parishes and four towns. Known more generally as the School Committees, their members were elected and empowered to provide elementary education for all with immediate effect. They took over many of the elementary schools managed hitherto by the Church. At this time, around 70% of all children in the whole of the Rushen Parish aged 7-13 years were enrolled in school. The Island-wide figure was estimated to be 75.6%.[24]

The inaugural meeting of the Rushen School Committee was held on 25th July 1872. The Captain of the Parish, Mr J. J. Clucas, was elected as chairman with Vicar G. W. Kilpatrick as Vice Chair, thus ensuring a continued presence of the Church in decision making *de facto*, if not *de jure*. The other members in attendance that day were John Kermode, Thomas Qualtrough, Thomas Sansbury and Henry Kelly.

The Committee discharged many responsibilities and wielded considerable power in the community. It raised education revenue from local rates, enforced compulsory education through the imposition of fines, collected 'school pence' from the children, paid for repairs to school buildings, purchased school books and granted fee waivers to those households too poor to pay the school pence. It identified and purchased land for the building of new schools, dwelling houses for teachers and school extensions and hired, paid and, occasionally, fired teachers.[25] In 1876 it gave notice to Mr Grindley, the master of the National School 'for not having managed (the) school well for several months'.[26]

By 1881 there were 158 children aged 5-14 years living in the census district of Port St Mary village, of whom 93% attended school,[27] a considerable increase over the figure of 50% just thirty years earlier. The enrolment of boys was slightly higher than that of girls (95% vs. 90%).

Rushen Girls' School, established 1798, with modern extension.

Rushen Parochial School for Boys, Church Road, opened 1861, now a private residence.

Port St Mary Boys' School, established 1880, with modern extension and windows.

High School for Girls. Castletown, opened 1875.

1879–1929

By the late 1870s a number of changes were afoot in the Port. The railway had arrived (1874), increasing communications of all kinds between the country districts and Douglas, the new capital. Children were able to travel further afield for their schooling – to Castletown and Douglas, albeit for the payment of fees. Regular steamship sailings between Liverpool, Whitehaven and Douglas facilitated the travel of boys from well off families 'from across' to enrol at King William's College and of elite Manx boys to enrol at schools 'across'.

A new boys' school for Port St Mary [8]

Following the 1872 Act, the Port St Mary National School for boys and girls was replaced by the Port St Mary Boys' school in 1880 on land purchased by Mr James Blythe. The new building was erected on the southern corner of the promenade and Station Road with a loan of £400 from the Oddfellows Harbour of Peace Lodge. Mr Cornelius Squires was appointed as Master of the Port St Mary National School in 1877, moving on to become the first head of the new Port St Mary Boys' School. By now all girls aged seven and over attended the Girls' School at the Four Roads. The National School building continued to be used for village meetings of various kinds, including the inaugural meeting of the Port St Mary Village Commissioners in 1890, by which time the building was known as The Rushen Hall.

Port St Mary Boys' School.

Inspections, non-attendance, payments in kind

Schools were visited regularly by education officers. Periodically the Secretary of the Central Board of Education travelled from Douglas to make a 'visit of surprise' to the schools. Visits of lesser surprise were made by Her Majesty's Inspectors (HMI) from England.

Non-attendance was enforced by the Committee. In 1879, for example, it considered nine cases of boys around twelve years of age, seven of whom had gone fishing to Kinsale. Parents were summoned. Charles Clague's son, not yet twelve, had gone fishing because 'the family is delicate... he wanted the boy to earn to help other family members'. The case of James Hudgeon was more complex. Hudgeon informed the Committee that he had three sons. He had sent his youngest son, aged eleven, to the Fisherman's Association to earn some money in order to send his eldest son, who is 'liable to fits', to a trade. He stated further that his second son is a 'cripple' and continues to attend school.[28]

'Payments in kind' were sometimes offered to the schoolmaster instead of fees paid in cash. Thomas Watterson recalled that the fee at Quilliam's school (the Boys' Parochial school) was 1d. per week. One day he took a note from his mother 'to ask if the schoolmaster would have a goose instead of fees for the Xmas quarter. He said he would take it'.[29]

The 1892 Education Act

The 1892 Education Act removed the obligation of parents to pay fees (quarterage) for state-supported elementary education. The passage of the Act was not without controversy. Reform-minded MHKs felt that the masses needed to be educated and instructed in their new functions. Landlord politicians baulked at the idea of being asked to pay an extra tax for fee-free education for the young, especially in the 'agricultural districts', which included Rushen. Such young people, it was felt, did not require education and should not be educated 'beyond their station'. The Act would only result in emigration to towns or to other countries. However, Governor Walpole judged that the centre of political gravity had shifted from the 'classes to the masses'.[30] School fees were abolished.

The Central Board of Education was increasingly exercised about the provision of education for five to seven-year-olds. After some deliberation the Rushen School Committee built an Infants' School in Port St Mary adjacent to the Boys' school [10], and in Port Erin, on the corner of Station Road and Droghadfayle Road. The Infants' Schools opened in 1896 and 1898 respectively. One who attended the Port St Mary Infants' School recalls:

> *(They) taught us how to knit. We had thick needles and thick wool and we knitted a little doll's hat... And I can remember we were saying... we'd only be about five, 'needle in, thread around, catch, take it off... And that was the way you learned to knit ...We used to have little concerts ... and Miss Sansbury would be there, she'd be making hot cocoa, cold days, there was always a fire going.*[31]

Rushen Girls' School, Four Roads.

Rushen Boys' School, 1900 with Headmaster, Mr William Cubbon on left.

The big sand tray, the rocking horse, the biscuits and the gooseberries stood out in the memory of another:

> *...when you'd practised (writing letters in the sand tray) – well, you could just rub it out, couldn't you, it was no problem. Then you got your slate and your slate pencil and you could write with your slate... And ...when you could read, just your simple little books, well then you got a ride on the rocking horse. ... (And) ... Mr Prideaux had the grocer's shop opposite... Every now and again ... his head would come up over the wall and he'd fling in handfuls of broken biscuits and we all tore like mad and grabbed. Hygiene didn't matter, you got your biscuit... you were thrilled to bits with that lot.*[32]

Despite the expansion of fee-free education for five years olds, some continued to pay for private schooling prior to proceeding on to King William's College, the Castletown Grammar School or the Buchan School. The Fieldby School, near the Four Roads, run privately by the Misses Whiteside offered private education into the twentieth century. And throughout the period 1879-1929, the Wesleyan and Primitive Methodist Sunday schools attracted large numbers of children. After its establishment in the late nineteenth century, St Mary's also offered a Sunday School.

Port St Mary Infants' School class with the prized rocking horse.

The 'Tin Tab' school [11]

In 1894 the Douglas Board Secondary School [9] opened its doors to boys and girls for a 'higher grade' education. And in 1896 there was an Island-wide enquiry into post elementary education. It was reported that Port St Mary parents were not overwhelmingly in favour of a 'higher grade school', and certainly not keen on such a school being located in Castletown, for which they would have to pay their children's train fare. However, they were interested in vocational education. Some parents of a 'goodly number' of boys engaged in the fishing season in Kinsale thought that an evening continuation school would be a 'boon... as so many of the boys engaged in the fishing idle their time away in the winter season'. But 'this class of children could not afford a high fee... (and) the subjects most suitable for them would be woodwork, navigation, agriculture, typewriting and shorthand'. For girls, a 'practical education in cookery, laundry work and housewifery would be a real advantage, Ports Erin and St Mary being pre-eminently holiday resorts'.[33]

Following the Higher Education Act (1907), four Higher Education Boards were established across the Island, including one for the South. In November 1910 the Southern Higher Education School [11] was opened for boys and girls aged fourteen and fifteen, admitted through examination, on a site opposite the Rushen Girls' School at the Four Roads. A temporary 'building' of iron and wood, the school acquired the epithet the 'Tin Tab' School and lay at the centre of what came to be known as 'The Rushen School Crisis'.

The Rushen School Crisis – 'the eyes of the Island were on Rushen'

The establishment of the 'Tin Tab' school was surrounded by dissent from the beginning. The Southern Higher Education District comprised the parishes of Rushen, Arbory, Malew and the town of Castletown. The school was intended to offer a more advanced education than that offered in the Elementary Schools, through practical subjects taught in a practical way – including practical mathematics, commercial subjects, woodwork, cookery, dressmaking and navigation. The decision to site the school in the parish of Rushen met with opposition from parents in Castletown and Malew who refused to send their children and whose School Committees refused to pay rates for its upkeep. Head teachers in the elementary schools in all the parishes of the South were unhappy about the establishment of a new school, not least because it was 'creaming' off some of the best pupils.

Following remarks made allegedly by the Chairman of the Council of Education (the central Manx authority at this time) during the Tynwald debate around the Vote for Education in 1911, matters intensified. The Chairman's remarks were interpreted by some as implying that elementary school education was of a lower quality than that offered by the Tin Tab and that the teachers' discontent involved an element of jealousy. Eight head teachers from the elementary Schools of the Southern District protested and wrote to the Chairman via an open letter to the Isle of Man Times:

We do not, as teachers, object to criticism of any action we may take in the cause of education, but at the same time we claim our right, as free citizens of a free country, to reply to any reflections made upon us and uttered in public, where our reputations as teachers are at stake.[34]

Older children at the entrance to the Southern Higher Grade School, otherwise known as the 'Tin Tab' school.

The teachers questioned whether the subjects on offer were in fact being taught at a higher level than in the upper classes of the elementary schools and they reminded the Council that cookery, cottage gardening and woodwork were already on offer in other Elementary Schools. They questioned the practices of the master of the new 'school' canvassing for pupils. They let it be known that one of the School Boards (also referred to as Committees) in the District had written to their teachers requiring children to sit an entrance examination without parental consent and they questioned the numbers of students allegedly enrolled in the school. They also questioned the costs to the ratepayer. The ratio of the teacher salary to pupil costs was more than five times that in the Elementary School across the road:

We have here in the South a waste of public money, where the School Boards have been so very careful over every penny spent on education. Really, it would have been cheaper to send all the children to King William's College.[35]

The teachers were invited by the Council of Education to apologise for writing to the press, which they duly did. The Council accepted the apologies but the Rushen School Board did not, regarding the three Rushen head teachers employed by them – Cubbon, Place and Cain – as insubordinate and inviting them to resign their positions. When they did not, they were dismissed. The school boards of the other parishes in the South did not see fit to dismiss their teachers. Having accepted the Rushen head teachers' apologies initially, the Council of Education members changed their minds, supporting the decision of the Rushen School Board instead.

The public were outraged. There were public meetings, letters to the press from Board members, parents and teachers, a 600-signature petition with and support for the teachers from the Isle of Man branch of the National Union of Teachers. On 7th October 1911 the Rushen School Board, led by Mr J.D. Clucas, H.K. C.P, resigned *en masse*. 'The eyes of the Island were on Rushen', wrote the *Isle of Man Examiner*.[36] Elections for a new board were called. Former members stood alongside a host of new candidates. Amid public debates and some 'disorderly scenes' candidates canvassed votes in what may have been the liveliest election campaign ever conducted within the Parish of Rushen (then as now). All members of the former Board were voted out. The teachers stayed in their positions.

The 1920 Education Act

The Education Act of 1920 abolished the School Committees and Higher Education Boards and replaced them with the Central Council of Education and the Isle of Man Education Authority. Parish parochialism in matters of education began to wane. While a number of children from Port St Mary attended the Tin Tab school from the age of fourteen others attended the secondary school in Douglas after sitting entrance examinations at the age of eleven. By 1921, of 532 students enrolled in the Douglas secondary school, thirty-six were from the Southern Higher Education District, including Port St Mary.

The Amalgamation of the Rushen Schools in 1927 [12]

Given the 'Rushen School Crisis' and the mutual opposition of Castletown and Malew and Rushen to a combined school, a full-blown secondary school of the type available in Douglas for the young people in the South would remain a distant dream.

A different plan was afoot in Rushen: the merger of the three elementary schools of the Rushen Parish, the two Infants' Schools of Port St Mary and Port Erin and the Southern Higher Education 'Tin Tab' School. This would become the Rushen School, built on land at the Four Roads purchased from J.M. Clucas of Ballakilley Farm. The site served the children of Port St Mary, Port Erin, Bradda, Cregneash, Croit-e-Caley, Ballakilpheric and on up the mountain to Scard. It offered education over ten classes – Infants 1-2, Standards 1-5 and Form 1-3. Children entered when they were five years of age and left when they were fifteen. Thus, a type of secondary education up to the age of fifteen was established, even though the official leaving age was still only fourteen. The new school opened for teaching on 4th April 1927.

People of Port St Mary

Photograph below: Miss Essie (back row) with the Rushen Girls' School choir, after winning the prize for singing in Manx Gaelic in c.1910.

MISS ESSIE CAIN

Miss Essie Cain was the headmistress of the Rushen Girls' School at the Four Roads from 1905-1913 and hence an important figure in the daily lives of girls aged seven to fourteen who lived in the Parish.

Born and raised in Castletown, Essie left school aged thirteen and commenced a teaching apprenticeship as a pupil-teacher at Hanover Street School in Douglas. On completion of her apprenticeship she continued to teach at the same school until taking up the headship of the Rushen Girls' School in 1905. She held certificates and diplomas in Physiography, Hygiene, Domestic Economy and St John Ambulance, all of which were sought after qualifications for the education of girls at this time. She took a great interest in the Isle of Man Industrial Guild and in music, and entered her pupils in many music competitions, with great success, part of a long tradition of music in the Rushen schools that continued throughout the twentieth century. Alongside her full-time work in Rushen she served the children of Castletown as a teacher and the librarian of the Castletown Wesleyan Sunday School. A member of the Wesleyan church choir, she also looked after the musical requirements of the Queen Street Mission room for eleven years.

Miss Cain was a key figure in 'The Rushen School Crisis' and the debate about post elementary education in the parishes of the South. Along with seven fellow schoolmasters and mistresses she co-signed an open letter to the Chairman of the Council of Education via the *Isle of Man Times*, in which they expressed their discontent with aspects of recently opened Southern Higher Education 'School' – otherwise known as the 'Tin Tab'. They repudiated an implied criticism made in Tynwald of the quality of work in the higher classes of their schools. They went on to suggest that their work was as effective and certainly more cost-effective than that offered in the Tin Tab. The Council of Education demanded an apology: all eight headteachers apologised. However, the Rushen School Board did not accept the apologies of the Rushen teachers and invited them to resign. They declined and were dismissed. A public outcry ensued – public meetings, letters to the press, a petition signed by more than 600 persons. The Rushen School Board was forced to resign *en masse*. Essie and her co-signatories – James Place, head of the Port St Mary Boys' School and William Cubbon, head of the Rushen Parochial School for Boys – were reinstated.

Probably as a result of her vigorous defence of teachers and education standards – her 'resolute attitude for the rights of teachers' – Essie was the first elected woman chair of the Isle of Man Branch of the National Union of Teachers, in which capacity she represented the Island's teachers at the National Conference held in Weston-super-Mare in 1913. She died later that year, aged 54.

The purpose-built school had been designed with a rural-oriented curriculum in mind and the headmaster, Mr Wilfred E. Kelly, from the parish of Andreas, was selected, in part, for his knowledge of horticulture. All the classrooms faced south with access to garden plots and there was also a large area to the rear for vegetable cultivation. There were eleven teachers, including the head and 365 children – 'the same number as the days in the year' as Edythe, the little girl at the beginning of the chapter, recalled. It was probably the largest Island 'country school' of its day.

Secondary Schools in Castletown for Port St Mary boys
Throughout this period a few boys proceeded to the Castletown Grammar School and King William's College. Willie Bridson attended the Port St Mary Boys' school before moving on to the Grammar School in 1897 at the age of twelve years.

> *What a change! I had to rise at six o'clock and walk to the station – a distance of over a mile – for we lived in the last house but one in Lime Street. There was half a mile from Castletown Station to the Grammar School. There we managed to dry ourselves out before a large stove after a wintry passage. The Master was J.H.W.T. Wicksey, a very capable master, I found, who took a great interest in the boys who showed that they were anxious to learn. School went on till one o'clock, then from two until five o'clock when we had to wait impatiently for the train at 5.45pm to take us home. There were actually half a dozen boys from Port St Mary and Port Erin. I was …away the round of the clock.*[37]

The Castletown Grammar School closed in 1931.

1930–1979
During World War II a number of Port St Mary people who had attended the Rushen School together during the 1920s were killed in action or captured as Prisoners of War. Some families lost all their sons of call-up age and many were left bereft with small children. The Town Hall was used as the Air Raid Precaution centre and was manned day and night.

In 1943 Mr Wilfred E. Kelly retired and was succeeded by Mr Percy Cubbin. The school log books of the time indicate that non-attendance at school was a continuing concern. Childhood illnesses of diptheria, whooping cough, scarlet fever, mumps and the usual coughs and colds were common causes of non-attendance. The desks and books of those who were unfortunate to contract scarlet fever were fumigated. Heavy snow and bad weather generally affected attendance, especially that of the children from Ronague, Ballakilpheric and beyond.[38]

Some school activities reflected an island at war. Ministry of Information films were shown in the school. Clocks were put on an extra hour in May 1941. Gas mask drills were held and children warned of the dangers of mustard gas. The oldest children were allowed to leave school a few weeks early 'owing to the war there is a great demand for child labour.[39] Every September the school closed for a day or two for the national effort of picking blackberries and rose hips. For example, on 15th September 1941 the children and staff picked a total of 214 pounds of blackberries, collected the following day by the Rushen Abbey van. Scrap metal was sold and added to a collection from staff and students that resulted in a cheque of £10.00 for the Prisoners of War fund. An extra holiday was granted in June because the school had smashed its fundraising target for 'Salute the Soldier' week.[40] On other days cocksfoot grass and foxgloves were collected for war measure purposes.

Some children aged eleven sat the scholarship examinations for entrance to the Douglas Secondary Schools, King William's College and the Buchan school. By 1943/44 more than half the thirty-three pupils enrolled in the relevant class were proceeding to the Douglas High Schools for Boys and Girls or to King William's College and the Buchan, the majority travelling daily from Port St Mary on the 7.10am train, returning on the 4.30pm train from Douglas.

Port St Mary Schools for Aliens [13]
As we have seen already in the Introduction, WWII brought a number of 'enemy aliens' to Port St Mary (see also Chapter 7). Hotels and boarding houses on Port St Mary promenade were requisitioned as a camp for 'alien' internees. One of the internees was Minna Specht, a German schoolteacher, who had fled to Denmark and then to Wales and Bristol, from where she was interned on the Island. She opened a kindergarten school for internee children up to age six years in the former buildings of the Port St Mary Boys' and Infants' Schools; and a school for the six to sixteen-year-olds in the

Rushen School Boys' football team, School League champions 1933 (with Headmaster Mr W E Kelly, centre).

'Cornaa' boarding house across the road. Adult education classes were also established in Port St Mary.[41] If the camp in Hutchinson Square internment camp in Douglas became known as 'the university' then the courses on offer to Port St Mary internees might warrant the epithet of a university college or college of further education. The adult education curriculum included Greek, German literature, British history, reading Shakespeare, problems of life and mathematical training plus vocational courses in glove and dressmaking and shorthand and typing.

The post WWII years

Rushen School was closed for two days on the 8th and 9th of May 1945 to celebrate Victory in Europe and on 23rd May two dozen 'Victory' trees were planted in the school grounds by the teachers and children. The trees planted were, appropriately, *Abies nobilis* (the noblest of pines), Sitka spruces and Victory Laurels.

The expansion of secondary education for all was on the horizon. In the first phase of expansion all children aged 11 years and over from the East, the North and the West of the island were admitted to secondary schools in Douglas and Ramsey. Children in the South had to wait another few years. At this time too, the Sunday Schools attached to the chapels and church were well attended.

Castle Rushen Secondary School [14]

Castle Rushen Secondary School admitted its first students on the 1st September 1948 and it was opened officially by the UK Government's Home Secretary, the Hon. Chuter Ede, on the 6th May 1949. The site for the school, in Arbory Street, Castletown, was purchased from the Royal Naval Air Service (the air arm of the Royal Navy operating from Ronaldsway airport). The school was a collection of concrete huts joined together by newly built corridors. The new school acquired the epithet 'Shanty Town'.

The official school name was the subject of much discussion within the Education Authority and with the parents of Castletown and the Rushen Sheading. Castletown High School and Castle Secondary School were both considered. Mrs Cubbon of the

Boys from Mount Tabor Sunday School entered Port St Mary Carnival dressed as the village lifeboat crew c.1954.

Education Authority thought that the term Castle 'rather savoured of dungeons' while Mr W. T. Kneale, Chairman of the Higher Education Committee, thought that a 'secondary' school was a definite type of school and the term 'high' school should not be contemplated. Eventually the name Castle Rushen Secondary School was chosen. The inclusion of Rushen indicated that it took in the area beyond Castletown and the reference to the Castle captured its Manx flavour. However, it would not be long before the name of the school became Castle Rushen *High* School.

The first headmaster was Godfrey Cretney, a Manx man, who served until 1955. The center mistress, Miss G M Wells, assumed the position of Acting Head until the arrival of Mr J R (Jack) Smith, originally from Wallasey, a former Lieutenant Colonel in the Irish Guards and Kings Regiment and Head of English at Stretford Grammar School. In 1976 he was succeeded by Mr Harry Taverner, previously Head of English in North of England schools and Deputy Head of the Douglas High School for Boys. When the school opened in 1948 there were 147 boys and 116 girls on roll. For a period of three years, some of those who had commenced their education from age eleven in Douglas, continued to travel there until completion. The first head boy of the school was Alan Cregeen from Port Erin; and the first head girl Barbara Kennaugh from Castletown. Greeba Creer from Port St Mary was head girl from 1949–1952;[42] and Ian Cottier from Port St Mary was head boy 1953-54. In 1958 enrolment had grown to 465; by 1976 it was 764.

The school was 'comprehensive' and 'bilateral' in the sense that it admitted all children regardless of ability, class or creed and offered two curriculum streams, one more academic than the other. It stressed the development of character, through cultural activities and sports as much as academic success. The school's motto, suggested by Mr John Gell, the handicrafts teacher and Manx scholar was *Lhiat myr toilliu*, to thee as thou deservest. It was remembered by the 'more mischievous pupils' as 'let me tell you!'.[43]

At the school's first Prize Day Mr Cretney described the organisation of pupils in these terms:

> *While there was segregation in the classroom of those quick to learn*
> *and those not so quick, and of the clever and the practical, there was*
> *no such distinction outside the classroom and it was there they aimed*
> *at building up the respect and understanding between those who*
> *would later form the adult population.*[44]

This mixing outside the classroom would take place through sport (football, hockey, cricket, cross country, athletics and later netball), assemblies, the school choirs and orchestra, the playground and a range of school clubs. The school's early days are remembered by former pupils as a happy time when teachers and pupils worked together to make a success of the new school.[45] On leaving Castle Rushen High School Godfrey Cretney moved to England to head up the newly created comprehensive Regis School near Wolverhampton. He was knighted in 1966 for championing the comprehensive system in England, an achievement influenced greatly by his pioneering years in Castletown.[46]

Academic success was certainly encouraged and by 1959 the school was able to boast with pride of the six students who had gained admission to North of England universities, one girl and five boys, at least two of whom were from Port St Mary.[47]

Ten years later Mr. Smith announced at the Prize Day held in November 1958 that 'Shanty Town has been condemned'.[48] A new school planned in accordance with the latest requirements of the Ministry of Education with facilities for the teaching of science, a medical inspection room and a kitchen for the school meals service would be built on land adjacent to Shanty Town. The new school opened in 1962.

Rushen Primary School boys' choir, 1957.

Rushen Primary School sports day c.1956. Girls' potato race.

The Rushen Primary School – 1948 to 1979

Now a primary school, everyday life at the Rushen School for the five to eleven-year-old children changed a little. The younger children struggled to maintain the gardens in the way the older, stronger children had done, an issue on which Inspectors' reports would comment periodically during the next ten years. The gardens were simplified over time. Three now-empty classrooms were refashioned to create a larger room for the Infants and a kitchen and dining room from where daily hot meals were served. After the end of the war swimming at the Port Erin baths had resumed. The children were taken by their teachers to the baths for swimming lessons, for which Education Authority paid the charge of 2d per head. The 'Port Erin and country' boys and girls swam on Fridays between 11am and noon; the Port St Mary boys and girls on Fridays between 3pm and 4pm.

Headmaster Cubbin retired in March 1953. He was succeeded by Mr William F. Little, previously Head of Braddan School and before that a teacher at Murray's Road Elementary School in Douglas, prior to serving in the Manx Regiment during WWII. One of his first tasks was to organise the Coronation of Queen Elizabeth II celebrations held at the school on 2nd June 1953. Sports competitions, a Commonwealth pageant, country dancing and a tea were followed by two days of school holidays. Several Royal visits would follow. For example, on 9th August 1955 the Queen and the Duke of Edinburgh visited Castletown and Mr Little took the children by train (on a very wet afternoon!). On 6th July 1963, Queen Elizabeth the Queen Mother visited Rushen Primary school.

Rushen Primary School girls' choir, after winning the Vancouver Shield at the Manx Music Festival in 1960. Miss Phyllis Kennaugh on the right and Miss Theresa Watterson (pianist) on the left.

The Queen Mother visits Rushen Primary School on 6th July 1963, hosted by Headmaster W.F. Little.

Inspection reports commented favourably on the school's leadership and the higher than average number of teachers with specialised skills in embroidery, dance and music. Music was a major part of the school life and continued a strong tradition that had started in the 19th century in the Girls' school. The trip to Douglas on Mr Corlett's coach on 7th May 1960 for competitions in the Manx Music and Drama Festival was a day to remember. The school won first prize for its action song, girls' choir, mixed choir, boys' choir and percussion band. And because the girls' choir achieved the highest marks in all the children's classes it was awarded the Vancouver Shield, a very proud day indeed for the school and for Miss Phyllis Kennaugh, the music teacher. This reinforced the strong musical tradition of the school and echoed the successes of the Rushen Girls' School choir of an earlier generation and described earlier.

Mr Little retired in 1974 at which point the school was divided into two – an Infants' School (for which a new block had been built in 1972) and a Junior school. Mr Roger Haines headed the school for a term before Miss Audrey Barker assumed the Headship from 1974. The Junior School was headed by Mr Denis Lewin. Miss Barker recalls leading a number of innovations in the Infant's school. Although the classrooms in the new 1972 building had been built 'open plan', in line with the educational thinking of the time, the spaces within the open plan tended to be used by teachers for single grade group teaching with dedicated resources and materials in the traditional way. Over time teachers began to share resources and expertise and to use space flexibly. The curriculum was organised around three main topics, with one of the three reflecting a Manx theme in the traditional way. Maths and English were integrated within topic teaching where possible. Dependence on textbooks was reduced and television was introduced as an educational medium. Assessment practices emphasised individual student progression rather than student comparison and competition.[49]

The two schools were recombined in 1993. Miss Barker assumed the headship of both until her retirement in 1997. With the expansion of the population of Port Erin enrolment numbers had grown in the Rushen Primary School and a separate Port St Mary Primary School opened in September 1993 on a site diagonally opposite that of the Port St Mary Boy's School built over a hundred years earlier.[50]

Ambitions achieved and exceeded

A long view of the history of schooling in Port St Mary suggests that despite legislative measures dating back to the seventeenth century, compulsory education for all was not achieved in practice until towards the end of the 19th century. Parallel schooling tracks for the rich and poor established in the 17th century were reinforced through the establishment for the rich of King William's College in the 1830s and the private High School for Girls (later the Buchan) in the 1870s. The socially inferior track comprised the Parochial schools for boys and girls, Port St Mary National School, Port St Mary Boy's School, the Infants' School and the Sunday schools. The two tracks underlined the social class divisions of the times, confirming the Manx proverb *Ta ynsagh coamrey stoamey yn dooinney berchagh, as t'eh berchys yn dooinney boght.*

The principle of fee-free education for the very poorest was established by the parochial schools from the mid seventeenth century. Important legislation in 1872 shifted the control of schools towards the state, and abolished school fees in 1892. The 1920 Education Act signalled greater government control over education, moves to amalgamate small schools into larger units and the waning of parochialism in education.

Secondary education had a faltering start with the establishment of the Southern Higher Grade 'school' in 1911 and its subsequent incorporation into the Rushen School in 1927. Not until 1948 did the South have its own secondary school, separated from the 'feeder' primary schools. The 1949 Education Act consolidated a series of post war measures designed to provide education for all to the age of fifteen and the expansion of opportunities for post-secondary education through a college of further education and a scholarship scheme for entrance to universities 'across'.

Social class divisions between the fee-free schools and the fee-paying schools remain to the present day. However, from the early 1900s, the boundary between the two tracks of education – one for all and one for the few – became blurred. A few students from less well-off families could, on the basis of excellent performance in scholastic examinations, enter King William's College, the Buchan School and the Secondary School in Douglas. Social mobility based on academic merit was in its infancy. Within the government secondary school, divisions based on academic merit were institutionalised through 'streaming'. Scores on verbal reasoning tests administered at the end of the primary school were used to allocate students to academic 'streams' in the first year of secondary. So while social class remained the main marker of difference between the pupils in the fee-free and fee-paying schools, 'academic merit' rather than social class became the main marker of difference within the government school.

In most respects, Bishop Barrow's seventeenth century vision of elementary *education for all* has been realised, albeit with a continuation of a separate track *for the few*. In other respects – not least secondary education for all and access to university for the many – his vision has been exceeded *erskyn towse* – beyond all measure.

Port St Mary Promenade in early 20th Century.

Classic colour poster of Port St Mary.

Tourism: Not for the Tripper

CHAPTER 6

HUGH DAVIDSON MBE

How tourism developed in Port St Mary

The phrase 'Not for the Tripper' comes from Port St Mary's 1909 Guide:[1] 'Those visiting Port St Mary .... will not be troubled by the Tripper as the inhabitants do not cater for this class of visitor. It is par excellence a family resort.'

One would like to think the Guide was not being intentionally elitist, but merely pointing out that Port St Mary had no intention of entering the mass tourism market and avoided competing with the bright lights and boisterous entertainments of Douglas. Rather it was a place to enjoy beautiful scenery and healthy outdoor pursuits.

For the South, the railway link with Douglas (1874) was the key change which opened up tourism, since Douglas was the main landing stage for visitors, and buses or coaches with useable roads only became widely available in the 1920s.

Port Erin was the first Southern community to develop tourism and the imposing Falcon's Nest Hotel was built in 1861. Castletown never became seriously interested in the visitor accommodation market. Port St Mary fell between these two places in its level of commitment to tourism in the early days and was slow to develop.

A Guide to the South in 1869, by Edwin Waugh,[2] confirms that before the arrival of the railway there was little tourism activity in Port St Mary: 'The inhabitants are almost wholly engaged in agriculture and fishing.' By 1882, just eight years after the arrival of the railway, tourism had become a factor, as Broadbent[3] observes in a Guide to the town, but as a centre for excursions rather than a destination. In the summer about fifty horse drawn vehicles, carrying day trippers, visited the village each day.

There were two 'good' hotels – Miller's Commercial Hotel and Qualtrough's Temperance Hotel.

The advert for Miller's states that its beds were constantly aired and that there was good stabling & lock-up for horses. Visitors with dental problems could visit Mr Walter Anderson, chemist & surgeon dentist who, in his ad, 'Begs most respectfully to inform ... that he is now in a position to supply artificial teeth of life-like appearance, fitted without pain, extraction or springs'.

The transition from fishing village to holiday haunt was not easily achieved and there was friction between the fishing and tourism interests. J.J. Qualtrough, JP, Commissioner for almost fifty years, recalls that in 1891 there were about 100 fishing boats, but accommodation for only twenty-five visitors (in the Bay Hotel and the Ship Hotel, now The Albert). While fishing was declining, there was hope for a revival and some opposition to developing tourism. An important first step was the laying of a modern water supply in 1886. Previously water had come from six public and several private wells.

There were two significant events in 1888. One was the building of Port St Mary's first major hotel, a redbrick pile with more than forty bedrooms. It was aptly called The Cliff Hotel and is now Carrick Bay Apartments.

Next was the laying of the foundation stone of the first house to be built on the new Promenade. This was part of the Ballacreggan Estate, purchased by Mr George Cary, proprietor of the Calf of Man. Port St Mary Promenade, the hub of the village's tourism, was built in the last decade of the nineteenth century and the architect was George Kay of Ramsey. Cronk Road, the location of many future boarding houses, was laid in 1894. By 1909 the Guide warns visitors that there is a 'need to book in advance since during the height of the season it is almost impossible to secure rooms.'[4]

In 1915, the Perwick Bay Hotel was founded and run by Thomas Clague (1851–1915), a successful Southern tourism entrepreneur. What eventually became the Ballaqueeney Hydro started modestly in 1914 with the rental of a single boarding house by the Kelly family.

The glory days of Port St Mary Tourism were from the mid-1930s until the mid-1960s, successful tourism decades for the Isle of Man too.

In the 1930s, Port St Mary's emergence as an Island tourism centre was completed by the expansion of Perwick Bay Hotel and the opening of its swimming pool in 1932; the third and most important extension of the Ballaqueeney Hydro in 1935; the construction of the Model Yachting Pool near the Golf Links in 1937; and the opening in the same year of The Point Hotel, designed in art deco style and with a sea view from every room.

During WWII, part of the village became a Women's Internment camp, mainly at Ballaqueeney and the Promenade but also other areas, which is discussed in the next chapter. From May 1946, Port St Mary was again a popular destination for visitors but by 1979, numbers had declined. However, the 1969 Regatta Program (see page 183) is an indication of how lively the town remained by that time, and Millennium Year in 1979 proved to be a very successful one for Port St Mary, coinciding with the visit of King Olav of Norway.

This chapter elaborates on these themes – examining how Port St Mary advertised and marketed its advantages over the years; visiting some of the main places visitors stayed in; exploring the area's main attractions; and making acquaintance with some of the interesting people involved in the history of Port St Mary tourism from 1829 to 1979.

How Port St Mary marketed itself across the decades
Based on an analysis of annual guides between 1882 and 1977, it's clear the village was skilfully and consistently marketed across many decades.

As early as 1882, it was emphasising health benefits: 'Sewage is discharged into the sea but is at once swept away by the strong tidal currents. These excellent sanitary arrangements have made Port St Mary one of the healthiest localities on the Island.' In 1891 the Commissioners retained the services of Alfred Havilland MRCS, who was apparently an expert on seaside health.[5] As for other resorts on which he reported, this

33639. PORT ST. MARY. NEW PROMENADE.

qualified surgeon wrote a brief but favourable opinion on the advantages of Port St Mary as a health resort, his endorsement being used for many years.

The Promenade, early 1900s.

By 1909,[6] the village had developed its health proposition even more strongly, contrasting Port St Mary's bracing climate with the 'stuffy, pent up valleys' which its visitors had to tolerate for the rest of the year: 'The Isle of Man has a sea-girdle around it, of a width of 16 miles … which endows it with its exceptional climate so favourable to the invalid … there are no stuffy pent-up valleys where prevailing winds are excluded'. It continued, courageously, to make the wind a selling point, as in 1955:[7] 'The bracing breezes on the hillside … make the atmosphere genial, invigorating, and ideal for relaxation and freedom from care'.[8]

Port St Mary identified very early that it needed to differentiate its offer from that of Douglas, emphasising that it was both a place to stay and a centre for exploring the many outdoor and heritage attractions in the South. The 1959 Guide pointed this out forcefully without naming Douglas, claiming Port St Mary 'makes no apology for its lack of bright lights, blaring music or tinselled pageantry. The general atmosphere is one of pleasant contentment and soothing relaxation. It is the ideal holiday resort for the whole family'.

Over the years, Port St Mary gradually developed a visitor proposition which combined the old-world charms of a fishing village with the advantages of a fresh, modern seaside resort. The older part was clustered around the harbour and Alfred Pier and was the southern HQ of the Manx fishing fleet. According to the 1938 guide, the more modern part 'rims two delightful sandy bathing beaches, spread over two headlands and reaches out to Perwick Bay'. The two sandy beaches were of course Chapel Bay and Baie Ny Carrickey, and the stony Perwick Bay was still being promoted as 'the third bay' as late as 1959.

This clear and convincing double theme was continued for decades and the 1959 Guide described the village as a 'romantic old-world fishing port where the sands of time run slowly … and a modern thriving holiday resort'.

By 1909, hotels focused on the range of attractive outdoor pursuits like golf, tennis, boating and 'unsurpassed' fishing.

Port St Mary Beach scene 1960s.

In 1926 the emphasis on outdoor activities continued, but there was also mention of dancing, motor tours, full drinks licenses, and in the case of the Golf Links Hotel, private garages and parking spaces. The car was already making its presence felt. The Ballaqueeney Hydro was the only hotel to offer electric light.

By 1938, hot and cold water (H&C) in every room and electricity throughout was available in many of the larger establishments like the Ballaqueeney Hydro, which also advertised two passenger lifts, dancing (with an excellent orchestra), private bathing pontoon, and fresh produce supplied daily from its own farm. The Perwick Bay also featured its private beach and open-air swimming pool.

Perwick Bay Swimming Pool.

By the 1950s H&C, though now widely available, was still a selling point. Larger hotels typically only had one bathroom per seven to nine rooms, but in those days many people only bathed weekly. Emphasis in the 1950s and 1960s shifted to availability of lounges, then TV and entertainment rooms (ping pong, billiards), nearness to the beaches and outdoor attractions, and quality of food and bedding. In 1955, Perwick Bay Hotel was offering central heating.

In the 1971 Guide, the Bay View Hotel advertised 'rooms with private showers', but this remained unusual even in the late 1970s. The days when most hotels and boarding houses had en suite bathrooms were still some way off.

Notable hotels and boarding houses

The prime locations for Port St Mary boarding houses were the Promenade, Bay View Road, and the Cronk. A typical boarding house would have one bay window, occasionally two, and accommodate eight to twenty guests, with one to three bathrooms. There would be a dining room for breakfast and high tea, and a lounge in larger boarding houses. Meals were at set times.

Only four hotels in Port St Mary could accommodate more than fifty people – the Cliff Hotel (later Carrick Bay Hotel); Ballaqueeney Hydro, which after 1935 could accommodate 300 guests; Mallmore, on the Promenade; and the Point Hotel, which opened in 1937. The Perwick Bay Hotel fell just below the fifty mark.

In the glory says of Port St Mary tourism, from the mid 1930s to the late 1960s, the number of summer visitors sleeping in the village was about 2,000, mostly staying for two weeks. There would have been almost twice as many visitors in the summer as locals.

THE CLIFF HOTEL. The owner and builder was Frederick Callow.[9] Three of the five storeys were at road level, the other two below this on the shore side. These contained the dining room (first floor) and lounges.[10] In earlier days, each had its own extensive balcony.

While not beautiful, the Cliff Hotel had a certain grandeur, with turrets, a tower, and spacious balconies high above the sea, later used for afternoon teas with dramatic views.

By 1909 the name had been changed to the Golf Links Hotel, capitalising on the new Port St Mary Links opened in 1905, but some distance away. In the 1930s basins with hot and cold taps had been installed in every room and by 1951 the name had been changed to Carrick Bay Hotel. It had thirty bedrooms with phones, at a time when few households had them; a spacious vita-glass sun lounge overlooking the sea; lift to all floors, and it was 'convenient for bathing, golf, tennis, bowls, motor boat cruising (the hotel owned its own boat) and fishing'.

Unfortunately, as the advertisement below demonstrates, it was difficult to present the hotel attractively. Whether the five-storey view facing the sea or the three-storey view from the road was used, the hotel had a bleak and unwelcoming appearance.

From the mid 1960s the hotel disappeared from the village guide and in the 1980s it was converted into apartments, known as Carrick Court.[11]

The Cliff Hotel, renamed The Golf Links Hotel in 1909.

Golf Links Hotel

Port St. Mary

FULLY LICENSED.

Commanding Splendid Land and Marine Views.
Private Garages and Parking Ground.

Tennis Courts and Golf Links three minutes from Hotel.

Boating.   Bathing.   Dancing.
Fishing in Bay Unsurpassed.

ENTIRELY NEW MANAGEMENT.

The original lift is still operational. It recently broke down, and the diagnosis was that the oil in the gear shaft had not been changed since 1946. The lift is now working well again.

The Point Hotel, now apartments. (photograph with permission from Peter Killey)

THE POINT HOTEL was the last significant hotel to be built – in art deco 'Moderne' style. It opened in 1937, had twenty-four bedrooms, each with a sea view. The hotel was licensed and full board, including accommodation with four meals daily, cost 10/6d per person per day (£36 in today's money).

The Point Hotel was owned and managed by the Summers Christian family from 1937 until the mid-1960s and thereafter by Mr & Mrs McCutcheon until it closed and was sympathetically converted into apartments. Unlike the Promenade boarding houses and the Ballaqueeney Hydro, the Point Hotel was never occupied by internees in WWII, because it was outside the boundary of Rushen Camp.

THE PERWICK BAY HOTEL[12] (originally THE "PERWICK HOTEL") was built by Thomas Clague (1851–1915) in about 1911 and developed in three stages. The original building was twin gabled with two colonial style open balconies and resembled a large country house, facing south towards the sea and high above the beach below.

During the 1920s a large accommodation block was built above the original building, connected by a covered passage.

The sun parlour of Perwick Bay Hotel.

Before the swimming pool was built, the south-facing open balcony was enclosed and the resulting sun parlour became a flagship feature of the hotel.

The third major development, in 1932, was the addition of a swimming pool, down a steep slope below the hotel, facing the stony beach and partly compensating for it. The pool was 100ft long and 40ft wide, with pavilion, refreshment room and sunbathing terraces. It was opened on 27th July 1933 by His Excellency the Lieutenant Governor Sir Claude Hill:[13]

> 'The Governor confessed that when he was first approached regarding opening the Baths, he had some anxiety lest he be expected to appear in a bathing suit and plunge into the Baths, because when he opened a Golf Course it was usual to hit a ball off the first tee. He assured them that nothing would have induced him to do this, because he anticipated that it might be a day, such as it turned out to be, when it was rather chilly...'

In 1935, twenty-one new bathing huts were added. The pool was not heated but the location was a suntrap with wonderful views.

The hotel name seems to have changed to the Perwick Bay Hotel in the 1920s. It differed from most other local hotels and boarding houses in being open all year round. The hotel made a feature of Christmas and Easter, marketing its advantages to non-residents especially for lunch or afternoon tea in the Sun Parlour. It hosted many local events for lunches or dinners and Graham Shaw, in his earlier days as a chef, recalls cooking a dinner for 150 guests. There were wedding receptions too, and mhelliahs for Rushen Silver Band. Especially in the 1930s, under Mr Scrimgeour, Perwick Bay Hotel became a prestigious location.

During World War II (1939–1945), servicemen were billeted at the hotel and a room set aside specifically for officers. The hotel was not considered suitable for internees due to its remote location. However, it remained open to visitors for meals, and functions continued to take place.

The hotel experienced difficult times in 1945-53 despite the booming island tourism industry, and had a variety of licensees. It was bought in 1953 by the Pye family and the new licensee was David Selwyn Pye, 23 years old 'who had seven years' experience in the catering trade'.

From 1960 until the mid-1970s local sisters Mona and Mary Quillen owned and ran the hotel. The final owners, from 1978, were Ken and Margaret Ives. Ken retired in 1988, having become concerned about subsidence and he sold the property to Roy Kermode who built apartments on the site.[14]

The hotel was distinctive and atmospheric. At its peak, it had twenty-four guest rooms. There were thirteen acres of gardens, brows and pastures, inhabited by a variety of animals, some, like the goats or geese, quite aggressive towards guests winding their way down the path to the swimming pool below.

It's doubtful whether the Perwick Bay Hotel was particularly profitable to its owners. The building was expensive to maintain, the beach stony, and, together with the swimming pool, could only be accessed via a steep and winding path. Also, the pool area was not licensed.

Today there is little trace of the existence of either the hotel or the swimming pool, only memories.

BALQUEEN HYDRO.[15] The hotel evolved through four names. First 'Ballaqueeney', linking up with the farm of the same name owned by the Kelly family. Then, in the late 1920s, it became Ballaqueeney Hydro, to avoid confusion with the farm. In 1946, the name was changed to Balqueen Hydro. And finally, in 1970, following the sale of the Balqueen Hydro by the Kelly family in 1965, the name had to be changed as a condition of the sale and became the Bayqueen.

In its heyday from the mid-1930s to the mid-1960s, the Balqueen Hydro was one of the leading family resort hotels in the north of England and usually full, from 1st May to the end of September each year.

The hotel originated from two boarding houses separated by a large gap. In 1914 Mr W.A. Kelly rented the left-hand house from the Lewthwaites and when that traded well, the right-hand one from Sir Hall Caine, the famous author. Later, he bought both.

In 1926, the double bay boarding house was extended from two bays to three and the space between the two houses filled with an attractive new building which comprised a large ballroom in art deco style, rooms above and a balcony built along the front. This balcony was very popular for sitting, promenading, and dancers would do the Hokey Cokey and Conga all around it.

Walter Kelly visited the USA with his parents in 1932 to review the latest in American hotels, especially the new Waldorf Astoria[16] in New York, then the largest hotel in the world with 1,500 rooms.[17]

His family commissioned Alec Davidson FRIBA, FRICS to design an extension.[18] Alec had himself worked as an architect in New York for six months in the late 1920s, after completing his thesis at Liverpool University on designing 'an imaginary new hotel on Fort Island, Isle of Man'.

The thesis gained a distinction and was featured in *The Architects Journal*. This, along with the Kellys' visit to New York, greatly influenced the design for the extension, with two large towers, which is now registered.

This extension added fifty more bedrooms, in addition to a new reception hall with terrazzo tiles laid by Italians who came over to do the work, a mezzanine floor above the new reception area, lifts, and a dining room to seat 400. The builders were McArds, and Arthur Cross and his family built the elaborate ceilings.

The building dominated Chapel Bay for sixty-six years until the right-hand half (the pre-1935 portion) was demolished in 2002.

After the Kelly family sold the hotel and property in the late 1960s it was owned and run by various companies until bought by Victor Sharma. After a few years of continued operation, it closed in the mid-1980s.

Back in happier days, the 1955 brochure said: 'Sunny balconies, the large dining room, ballroom, lounges, billiards room and the fine entrance hall combine to ensure the comfort of guests.' There were four set meals, yet no one appeared overweight. Food was fresh and high quality, sourced daily from Ballaqueeney Farm or local suppliers.

The hotel appealed to families and was unlicensed. Many guests stayed year after year, sometimes twice a year. The orchestra under Harold Moorhouse played four nights

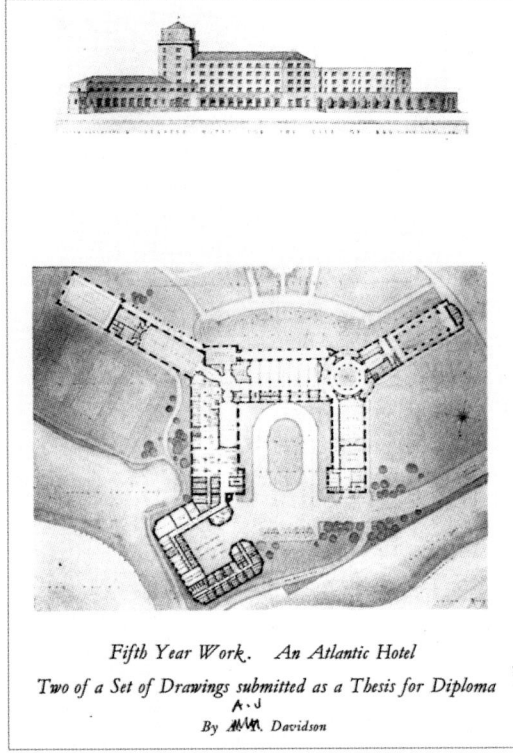

Fifth Year Work. An Atlantic Hotel
Two of a Set of Drawings submitted as a Thesis for Diploma
A. J
By A̶W̶M̶ Davidson

Imaginary new hotel on Fort Island: Drawings for Alec Davidson's thesis.

Stage 3 – Balqueen Hydro, final result.

*Fred Hoyle,
Entertainments
Manager with
guests.*

weekly for dancing in the ballroom. Thursday was Fancy Dress Gala Night, while on Sunday guests did concerts or there were sometimes visiting performers.[19]

There were ninety summer staff including five permanent farm staff. Typically, fifty would be local and the forty from 'overseas', mainly from Liverpool and Ireland, and recruited personally by Walter Kelly each year. About ten local staff were retained for the whole year, doing repair and improvement work in the winter.

Many visiting staff got married to local people and settled in the Isle of Man. Barbara Guy from Manchester met her husband John Guy in that way. Barbara worked in 1970 as a waitress for £7 per week plus tips, free board and lodging, banking her wages and living on tips. Each waitress was responsible for an area with tables for twenty guests.[20]

BALQUEEN HYDRO, PORT ST. MARY, ISLE OF MAN

*The Ballaqueeney
waitresses.*

MALLMORE. This brief account is based mainly on an interview with Adrian Bashforth,[21] the nephew of Miss E.B. Qualtrough (1912–1993) whom, it's thought, worked at Mallmore for sixty years. This period spanned from 1928, when her father bought Mallmore, until her retirement in 1990. There was a brief break in WWII when she worked in a local bank.

Mallmore was built as part of the original Port St Mary Promenade in the 1890s.

William Samuel Qualtrough, who was in shipping, owning and operating schooners in Port St Mary, bought Mallmore in 1928, but died ten years later. His wife, Harriet, with help from her daughter Beatrice (Miss E.B) operated Mallmore until her death, aged 76, in 1956.

The original Mallmore consisted of two bays. The only other boarding house with two bays on Port St Mary Promenade was Southlands, next door to Mallmore. In 1953, Harriet bought Southlands from Mrs Mary Eslick,[22] and then Cronk Wyllan, which had one bay.

Adrian says that occasionally, in the high season, Mallmore was overbooked, and guests would be temporarily accommodated in the Qualtrough family home, taking meals at Mallmore.

Following the sharp decline of the Manx tourist industry in the 1970s and 1980s, the hotel was sold in the early 1990s after the death of Beatrice Qualtrough. The original Mallmore was sold to the Scripture Union in 1994; the previous Southlands was bought by Mr & Mrs Berry and the name changed to Aaron House; and Cronk Wyllan was purchased by Alan Leece, the builder.

At Mallmore's peak, at 1pm a maid would walk on to the Promenade ringing a bell to summon visitors on Chapel Beach to lunch. There was also afternoon tea in the lounges. The hotel had an older type of customer than Bayqueen Hydro. Unlike the Bayqueen, the Mallmore never had a ballroom.

The Mallmore in the 1950s.

Beatrice Qualtrough.

Adrian Bashforth remembers his aunt as kind and generous. On one occasion, he and his brother Eric were sword fighting in the dining room and accidentally despatched a light fitting with a swish of the sword, but the incident was treated lightly. In winters Beatrice occasionally went on holiday in the UK, sometimes staying with a relative in Liverpool, but she spent most of the off season redecorating & refurbishing Mallmore with family help.

CONCORD HOTEL. The 1926 Guide refers to 'the Carlton Boarding Establishment', which sounds Dickensian. The proprietress was Mrs Henderson (late of Yorkshire).[23]

Mrs Lilian Alway visited the Island on a holiday paid for by her grandfather in 1947. She saw a for sale sign on the Carlton and persuaded her husband to buy it. She changed the name to The Concord Private Hotel because 'concord' signified Peace. Mr Alway continued his butcher's business in Liverpool for about ten years thereafter, running it himself in the winter, and through a manager when he was in the Isle of Man during summer months. He then settled permanently in the Island.

Initially Lilian bought only two of the three bays at Concord, and purchased the third bay some years later. She ran the hotel for about thirty years.

Lilian and her sister were known as 'the beautiful sisters', and her sister became a Bluebell Girl, dancing at the Folies Bergère in Paris.

*Right: Lilian Alway
Far right: Lilian's sister, Daphne, at the Folies Bergère.*

The whole family was very musical, something her daughter, Daphne Murray, has inherited. Mr Alway played the cello and was a member of the Gaiety Orchestra.

Among other tasks, he sliced eggs for forty individual salads and on completion would twang the slicer like a harp, singing 'another week gone'. His daughter Daphne, as a waitress in her teens, could balance four plates of soup with saucers on her arms.

Lillian Alway played a leading role in the life of Port St Mary. She spent twenty-five years as a Commissioner, some as Chair, was a qualified State Registered Nurse, effective public speaker, and busy volunteer for many organisations.

Concord Hotel.

Concord Hotel was closed to guests from 1st October to 1st May, and the family lived on the lower floor. There were musical evenings for friends and Mr and Mrs Alway would usually drive to Germany or Switzerland for a three-week holiday.

How visitors spent their time

In the peak decades of Port St Mary tourism, the main attractions were scenic and active. The village was a hub for travel to other parts of the south through coach trips or by boat along the coast to the Calf of Man. There were outdoor events, tournaments, and photographic competitions, with the Regatta one of the highlights.

Time near and on the water. Chapel Bay would be filled with people – lying on the beach, sun bathing, playing games, paddling, and swimming. There was also plenty of sailing, row boating, and many boat trips. As early as 1882,[24] boats were always for hire, with experienced boatmen ready to row parties to Calf Island and the Chickens Rock Lighthouse. In the 1950s there were many sailings every day from Chapel Beach to The Calf.

Sugar Loaf Rock and The Chasms.

Scenic Attractions. The 1950 Visitors Directory describes some of these.[25] Visitors seemed more interested in caves & rock formations then:

- **Boating** – Port St Mary via Shag Rock (Perwick Bay), Noggin Head, the 'celebrated' Fairy Caves, The Hall, Sugar Loaf Rock and The Chasms
- **The Chasms** (300ft) – 'evidence of age-old cataclysm of nature, in one of the recesses of which is a small stone circle, possibly of the Bronze Age'
- **Mull Circle** – stone circle of Neolithic period, unique in the British Isles
- **Behind the breakwater** – limestone rocks scratched and grooved by glacial action while at the base a Neolithic floor was discovered in 1886
- **Black Head** – eastern projection of the Mull Peninsula. Perpendicular precipice rising 350 ft above the sea
- **Gansey Point** (Magic Bay) – The Smelt, lead smelting
- **Chicken Rock** – 122ft high, cost £100,000 when opened in 1875. Three lighthouse keepers always on duty, one onshore relief. All lived in Port St Mary

Land-based sporting activities: golf, tennis, and bowls were the main ones:

- **Golf** – The first 9-hole course was laid out by William Fernie on The Cronk in 1903 and this lasted until 1918 when the Club was wound up. From about 1920, a new 9-hole course was laid out on land belonging to Henry Cooil of Ballacreggan Farm between the Railway Station and Balqueen Hydro. By the early 1930s Mr Cooil 'had tired of visitors, particularly from the Ballaqueeney Hydro, and some locals sneaking over the walls at the far end of the course and playing the bottom holes without paying a fee', and the course was closed. The present 9-hole course was opened on 3rd June, 1936, and has flourished since. Very few places in the British Isles have had three golf courses in different locations.[26]
- **Tennis and bowls** – From the 1920s T.H. Qualtrough offered seven grass and three newly laid hard courts. There were tennis courts and a bowling green at Ballaqueeney Farm, near the Railway Station

Coach Tours: Corletts offered all-day Island tours, afternoon and evening tours and mystery tours. Millers ran coach tours, a taxi service, and rental cars.

Dancing: The Balqueen Hydro had a splendid ballroom with permanent orchestra, but it was open to residents only. The Perwick Bay Hotel also had a small ballroom. Visitors keen on dancing would often gravitate to Port Erin, where many of the hotels had ballrooms. The Belle Vue Hotel, later the Port Erin Royal (now demolished), was especially popular.

Cinema and Shows: Visitors could go to Port Erin Cinema or one of the many in Douglas. The big shows all took place in Douglas at the Gaiety, the Palace, or Derby Castle.

People of Port St Mary

THOMAS CLAGUE Senior (1851–1915) – A true entrepreneur

Mr W.A. KELLY & Mrs ANNIE KELLY[27]

Thomas Clague played a leading role in the life of both Port St Mary and Port Erin and was one of the great entrepreneurs during the early days of Southern Tourism. A successful farmer and butcher, he ran businesses in both villages with his son Thomas Clague Jr. He built and ran the Belle Vue Hotel (name changed in 1980s to Port Erin Royal) in Port Erin, and the Perwick Bay Hotel from the early 1900s.

Together with other investors he opened the Calf of Man as a visiting resort, but this did not prove lucrative. He became sole proprietor of The Calf and sold it to Mr Haigh of Huddersfield for £2,650 in 1911. Mr Clague was also one of six subscribers to the first Port St Mary Golf Club in 1903, describing himself as "Farmer", and became an ardent supporter. He was also central to building a Golf Course around Bradda Head, sponsoring its first competition in 1896.

However, he came to a sad end. In a spirit of public duty, he tried to restrain the drunken proprietor of the Albert Hotel in Port St Mary. After a violent struggle, Mr Clague died as a result of having a weak heart. Seven hundred people attended his Funeral.

Annie Kelly (1884–1972) was an outstanding business woman and had exceptional drive. Her husband, W.A. Kelly, initially a farmer, partially lost his sight in an accident with a lime spraying pump when treating apple trees. This limited his ability to work the farm. They decided to keep Ballaqueeney Farm, which has been owned by the Kelly family since the sixteenth century, but to enter the then fast-growing boarding house business in 1914. The farm provided fresh supplies to their boarding houses (two initially) daily, as a captive customer, and in turn, this became an important selling point for visitors staying there – a clever example of vertical integration.

W.A. Kelly MHK was a farmer, hotelier, and Member of the House of Keys for Rushen from 1928-29 and 1931-46. He chaired the Board of Agriculture and pioneered the introduction of the Bovine TB Eradication Scheme. He was also a Methodist Lay Preacher and expert horticulturist.

Together, Mr & Mrs Kelly guided the Balqueen Hydro through its three major stages of development from 1913 to 1936, when their 26-year-old son Walter took over (see below). During WWII, when Walter was away, they returned to run the Balqueen, first as part of the Rushen Women's Internment Camp, then, when that moved to Spaldrick (Port Erin), as an Officer Cadet Training Camp for the Royal Pay Corps.

According to Robert Kneale, who worked as a

People of Port St Mary

porter at the hotel and helped at the farm, Mrs Kelly was firmly in charge, and he always referred to her as 'Madam', which was apparently how she wanted to be called. Robert said she was a good organiser, strict but kind, and during WWII she often had to go up to talk to the internees to keep them in order.

MR WALTER KELLY, OBE, JP (1910–1969)

Walter was modest, charming, well-liked and highly respected by guests, staff, and locals alike. He took over the Balqueen from his parents in his mid-twenties but was well-prepared, influenced by training at the Mayfair Hotel and the Dorchester in London.

Walter developed the Balqueen Hydro into a first-class hotel offering an excellent holiday experience at reasonable prices from 1936 until WWII, then from 1946 to 1965 when he retired for health reasons.

In WWII, he rose to Lt Colonel in the Royal Army Service Corps. His wife Betty, who also played her part in the Balqueen's success, said she once enquired about what Walter did to receive his OBE. He replied: 'For the feeding of one million people in 1943-44 after the Allied invasion of Southern Italy' (he was the Colonel in the RASC responsible for supply lines for troops and civilians after the Anzio Beachhead Invasion). This gives some measure of his calibre.

Walter returned from WWII service in March 1946 when the hotel had not yet been de-requisitioned from war use, but somehow, he and the staff managed to open the hotel to their enthusiastic visitors on 1st May 1946.

He appears to have been a very good 'hands-on' managing director, supervising every meal. Each night Walter stood in the hall at dinner time, greeting and chatting with guests. He selected most members of staff and was a skilful and motivating manager of people. The hotel seems to have had well designed processes and high standards. There was low staff turnover, and many guests returned year after year, sometimes twice a year.

JAMES SCRIMGEOUR (1872–1958)[28]

He was always known as 'Mr Scrimgeour', not 'James', retaining a respectful distance from staff. He became a leading figure in the South during the 1930s and beyond, developing the Perwick Bay Hotel into a

People of Port St Mary

prestigious location for events and an attractive place to stay for visitors.

Mr Scrimgeour was a cotton mill owner in Lancashire, an industry in crisis in 1930, badly affected by new foreign competition and the Great Depression.

During the 1920s, 800 Lancashire Mills closed, and more than 300,000 jobs were lost.

Many of Mr Scrimgeour's family and friends were affected, and some committed suicide. In 1930, the family clubbed together to form a private limited company, with finance to buy the Perwick Bay Hotel. It was to be managed by Mr Scrimgeour, with his friend, Charlie Pearce.

His first wife died young, leaving him with five children. His second wife, whom he married in the early 1920s, was two decades younger. She and their daughter Eileen also worked very hard at the hotel. Eileen (b.1923) worked in many Port Erin hotels, married Alan Swales in the 1950s and helped their son Philip build up the very successful A.C. Swales flooring business in Laxey. She retired aged 86.

Mr Scrimgeour seems to have been a man of courage and enterprise, and it had always been part of his vision to turn the Perwick Bay into a resort hotel, with in-house entertainment and a swimming pool below. The new swimming pool opened in 1932 and pool users had to pay 2/6d per week to use it. But the pool closed after teatime and many locals have memories of bathing free, some even skinny dipping at midnight. Mr Scrimgeour knew this but felt they did no harm. He was 58 when he arrived on the Island, and retired in 1945, aged 73, when the hotel was sold.

Miss Furmston, Ivy Ward, and her daughter Jane Fargher, 1962.

MISS FURMSTON – Linen Keeper at the Balqueen[29]

Miss Furmston was engaged to be married and planned to emigrate to America with her fiancé. They arranged to meet at the *Titanic*'s berth in Southampton, but Miss Furmston missed her bus – and therefore the ship. Her fiancé, however, decided to go ahead without her. He drowned in the disaster on 15th April 1912.

We know nothing of Miss Furmston's life between 1912 and May 1930 when she became linen keeper at the Balqueen Hydro. She was perhaps around 40 years old on arrival and spent about forty happy years at the hotel. Jane Fargher, the daughter of Charlie Ward (see below), has the first page of a letter by Miss Furmston describing her job. It is remarkable that someone who experienced such drama could settle down to a life of quiet routine. Here is an excerpt from the letter:

'Since 1930 I have been Linen Keeper ... and have had a very happy time here. When the Hydro was enlarged in 1935, I had a very nice large room given over for linen ... and it is very convenient and pleasant, with large shelves for all the different things to keep for the bedrooms and dining room and the

People of Port St Mary

waitresses and kitchen staff. During my time here we have only had three new Head Housekeepers ... and they were very nice.'

Mrs MAY ADDISON (1916–2003)[30]

May was born in Birkenhead, one of five girls. Times were hard and they used to watch the Manx boats going up and down the Mersey every day. In 1936 they came to the Isle of Man for summer work; one worked at the Point Hotel, two worked at Mallmore and two at the Ballaqueeney. Three of the sisters married Manxmen, including May, who married Tom Addison, a baker at the Ballaqueeney.

After the War, Tom came back to his old job as baker and May worked as a chambermaid during the season for many years. Tom was on the full-time staff at the Balqueen and in the winter worked on general maintenance and decorating the building. When the Balqueen was sold by Walter Kelly, Tom worked there for another three years, then moved to Martin Baker's ejector seat factory at Ronaldsway. May and Tom's daughter Margaret married Alex Downie, who became an MHK and Government Minister.

Several mothers and daughters and sisters in the same families came year after year, from Liverpool and Ireland in particular, to work the summer season at The Balqueen. Many visitors were regulars too. They knew so many staff it was like being home from home.

Mona Quillen on her 100th birthday with Laurence Skelly MHK and Juan Watterson SHK.

MISS MONA QUILLEN (1915–2017)[31]

Mona's father was a stone mason and travelled to The Calf to fix the lighthouses there. She wanted to teach, but there was not enough money in the family for that. So, aged 14, she started work in the Allendale Cafe in Port Erin as an apprentice baker.

In 1932, Mona and her sister Mary moved to Cronk Wyllan, a guest house on Port St Mary Promenade. But Cronk Wyllan only had twelve bedrooms with not enough profit to justify expansion, so they sold it in 1960 for £990 and bought the Perwick Bay Hotel for £8,000 with a mortgage.

Mona and Mary built up the business with functions, weddings, and public meetings. Mona focused on the cooking and Mary ran the front of house. No one ever got drunk. Mona said, 'If people had a lot to drink, they were told to have a rest and sit quiet for a while'.

Brian Cooil recalls that the two sisters had nicknames. One was called 'yes, yes, yes', and the other, 'no, no, no'. He is not certain which was which, but suspects that Mary, who was quite shy and inclined to assent, was 'yes, yes, yes'.

People of Port St Mary

In 1976, Mona and her sister took out another loan, and unfortunately ended up having to sell the hotel for what sounds like a knock down price.[32]

They were very unlucky to have had a mortgage in the 1970s, a decade of very high inflation when borrowing costs would have escalated.

Mona and Mary continued to work in the tourist trade for some years. At various times Mona worked at the bar of the Belle Vue Hotel when Gil Robertshaw (Chris Robertshaw MHK's father) was manager, and at one point she ran the Carrick Bay Hotel but left after a year 'because the profits were not much'. The sisters travelled to many parts of the world when they took annual holidays while running the hotel and settled in Port St Mary when they retired.

Mona continued to live at her bungalow and a very well-attended celebration of her 100th birthday took place there on 26th March 2015, with visitors including the Lieutenant Governor.

Charlie Ward as Head Porter (2nd from right).

CHARLIE WARD (1913–1980)

Charlie started work at Ballaqueeney Hydro aged 14. He began as a junior porter and worked his way up to head porter. He served in WWII in North Africa and returned to the hotel after the War. Subsequently his first wife died and he married Ivy, a waitress at the Balqueen, who is pictured earlier in this section with Miss Furmston.

Charlie was a good organiser, and as Walter Kelly's wife Betty says, he was: 'always very reliable and dependable'. He became a key player at the Balqueen and when Walter Kelly retired for health reasons in 1965, Charlie became joint manager with Bobby Littler (see below). In total, excluding the War years, he worked for more than 40 years at the Balqueen.

BOBBY LITTLER

Bobby was an insurance agent in Southport, pre-WWII, when he served in the Manx Regiment.[33] In 1948, Walter Kelly invited Bobby to be bookings and assistant manager at the Balqueen. His main job was to keep the hotel full from 1st May to 30th September. Betty Kelly says he did this brilliantly, with military precision – he had a vast diagram across the wall of his office showing the bookings status of every room throughout the season.

Bobby trained in the winter at the 5-star Mayfair Hotel in London and holidayed most years in Baden Baden, a stylish Spa Town in Germany. He had a slightly military style, was very well dressed, impeccably polite and highly organised. Like Walter Kelly, he was greatly liked and respected by guests. When he died, Bobby left £50 in his will to everyone who had worked at the Balqueen between 1948 (when he joined) and his retirement

People of Port St Mary

(1970s). Many local people successfully claimed their £50 from Bobby's advocate. Bobby was a distinctive personality and two reminiscences give a flavour of this:

Sir Miles Walker, Chief Minister 1986–1996: '*I used to deliver one pint of milk each day to Bobby Littler's house, next door to The Moorings (now Chapel Bay House) where Walter and Betty Kelly lived. Bobby was polite but pedantic. He insisted that his pint was always to be placed on the left side of the doorstep, not the right, and when there was any deviation from this process he was quick to point this out.*'

Edwin Looney, who was lift boy at the Balqueen in 1955: '*At the Bayqueen, Walter Kelly was the boss, delightful, very hands on. Bobby was second in command, unflappable. The Bay View Hotel in Port St Mary was Bobby's favourite evening place. After dinner was completed he was usually there. At the Bay View he was friendly and relaxed and would talk to me. But he was very different on duty – formal and correct.*'

JOAN ESLICK (1926–2006)

Joan Eslick was born in Port Erin to Mary and James Eslick. Together with her relatives, Mary bought Southlands Boarding House on the Promenade. Mary and her family eventually sold Southlands as she was looking for a smaller boarding house and bought Manchester House in the High Street with good views of Chapel Beach below.

Joan grew up in Port St Mary, attending Rushen Primary School junior and senior schools. During the summer holidays she would take a container to the wishing well on the hill leading down to Chapel Beach and fill the jugs for the guest tables with wishing well water.

In WWII Joan joined the RAF and became a wireless operator stationed at Plymouth and in Scotland in Coastal Command. When Joan returned after eight years in the RAF, she became the head receptionist at the Balqueen Hydro working alongside Walter Kelly and Bobby Littler.

Joan met and married her husband, Karsten Kjolner, who was running the Brobourn boarding house in Port Erin. Karsten was Norwegian and shared his time between the boarding house, where he would prepare all the food, and travelling back to Norway whaling, when the summer season was finished.

They had two daughters, now Alison Graham and Jane Saywell of Rushen Heritage Trust.

With encouragement from Joan during their summer holidays, daughters Jane and Alison would collect scallop shells from the factory on the harbour, paint scenes of boats, seagulls, and hills, and sell them to the visitors who would decant from the coaches opposite Mount Tabor Church. Visitors were very pleased with their 6d genuine locally collected and prepared souvenir of Port St Mary, as were the girls, having made a little pocket money from their efforts.

Joan Eslick shaking hands with Princess Marina.

PORT ST MARY REGATTA PROGRAM
1 August 1969

Morning on the Beach

9.30   Sand modelling for 7, 10, 14 year olds

10.30   Novelty Dog Show

           1. Waggiest Tail   3. Cheekiest little beggar

           2. Most soulful eyes   4. Owner in best condition

11.00   Bonny babies

11.30   Beach fashions

           1. Under 5   3. Boys

           2. Girls   4. Ladies

12.00   Bay Swim, Inner Harbour to Chapel Beach

12.30   Water Ski demonstration

Afternoon in the Harbour

2.30   Yacht Racing

2.30   Aquatic Sports

4.30   Presentation of Prizes

Evening at Happy Valley

6.45   Manx Folk Dancing – Town Hall Green

7.00   Fancy Dress assembly at Mount Tabor

7.15   Parade to Happy Valley, Rushen Silver Band

7.30   Judging of Fancy Dress

8.30   Pinta Competition for men over 18. 1st Prize: 1 gallon of beer

        Barbeque Band Concert

9.00   Regatta Dance

        The Infinity & Teddy Palmer Trend of Belfast. Up to 12.45

ADMISSION: 7/6d (38p)

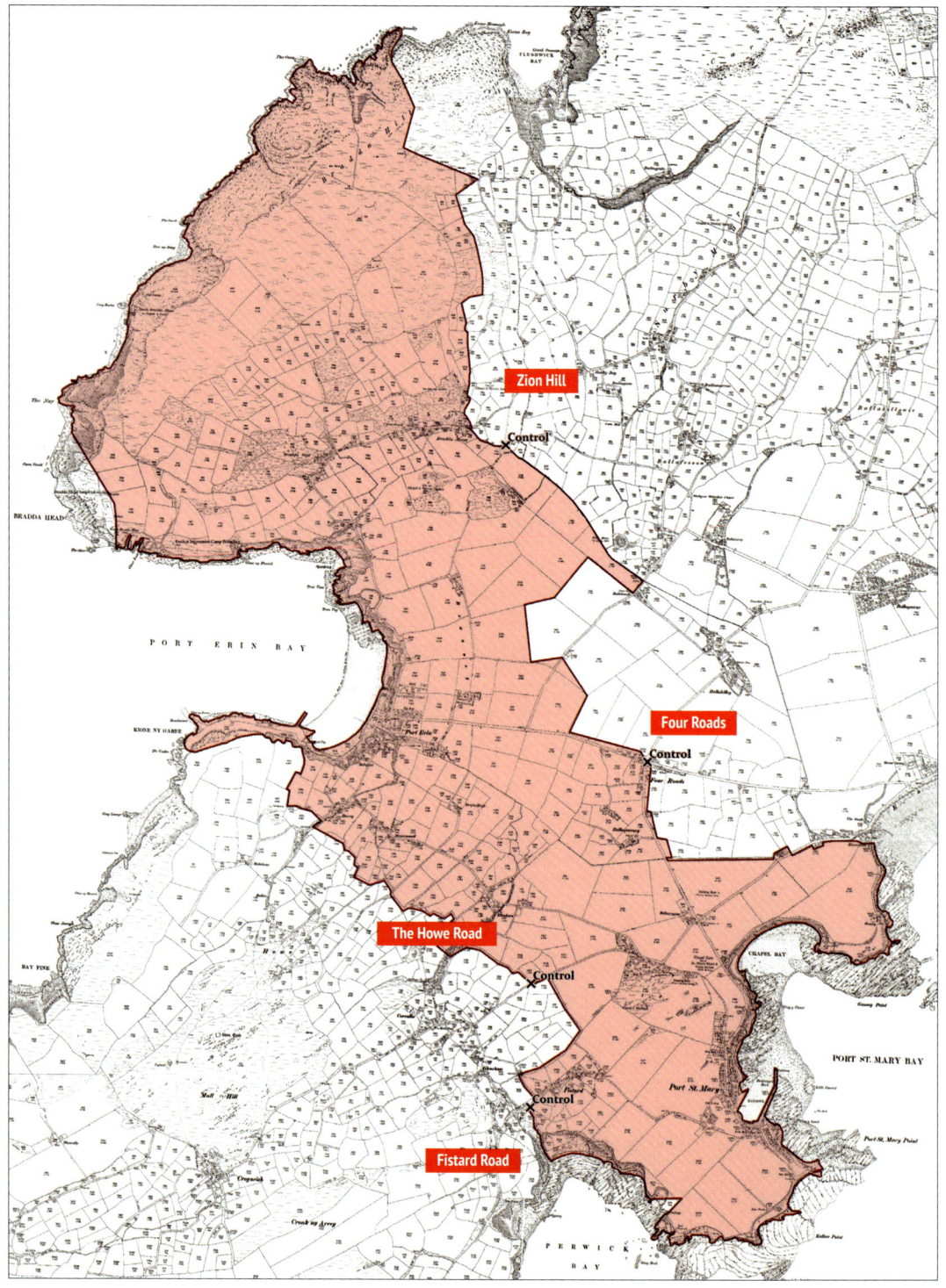

Enemy Aliens in Port St Mary

CHAPTER 7

DOREEN MOULE

How the Internment Camp came into existence

When World War II broke out in September 1939, there were more than 70,000 'enemy aliens' in Britain. Enemy aliens are defined (by *Collins English Dictionary)* as 'natives, citizens or subjects of one country living in another country with which it is at war and viewed as suspect as a result'.

It was a major concern that some of them may be spies or willing to collaborate with the enemy in the event of an invasion. Consequently, the decision was made by the British Government that all Germans and Austrians over the age of sixteen should attend one of the 120 tribunals set up by the Home Office in different regions throughout Britain. The panels presiding at these tribunals were made up of people like judges, magistrates, Justices of the Peace and civil servants. Their role was to categorise the enemy aliens into one of three groups:

- 'A' – pro-Nazi supporters, immediately interned as **high security risks** (569 initially identified in this group)
- 'B' – '*doubtful cases*', who were subjected to restrictions and supervised (approximately 6,700)
- 'C' – who were free to continue their lives as '*no security risk*' (about (90%, or 66,000)

About 55,000 of category 'C' were acknowledged as 'refugees from Nazi oppression' and most were Jewish.

By February 1940, the tribunals had completed their work with 73,000 individuals having been assessed. Category A internees were quickly interned in several camps around Britain.

After the failure of the Norwegian campaign, in the spring of 1940, there was a heightened fear of spies and 'fifth columnists', resulting in greater antagonism towards enemy aliens. Influenced by strong media pressure and poor progress in the war, Winston Churchill reputedly said, 'Collar the lot!', so the vast majority of the 73,000 were interned even though many of their families had lived in Britain for decades.

Most internees were loyal to Britain and opposed to Hitler. They wanted Britain to win the war, because if the Germans won, most of them, especially the Jews, would be sent to concentration camps.

Little consideration seems to have been given to dependent children, with some accompanying their mothers or having to be left with family or friends. If such arrangements were not possible, some children were taken by police to children's homes.

Opposite: The position of the main control points as outlined in the Order for Control of Highways.
(Reproduced by permission of the Treasury of the Isle of Man. ©Crown copyright reserved)

Many of the children were reunited with their mothers in the internment camp some weeks or months later following protests to the Commandant and the Home Office.

Why was Rushen chosen for the Internment Camp?

During WWI there had been an Internment Camp at Knockaloe, near Peel, in which more than 23,000 men were interned. Despite it having been decided after WWI that the policy of internment should be avoided in future, when the tide turned against the Allies in WWII, it was decided to adopt a similar policy, and the Island was once more considered as safe and secure and a better place to house internees in the long term than in the temporary camps set up in mainland Britain. The first camp for men was opened in Ramsey on 27th May 1940, followed by others in Onchan, Douglas and Peel, but, for the first time in Britain, women were interned. A separate camp was therefore required and Rushen, which covers the greater part of the south of the Island, and could easily be sectioned off, was designated as the Women's Camp.

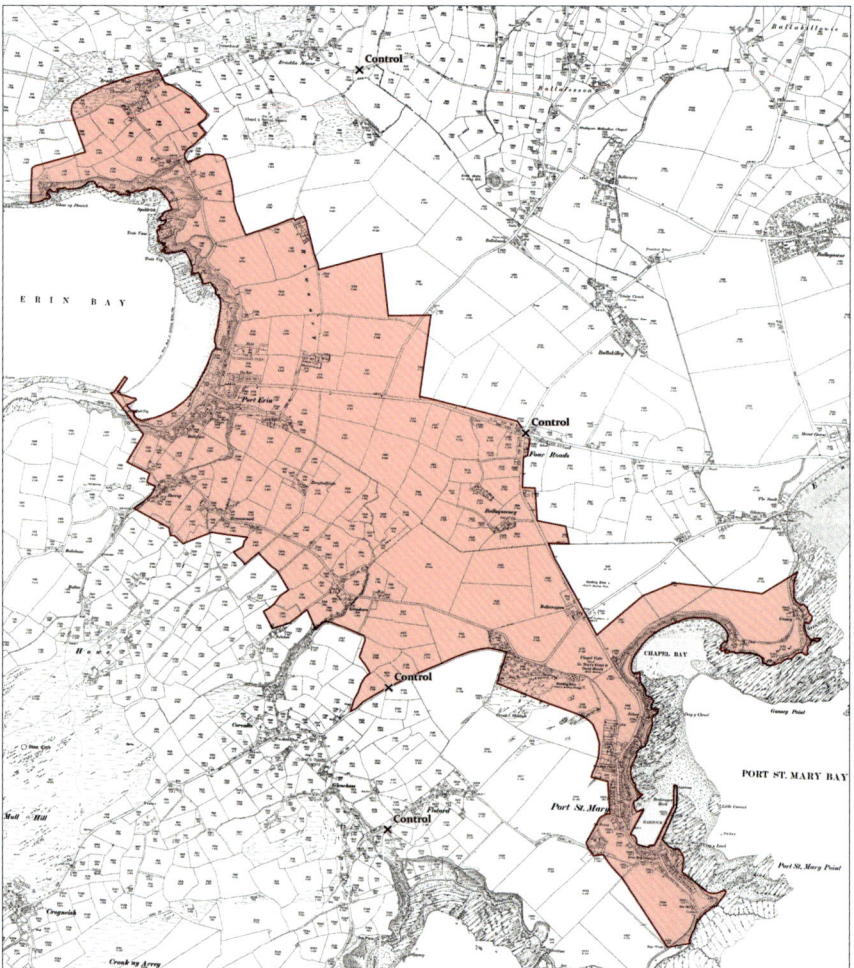

The Married Camp (Camp Y) and Camp W for the unmarried women and those not to be reunited with their husbands. 1940/377. The Defence (General) Regulations (Isle of Man) 1939 Control of Highways – Port Erin, Port St Mary and Parish of Rushen, 11.10.1940.
(Reproduced by permission of the Treasury of the Isle of Man. ©Crown copyright reserved)

As the map opening this chapter shows, the original area covered by the camp was considerable, but as internees were released back to the UK the area gradually reduced in size. Rushen Camp covered substantial parts of both Port St Mary and the adjoining village of Port Erin. Most internees were housed in Port Erin, the larger of the two villages. The map opposite shows the extent of the camp in 1941 when the married camp opened.

Who were the women internees?

Most were German or Austrian and from surrounding annexed countries. Later, when Italy joined the war, Italians were also interned. Some had come to Britain after WWI to begin a new life. They had settled into local communities, brought up their children as British and some had set up their own businesses. They were not expecting another war and had not felt it necessary to become naturalised British citizens.

However, there were others who were relatively new arrivals since 1933 when Hitler had come to power in Germany. Many were Jewish. The persecution of the Jews had become intense and widespread, so those who could had left Germany quickly. Others, whether for family reasons, age or because they failed to admit the threat until it was too late, stayed. There was a dramatic increase in refugee numbers from 1938 as the urgency to leave became more apparent, though by then it was difficult to leave Germany and there were significant restrictions on immigrant numbers both in Britain and other countries. Many of the refugees in Britain had to become accustomed to the difficulties of living in exile after having been used to a comfortable standard of living.

Some were fortunate and permitted to work, giving them limited control over their living standards. More than 20,000 women, the largest group, arrived in 1938 and 1939 on 'domestic' permits which were the easiest to obtain. To many – teachers, medical students and other educated women – this sort of work was unfamiliar. By the outbreak of war, only a few refugees were still able to reach Britain as the borders had been closed.

Arrival – Women aliens entering Douglas railway station to entrain for the charming resort of Port Erin, which is to be their place of detention until Germany is humbled. (Image courtesy of Manx National Heritage)

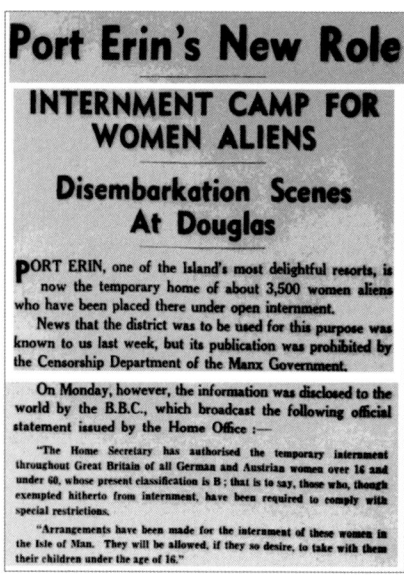

Port Erin's New Role

INTERNMENT CAMP FOR WOMEN ALIENS

Disembarkation Scenes At Douglas

PORT ERIN, one of the Island's most delightful resorts, is now the temporary home of about 3,500 women aliens who have been placed there under open internment.

News that the district was to be used for this purpose was known to us last week, but its publication was prohibited by the Censorship Department of the Manx Government.

On Monday, however, the information was disclosed to the world by the B.B.C., which broadcast the following official statement issued by the Home Office :—

"The Home Secretary has authorised the temporary internment throughout Great Britain of all German and Austrian women over 16 and under 60, whose present classification is B ; that is to say, those who, though exempted hitherto from internment, have been required to comply with special restrictions.

"Arrangements have been made for the internment of these women in the Isle of Man. They will be allowed, if they so desire, to take with them their children under the age of 16."

Local report about the opening of the internment camp. (Image courtesy of Manx National Heritage (Isle of Man Examiner 31st May 1940, p.5))

At this point, some 8,000 foreign domestic workers were given notice by their employers, who were afraid that they might be employing enemy aliens. It was the refugee organisations who came to the rescue of these women who had lost their jobs and, in many cases, their homes.

Local feeling about the Camp

Manx householders had been asked, in September 1939, to be prepared to welcome evacuee children, so it was, with some surprise, that the landladies of Port Erin and Port St Mary received the news that internees were to be billeted with them.

Joan Johnson, daughter of Reverend Harry Johnson (see Chapter 4), observed in her Memoirs, (Memories, Manx Museum Library) that the train carrying the internees went first to Port Erin where the internees were registered and as many as possible were billeted. It then returned to Port St Mary with the remaining internees, where approximately 800 were accommodated.

From the following extract, dated 28th May 1940, it would certainly seem that the station masters and railway staff knew little or nothing about the internees' arrival until the day before:

NOTICE TO STATION MASTER, TRAINMEN AND ALL CONCERNED
Special Trains will be run between Douglas and Port Erin TOMORROW, WEDNESDAY 29TH MAY for the transport of German Women to Port Erin. There will be two Special Trains in the morning and two later in the day. The times of departure of the Special Trains cannot be definitely stated as this will depend on the time of arrival of the Special Steamers and the interval necessary for transfer of Aliens from Pier to Douglas Station (courtesy of Manx National Heritage)

There must have been considerable animosity towards the internees on their arrival, because many of the local people would have perceived them as 'the enemy'. In addition, their arrival was on the very day when three Manx ships – *Mona's Queen III, Fenella II* and *King Orry IV* – were attacked at Dunkirk, with two being sunk and the third sinking the following morning. However, most people put their own feelings aside and treated the internees with kindness as they had been requested to do by the Commandant of the Camp, Dame Joanna Cruickshank.

EVERYDAY LIFE IN THE PORT ST MARY CAMP

Dame Joanna Cruickshank D.B.E., R.R.C. (1875–1958) was the first Commandant of the Camp. Before she came to Rushen Camp, she had had an illustrious career:

1907 she began her career at Guy's Hospital in London, later joining the Queen Alexandra's Nursing Service. She worked in India and was shipped to England with malaria, surviving when the ship was torpedoed in the Mediterranean

1918 she became Matron in Chief of the newly formed Royal Air Force Nursing Service (later the Princess Mary Royal Air Force Nursing Service) with responsibility for organisation of the entire service. She became the Air Ministry's representative on the Joint Voluntary Aid Council after establishing hospitals in Britain, Aden, Iraq and Palestine and receiving the CBE for her organisational skills

1931 she was elevated to Dame Commander of the Order of the British Empire

1938 she volunteered and was made Matron in Chief of the Red Cross Society

1939 she became Matron-in-Chief of the joint British Red Cross and St John of Jerusalem

1940 she retired from the joint British Red Cross and St John and was awarded the Royal Red Cross medal for exceptional service in military nursing, an honour shared with Florence Nightingale

When the Internment Camp was being established, Sir John Anderson identified Dame Joanna as being the ideal candidate for the Commandant's job. He was reluctant to approach her as she had recently retired. However, his private secretary suggested that he should approach her informally.

She agreed to take on this onerous task with just a staff of five and the assistance of local clergy wives. Within two days, she had requisitioned hotels, boarding houses and rooms in private homes, set up a registration system, established an office and received an unexpected influx of close to 3,500 internees and their children, who were all billeted by nightfall – an amazing feat of organisation.

Dame Joanna Margaret Cruickshank by Elliott & Fry. (© National Portrait Gallery, London)

She organised the Camp for a year, May 1940 – May 1941, at which point the Married Camp was established in Port St Mary. Dame Joanna believed that the camp was changing considerably as many of the internees were being released and the 'less friendly internees' remained. She was also concerned that the Home Office was considering moving the Class As to the camp and some Class Bs. She and her deputy, Miss Looker, had discussed this and agreed that:

> the whole character of the camp must probably change ... and we have agreed that we neither of us had the right kind of training or experience, and I think I may add, temperament or inclination to carry out a policy which may I suppose be increasingly repressive and where 'security' and 'intelligence' will be more and more the important side of the camp administration. We have no doubt in our own minds that we would not only much rather not have to be responsible for work of this kind for which we have no training or aptitude but also that we would be more useful in the national effort on the mainland doing work in which we are more experienced and for which we have better qualifications.
>
> (extract from Dame Joanne's resignation letter, May 1941)

Almost one year after taking the appointment of Commandant, Dame Joanna and Miss Looker left the Island for London. She attended reunions of the PMRAFNS and the annual inter-hospitals tennis tournaments. She never married and died on 16th August 1958, aged 82.

Chief Inspector Cyril Cuthbert (1902–1984)
Commandant from May 1941 to September 1945

Cuthbert at work. (Image courtesy of Manx National Heritage)

As a young constable Cyril Roy Mitchell Cuthbert was a keen amateur forensic scientist, who was enthusiastic about developing a more scientific method of crime detection at the Metropolitan Police HQ. Using his dental and medical knowledge plus a course of evening classes in chemistry, he purchased a second-hand microscope for 35 shillings and established himself as the scientific policeman. Although his superiors were sceptical, on a visit from Lord Trenchard, the Commissioner of Police, Cuthbert borrowed a white coat and was working at his microscope. As a result, the Commissioner deemed that a Forensic Unit was desirable for the Metropolitan Police and professional scientists were employed to set up a laboratory with Sergeant Cuthbert becoming the Forensic Unit Police Liaison Officer.

At the outbreak of war, Cuthbert, who was now an Inspector, was transferred to the Alien Tribunal at Bow Street Magistrates Court in London, as secretary. In September 1940, he joined the Alien Tribunal Administration Team in Douglas.

By 1941, both the need for tribunals and the number of internees was rapidly diminishing and Inspector Cuthbert transferred to Port St Mary, where he worked alongside Miss Wilson, a former prison Governor, who was developing Dame

Joanna Cruickshank's plans for a married camp. In May 1941, in the event of Dame Joanna's retirement, Inspector Cuthbert was given responsibility for the 162 couples who had moved into the Married Camp, with Miss Wilson as his Deputy, and he moved into the Ballaqueeney Hotel. Many of the landladies regarded him as a ladies' man and, as such, he was a significant change from the stern Dame Joanna.

His charming way with the landladies did not prevent Inspector Cuthbert being given a severe reprimand by the Home Office for altering documents which read 'Internees' to read 'Aliens'. A question was also asked in Parliament as to whether it was appropriate for a man to oversee a women's camp, but it was deemed to be acceptable as Miss Wilson was to be his Deputy in special charge of women's interests. The Inspector moved into a furnished house in St Mary's Crescent in Port Erin and when, in August 1942, the internee numbers dramatically reduced, the Married Camp was moved to the Spaldrick area of Port Erin.

After the War, Inspector Cuthbert returned to the Forensic laboratory at the Metropolitan Police in London, where he lectured to many police departments on his specialist subject, referring to cases he had seen investigated. After one of these lectures at Harvard University in the United States, he was made an Honorary Fellow. In 1951, after promotion to Chief Superintendent and receiving the King's Police and Fire Services Medal for distinguished service, he retired from the Police service.

He later occupied positions with the boards of several companies, travelling the world selling scientific instruments to India, Ceylon, Pakistan and Malaya. In 1958, he wrote *Science and the Detection of Crime*, a fascinating book, evaluating the work of the team of Forensic scientists at the Criminal Investigation Department. He died in 1984 in Haywards' Heath, Sussex aged 81.

The day-to-day running of the Camp

Under the supervision of Dame Joanna, the everyday running of the camp was overseen by members of the English and Manx constabularies. Volunteers had been called for from the Metropolitan Police Force in London, to support the Manx Constabulary, and there was no shortage of offers.

WP Sergeant Ivy Baxter was one of the volunteers and came to the Island in 1940. She stated that policing the Camp was, for the most part, without problems. If the Commandant had to attend meetings in London, Ivy, with support from seven WPCs and the Port Erin constable, was in charge of both the Port Erin and Port St Mary camps.

Amongst other roles, the constables were responsible for:
- ringing the curfew bell at the end of the day in the summer
- escorting the internees to tribunals in Douglas
- supervising internees who worked on the farms
- travelling (and staying) with any internees who had to travel to and from the UK for medical treatment
- searching parcels that arrived for the internees

Sergeant Ivy Baxter with three WPCs searching luggage and parcels at Port Erin Railway Station. (Courtesy of The Mayor's Office for Policing and Crime. (Heritage Centre))

- delivering pay and documents to all the camps each Friday

The hours of work were long, but there was a day off each week when they often went to Douglas to shop and have a pub lunch.

Health and Welfare

The diet in the south of the Island in the 1940s, even during the war, would have contained plenty of fresh produce including meat, vegetables, eggs and fish, especially herrings and kippers. Farmers and butchers called at the boarding houses with horse-drawn carts and wheelbarrows to sell off any spare commodities such as turnips, potatoes, bacon and butter. The landladies took good care of the dietary needs of the internees, making the rations go further with traditional Manx recipes for broths and soups. The internees themselves were resourceful and produced nutritious meals for the household from whatever was available. If the ingredients were accessible, they would make cakes such as stollen, introducing the landladies and their families to new recipes.

Internees were employed by the local farmers to help with crops, vegetable production and tending the livestock. Hens were kept and areas of land were turned into allotments, with many of the internees working the allotments to produce food for their households. They also bartered some of their produce with the locals in exchange for toiletries, clothing, confectionary or anything that was difficult to come by. However, if this activity was discovered, both the internee and the local would be taken to court!

There was rationing on the Island, and this did not finally end until 1952. Ration books were issued to residents of each district so that the local shopkeepers and grocers would be kept in business. Because of the availability of fresh foods, the general health of the people of Rushen, including the internees, was good and this was corroborated by the reports from various welfare groups visiting the camps.

There were clinics for the internees who had problems with hair and body lice when they first arrived, possibly because of the overcrowding. They would be treated with lotions and lice powder and the landladies and their families would be treated too. Bed linen and clothing had to be fumigated. Hospital care was available in Port Erin and maternity care was available in Port Erin and Port St Mary. If necessary, patients (especially new mothers) were taken under escort to Noble's Hospital and the Jane Crookall Maternity Home in Douglas. Local GPs surgeries, Dr Lewthwaite in Port St Mary, and dentists were used and medical professionals amongst the internees were allowed to assist local practitioners. Local Commissioners were under strict instructions regarding any infectious cases notified to them by the district nurses, local GPs and first aid posts, to ensure that the appropriate treatment was administered and paid for.

There was, however, some concern that while local residents paid for their health care, the Manx Government was reimbursed by the Home Office for the internees' care. Dame Joanna made the observation:

'Our own people would have to pay a high price for the treatment the Camp's maternity cases were receiving'.

Learning something new

The internees' main problem was boredom and the children needed structure to their daily lives. There were many highly educated women in the Camp including a number of educationalists. They approached the Commandant about establishing schools for the children and, where children were concerned, she was always supportive.

Minna Specht. (Image courtesy of Manx National Heritage)

One famous educationalist, Minna Specht, was instrumental in setting up a kindergarten in Port St Mary in the rear of Cowley's Café, a former boys' and infants' school on the corner of the High Street and the Promenade, for the children up to the age of six. Demand for places was high, so children could only attend either in the morning or the afternoon. Minna Specht also set up a school for 6 to 16-year-olds in the Cornaa Boarding House across the road from Cowley's Café.

Many of the children had been severely disturbed by their experiences and others were 'running wild'. In January 1941, Theo Naftel, a member of the International Cooperative Women's Guild Committee, made an official visit to the camp. In her report, she stated that:

everyone agreed that regular schooling has had a very beneficial effect on the children, they love school and are much brighter and less nervy since they have not been in such constant contact with the adult life in the hotels.

Erna Nelki. (Image courtesy of Manx National Heritage)

One of the internee teachers, also a psychologist and socialist, Erna Nelki, also approved of the educational provision made for the children. Writing in 1941 in the *New Leader*, the Independent Labour Party's magazine, she said:

The outlook of the majority of the refugees on the Isle of Man was anti-German. The children often refused to speak German. Most of them wanted an English

Below: Former infants' and boys' school in Port St Mary which, during the war, was Cowley's Café. (Courtesy of Doreen Moule)

Right: Port St Mary – Cornaa Boarding House, a school for six to 16-year-olds. (Courtesy of Doreen Moule)

school, with an English curriculum and English ideals. We tried to give them that. But for those who were willing to play their part in building up a new free Germany, we tried to give the knowledge which will help them in that task.'

The children were being prepared for their future, wherever that may be.

Adult education

Academic and skills courses for the adults were also catered for upstairs in the building at Cowley's Café. There were thirty different courses including British history, German literature, Greek, mathematical training, problems of life, and reading Shakespeare. Practical skills were also taught including dress and glove making, millinery and shorthand.

Entertainment

Music is an international language and many of the internees came from countries famous for their composers and their great works. Many of the internees were musical and several of them took a regular active part in the church services.

One such internee was Else Haefner, an operatic singer and organist who was born in Hanau, a town in Hesse, Germany. She was billeted in *Barrule* on Port St Mary Promenade. Else was a regular soloist and played a significant role in services at St Mary's Church. Her musical repertoire was mainly classical.

Choirs became an important part of the internees' social lives and the more artistic amongst them put on shows and musical evenings for both internees and locals to enjoy. Several of these shows took place at Port St Mary Town Hall with others at Mount Tabor Church Hall.

Religion

The churches in both Port St Mary and Port Erin welcomed the internees into their congregations and the women took an active part in services, particularly from a musical aspect with regular performances from individual soloists and instrumentalists.

Reverend Harry Johnson was the Methodist minister in Port St Mary. In early June 1940, he received a letter from War Registers International, which requested help concerning specific internees in Rushen Camp. War Registers International was a charity representing refugees throughout Europe.

Prior to this request, the Methodist Church had already contacted some of the internees, because many of them had attended the church services. As a result, Rev. Johnson and his own junior minister in Port Erin, Rev. Joseph Benson Harrison, plus the Anglican vicar and the Roman Catholic priest, began the pastoral care of internees. They were later joined by Deaconess Sister Emmeline Cheshire when she was appointed by the Home Office.

At first there was no specific provision for the Jewish internees, but several requests for a place of worship for them resulted in a synagogue being established, possibly in the basement of Port St Mary Town Hall.

Rev. Johnson's daughter, Joan, recalls in her memoirs that she believed the main aspects of internment to affect the women and children were 'separation' and 'bewilderment'. The effect of separation was a feeling of loss – of parents, partners, children. Some separations were resolved when children were restored to their mothers or partners joined them in the Married Camp. However, not all separations had happy endings, such as the sinking of the *Arandora Star* with the loss of many male internees on their way to Canada. It was several weeks before some internees had news about who had been lost or saved, and this was exacerbated by the fact that some internees had swapped identities with others who did not wish to or who were too infirm to travel, making it difficult to identify people accurately.

SS Arandora Star.

The bewilderment came from many of those having lived in Britain for many years, with British-born children (some of whom were fighting in the British army) and who were obviously anti-Nazi. They could not understand why they had been arrested as enemy aliens. They were even more bewildered that the Germans could attack the *Arandora Star* when it was transporting people of their own nationality.

To give solace and support to the internees, Rev. Harry Johnson organised services and discussion groups, with scripture classes for Protestant children. Christmas and Easter were celebrated as special times, with the internees sharing their customs with the local people. Joan Johnson stated that the musical evenings, talks and discussions about their travels and experiences 'broadened the outlook' of a twelve-year-old girl, as she was then. She also felt that a lot of good came from her interactions with the internees as she learned 'tolerance, open-mindedness to people of different backgrounds and about sharing love'.

The Opening of the Married Camp in Port St Mary

Many of the married women internees had husbands in other camps on the Island and they had made requests to the authorities to be able to meet up with them. After repeated protests about the meetings, it was decided at the end of July 1940 that meetings would be permitted on a monthly basis.

Women travelled to Douglas by train under escort and were coached to Derby Castle. Husbands travelled, again under police escort, to meet up with their wives at Collinson's Café in Port Erin or Ballaqueeney Hotel in Port St Mary.

However, many of the men had been sent to Canada or Australia in five shipments:

- *Duchess of York* (20th June to Canada)
- *Arandora Star* (1st July to Canada)
- *Ettrick* (3rd July to Canada)
- *Sobieski* (4th July to Canada)
- *Dunera* (10th July to Australia)

As a result of this 'transportation', many couples were never reunited. As mentioned previously, the *Arandora Star* was sunk by a torpedo and others on the *Dunera*, being transported to Australia, suffered appalling conditions and cruelty.

A deputation was appointed in January 1941 to discuss with Dame Joanna Cruickshank the formation of a 'mixed alien camp' and in March 1941, the Commissioners in Port St Mary were informed by Dame Joanna that 'the camp for married aliens would be in Port St Mary'. Rumours of this proposal had reached the ears of locals in January 1941 and a petition, signed by more than 100 rate payers, was received by the Commissioners.

The petition read:

Sir, We the undersigned rate payers hereby desire to register our protest against the village being turned into a mixed alien camp. We do not consider that their influence will be good for the native population, especially the younger people and children, and also object to male aliens being billeted on our womenfolk while the majority of the male population are absent on their various war duties, and we hereby request you, and the members of the Board, to make vigorous protest to the proper authority in our respective names.

On 8th May 1941, 169 married internee couples were moved into Port St Mary. Two days later, Dame Joanna expressed her concerns in her retirement letter to Sir John Moylan C.B., C.B.E., dated 10th May 1941 (see page 190).

Dame Joanna left the Island on 22nd May 1941 with Miss Looker, and the new Commandant took over. Chief Inspector Cuthbert, his deputy Miss Wilson and Mr Latham from Government Office, met with the Board of Port St Mary Commissioners when the proposed married aliens' camp was fully discussed, and the rate payers' petition was presented. The Commissioners' then received a letter from Government Office which read:

Sir, I have to inform you that the Home Office desire that a Camp for married internees and their families shall be opened at Port St Mary early in May, and they have appointed Chief Inspector Cuthbert of the Metropolitan Police to be Commandant of the Camp. It is proposed that this Camp shall be confined to the houses on the Promenade at Port St Mary and the fence will include two fields in the rear of the Promenade houses and will run out to the Point.

The Married Camp included the Ballaqueeney Hotel as well as the houses on the Promenade mentioned above. The Ballaqueeney Hotel, at that time, was the 'epicentre' of Port St Mary. Mr and Mrs W.A. Kelly had come out of retirement to run it while their son, Walter, was away in the Army. It became a Kosher house for the Jewish internees. The internees produced the drawing and inscription for Mrs Kelly at Christmas 1940. After the War, the Chief Rabbi in London wrote to Mrs Kelly thanking her for her kindness to the Jewish community in Ballaqueeney, arranging 'for them to have their food and a room where they could hold their own prayers and ceremonies'.

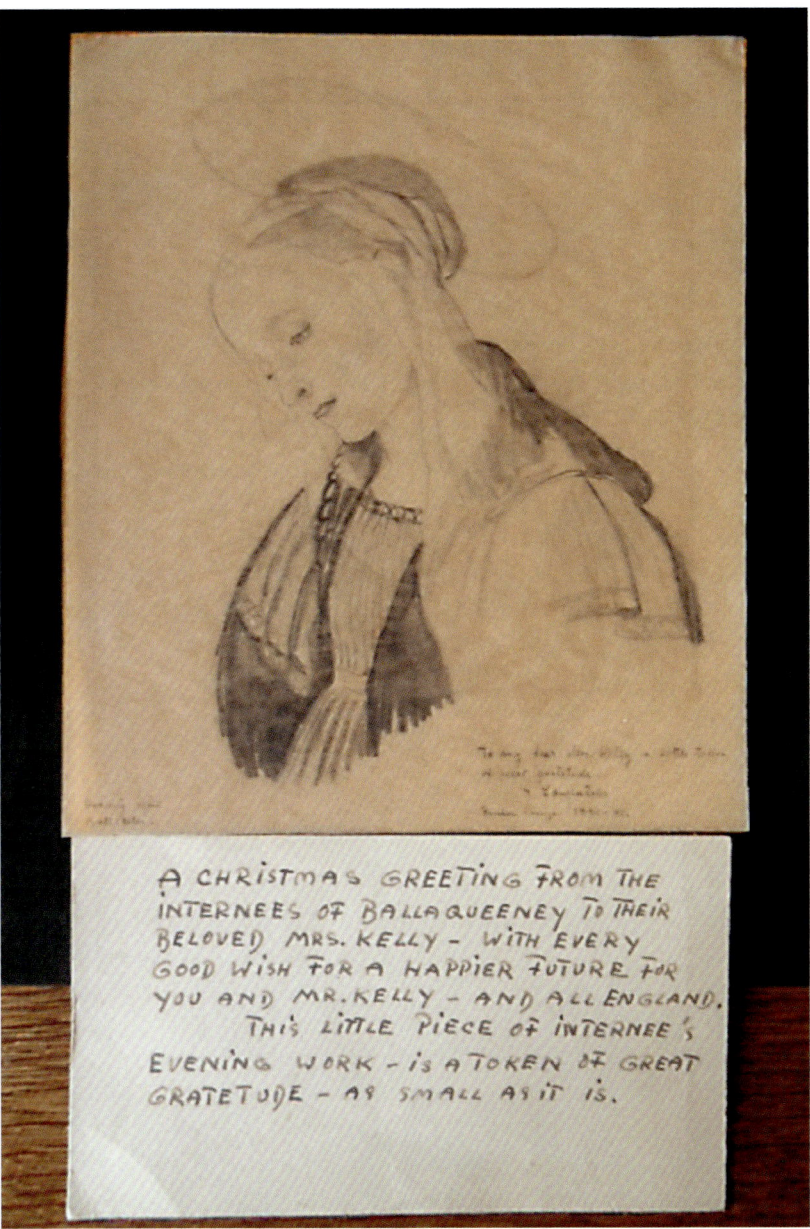

Christmas greeting for Mrs Kelly from the internees. (Courtesy of Mrs Betty Kelly)

A CHRISTMAS GREETING FROM THE INTERNEES OF BALLAQUEENEY TO THEIR BELOVED MRS. KELLY - WITH EVERY GOOD WISH FOR A HAPPIER FUTURE FOR YOU AND MR. KELLY - AND ALL ENGLAND. THIS LITTLE PIECE OF INTERNEE'S EVENING WORK - IS A TOKEN OF GREAT GRATETUDE - AS SMALL AS IT IS.

Life in the Married Camp

The atmosphere of the Married Camp seemed relaxed, with landladies and their internees sharing chores and the shopping. Some items of food were rationed, but radio and newspapers were more accessible, and many internees would spend the evenings with the boarding house and hotel owners. The children attended school as normal and school holidays were spent on the beach and in the outdoor swimming pools. Local

People of Port St Mary

MARY ESLICK (1895–1964)

Mary Eslick (née Brew) was born, one of eight children, in 1895 in Douglas. In the early stages of WWI, she and three of her sisters went to work in a munitions factory in Coventry. While in the UK, she met James Henry Eslick and they were married on the Island in September 1919. James had been invalided out of the war with shrapnel injuries and the effects of gassing in the trenches. At first, they lived and worked in Douglas, but later moved to Port St Mary when Mary took over the running, with other relatives, of *Southlands*, a boarding house on the Promenade.

When Mary was 39, in 1934, her husband died as a result of his injuries and she was left to bring up five children on her own. Life was not easy, but when the Home Office requisitioned the boarding houses and hotels to billet the internees, things changed, and she was paid 21 shillings (a guinea) per week for each adult internee. Although wartime was not easy for anyone, these payments improved Mary's situation.

Family members were apprehensive about accommodating the internees and were 'convinced that they would be murdered in their beds'. In fact, the internees were of great help to Mary, scrubbing down the stairs each week (carpets had been removed on the advice of the Home Office) and helping with the children on bath night.

Recollections from Joan Eslick (see Chapter 6), one of Mary's daughters, includes an occasion when Mary confronted internees sympathetic to Germany in an upstairs room who were cheering at the sight of the red skies above Liverpool from the fires during the bombing raids.

Joan also observed that:

> As Manx residents living in the same house as the then perceived enemy, it

could be described as a unique experience. We had German 'nannies' taking care of our everyday needs, German language tuition and no shortage of clothes such as knitted garments since they were prolific knitters.

When the married camp opened, several couples were billeted with Mary in *Southlands* and she made good friends with some of them including Dr Gerhard Bersu and his wife, Maria (more about them later). Another couple was Mr and Mrs Joester, who had lived in Hull for almost fifty years. They had not seen a reason to become British citizens but were arrested and sent to the Island as aliens.

children shared these facilities with the internees' children. Many stories are told of their experiences and many of them were mostly unaware of the war.

During the period of the Camp (1941–1942), permission was given for the establishment of various small industries. It is believed that one such industry, a concrete factory, was set up by one of the male internees with the purpose of keeping fellow internees busy. The factory produced bookends and other models which could be sold.

The number of internees was reducing and by Christmas 1941 there were about 400 men, women and children, but many of the workshops and classes set up during the first year for adults and children continued.

TWO INTERESTING INTERNEES FROM THE PORT ST MARY CAMP

Gerhard Bersu (1889–1964)

Gerhard became captivated by archaeology when he was a teenager and was fortunate enough to go on to live his dream by 1924, when he joined the German Archaeological Institute in Frankfurt, becoming its director in 1931. Under his leadership the Institute became adjudged as one of the world's leading archaeological organisations.

However, in 1937, he was forced to retire because of his Jewish parentage, so he emigrated, with his wife Maria, to Britain, where he won further accolades for his excavation at Little Woodbury in Wiltshire. As German nationals, the outbreak of war in 1939 led to their arrest and internment, Gerhard in Douglas and Maria in Rushen Camp, although for a while they were unaware that they were both on the Island.

Gerhard had a degree of freedom not experienced by the other internees, both in his excavations and around the camp. Normally strictly against the rules were visits to internees in other camps, but he was allowed to visit his fellow archaeologist, Paul Jacobsthal, most evenings in Hutchinson House, Douglas.

Whilst in the Married Camp, with sponsorship from the Society of Antiquities and co-ordinated by the Manx Museum, Gerhard and Maria carried out a highly successful programme of research and excavation, using parties of internees working under armed guard. It is understood that, as a token of appreciation for the work of this esteemed archaeologist, when visiting the sites they would drop a little box of his beloved snuff

 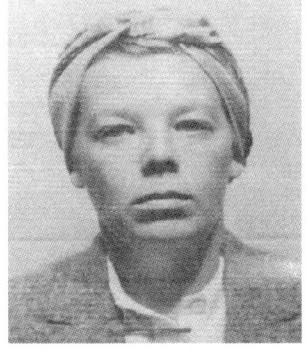

Gerhard and Maria Bersu. (Images courtesy of Manx National Heritage)

Edith Bach-Kaczynski. (Image courtesy of Manx National Heritage)

William Kaczynski. (Image courtesy of William Kaczynski)

into his Wellington boot. There is no record, however, that Maria, although an expert surveyor and draughtsman of the excavations, received any similar gifts! She was a rather stern lady and may have frowned on such favours. While interned, the Bersus discovered the Viking ship burial at Balladoole, and made Celtic discoveries at Ronaldsway, Ballanorris and Ballacagan. They remained on the Island after the war to complete the digs.

In 1947, Gerhard was invited by Eamon de Valera (a controversial figure during the war, as he trod a fine line between Nazi Germany and England) to become the Professor of the Royal Irish Academy in Dublin. He stayed there until 1950, when he returned to his former post at the German Archaeological Institute with the challenge of re-establishing, and physically rebuilding, the Institute in the new political system. He succeeded with his challenge and the new Institute was opened before his retirement in 1956.

Edith Bach-Kaczynski (1896–1975)

Edith Bach came from a musical family and in pre-War Berlin, when at the height of her musical powers, she was a coloratura soprano and performed across Europe. She was known as the 'Nightingale of Königs Wusterhausen'.

The Königs Wusterhausen transmitter, built in 1915, handled long, medium and short-wave broadcasts and on 22nd December 1920 made the first transmission of music and speech. Edith (pictured left) was a director of the radio company and her singing was the first to be transmitted from Germany to England. Regular weekly concert broadcasts were made and Edith was frequently mentioned in the BBC radio supplement. However, the result of the rise of Nazism meant that by 1935 Edith was banned from performing, simply because she was Jewish.

Edith had married Martin Kaczynski, a prosperous milliner, but after *Kristellnacht* (the night of 9/10th November 1938), he was arrested and taken to Sachsenhausen concentration camp. Edith managed to escape with their two young sons, William and Edward, who was only a baby and had been damaged at birth through lack of medical attention. Edith managed to get a work permit as a milliner for Martin and they were reunited, hoping to begin a new life in England. The reunion was short-lived, as they were arrested and interned in separate camps in the Isle of Man. However, happier times were ahead and they were reunited in the Married Camp in Port St Mary.

There is no evidence that Edith performed in any concerts while in the camp, but, as a diploma teacher, she did give singing lessons. When her son, Edward, first moved his paralysed arm, she announced to the internees that she would now be giving singing lessons for free.

After the war Edith, by now in her forties, tried to re-start her singing career. She contacted the BBC, but there was no interest. Resigning herself to a role as a wife and mother, but still enjoying her singing, she gave charity concerts in her local community and helped her husband in his millinery business. However, her family were sad that they had no recordings of her voice and could find none, but recently her sons have been astounded and delighted to discover that a record does still exist *(Der Rote Sarafan)*. They have given, to Rushen Heritage Trust, a DVD and a scrapbook of their mother's appearances at the height of her career. Once more the voice of the Nightingale of Königs Wusterhausen can be heard. In addition, a university house has been dedicated to her name, so her memory will live on.

Decline and close of the married camp

By August 1942, the number of internees in the Camp had decreased considerably and there was concern amongst boarding house owners on the Promenade and the owners of the Ballaqueeney Hotel that this was creating hardship for them, so they wrote to the Commissioners requesting financial assistance. These properties had been located inside the Camp boundary, and, with the internee numbers decreasing, they were unable to fill many of the rooms.

In Port Erin the number of single internees was also decreasing, and the boarding house and hotel owners were in a similar situation, so the same action was taken. As a result, the decision was made to move the Married Camp to the Spaldrick area of Port Erin, with the single women's camp focussed on Port Erin Promenade.

It was a busy scene in Port St Mary on 'moving day'. Lorries were loaded by more than 300 male and female internees with all their baggage and unloaded again at their new billets in Port Erin.

Once this move had taken place, the Ballaqueeney Hotel took on a new role and became an Officer Cadet Training Unit for the Royal Army Pay Corps where some of the landladies, who now needed to find other forms of income, went to work in the NAAFI. After considerable refurbishment, the boarding houses and hotels were again open for holiday trade. Some landladies were fortunate and obtained visitor bookings, but the tourist trade was slow in returning to the village, resulting in considerable economic hardship for many people.

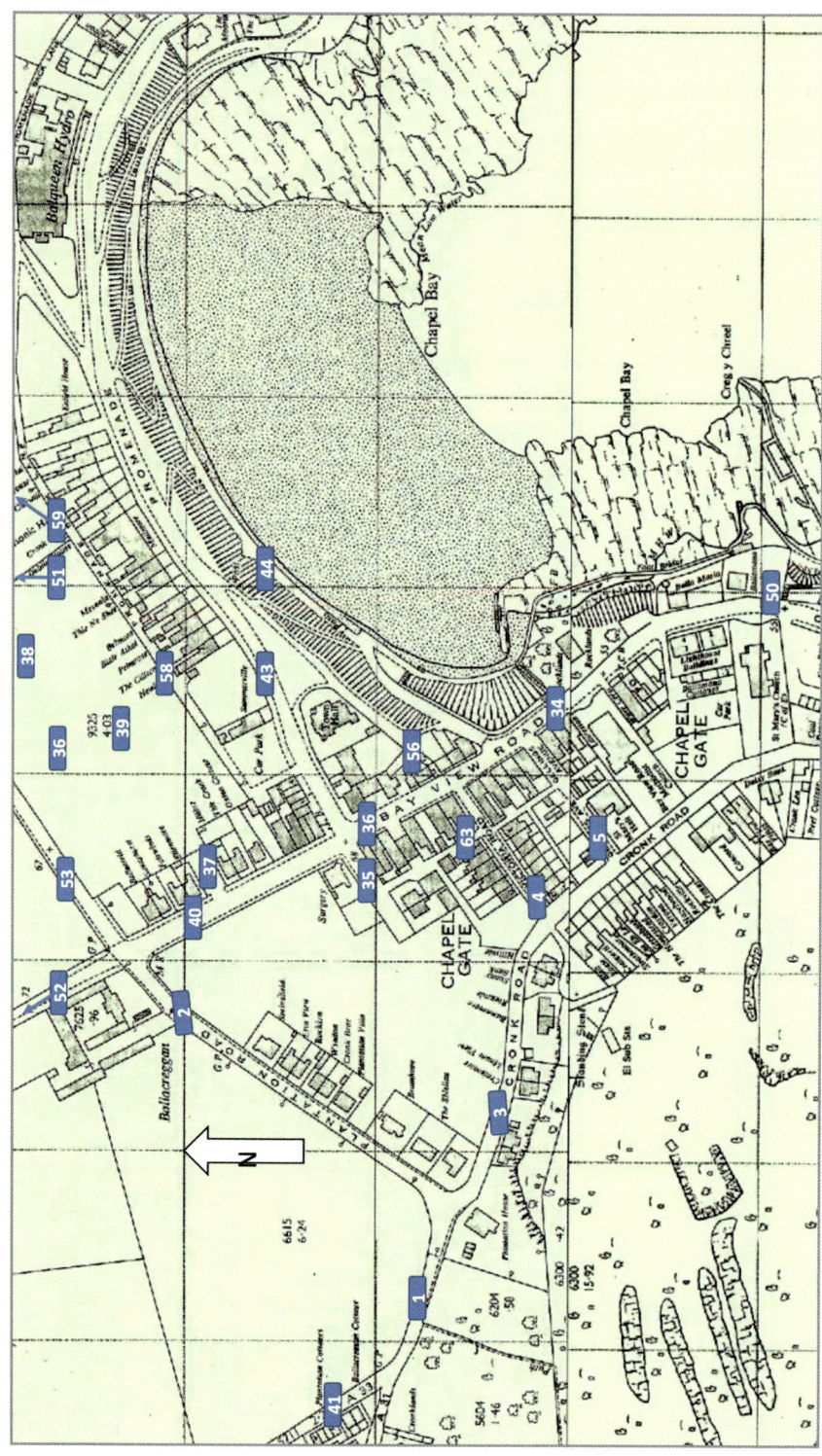

Streets, Roads, Avenues, Lanes and Guts

CHAPTER 8

STAFFAN OVERGAARD and JOHN W. QUALTROUGH

Place names raise questions – when you see a street sign, you often start to think about how it got its name. You might also start to wonder what year its name dates back to; history is often well-connected to street names.

The place names in Port St Mary also have a language context. The street names are bilingual, with the structure of the names including English, Manx Gaelic and old Norse combinations. An obvious English name could have a background in Old Norse or in Manx Gaelic.

Street names follow trends – Bay View Road was named in 1926, probably to fit the tourist expectations, while Flitter Street received the more elegant name of Loch Road. With the introduction of trains, we got Station Road, implying that you could reach Port St Mary in high fashion with the train.

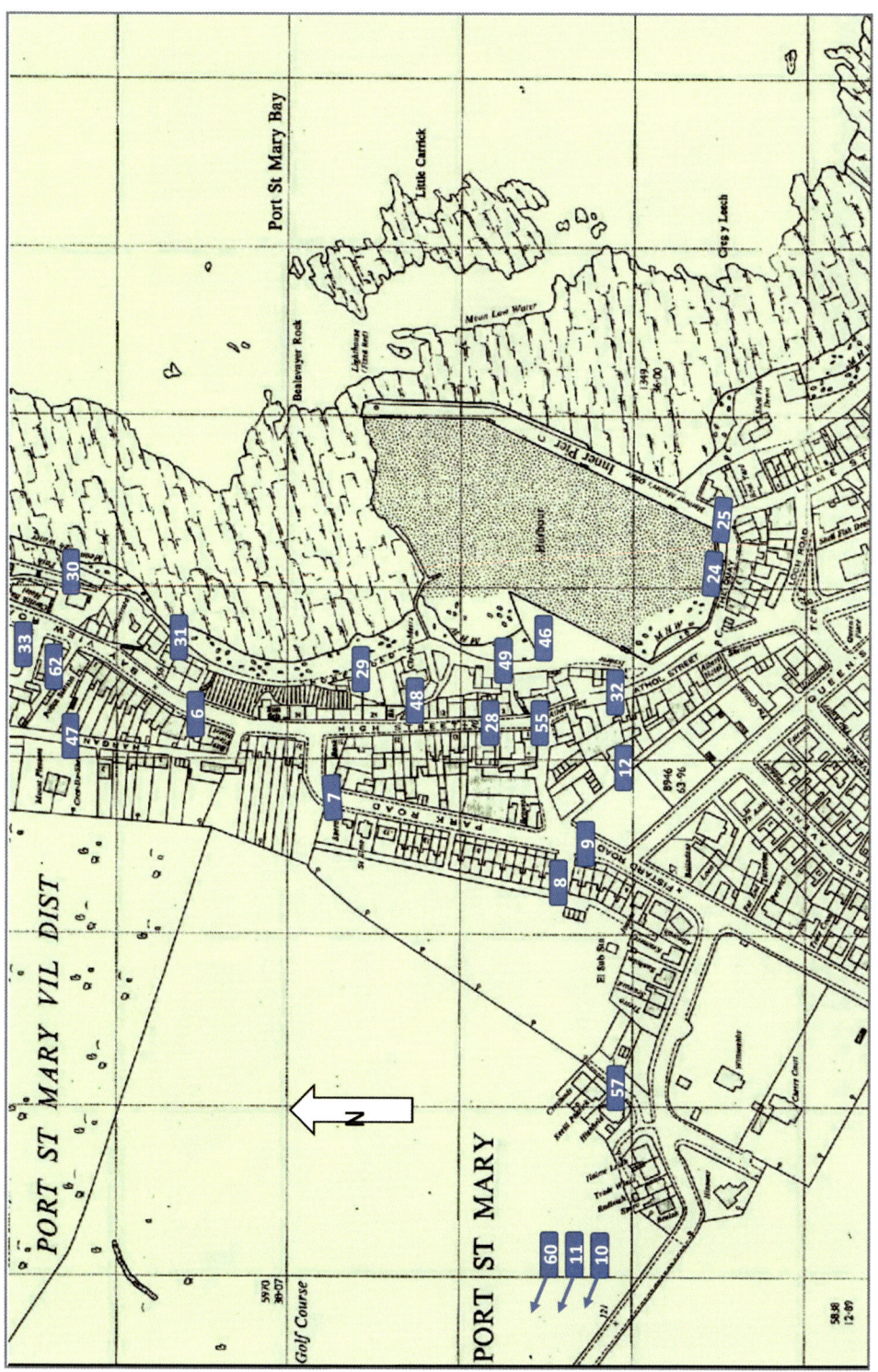

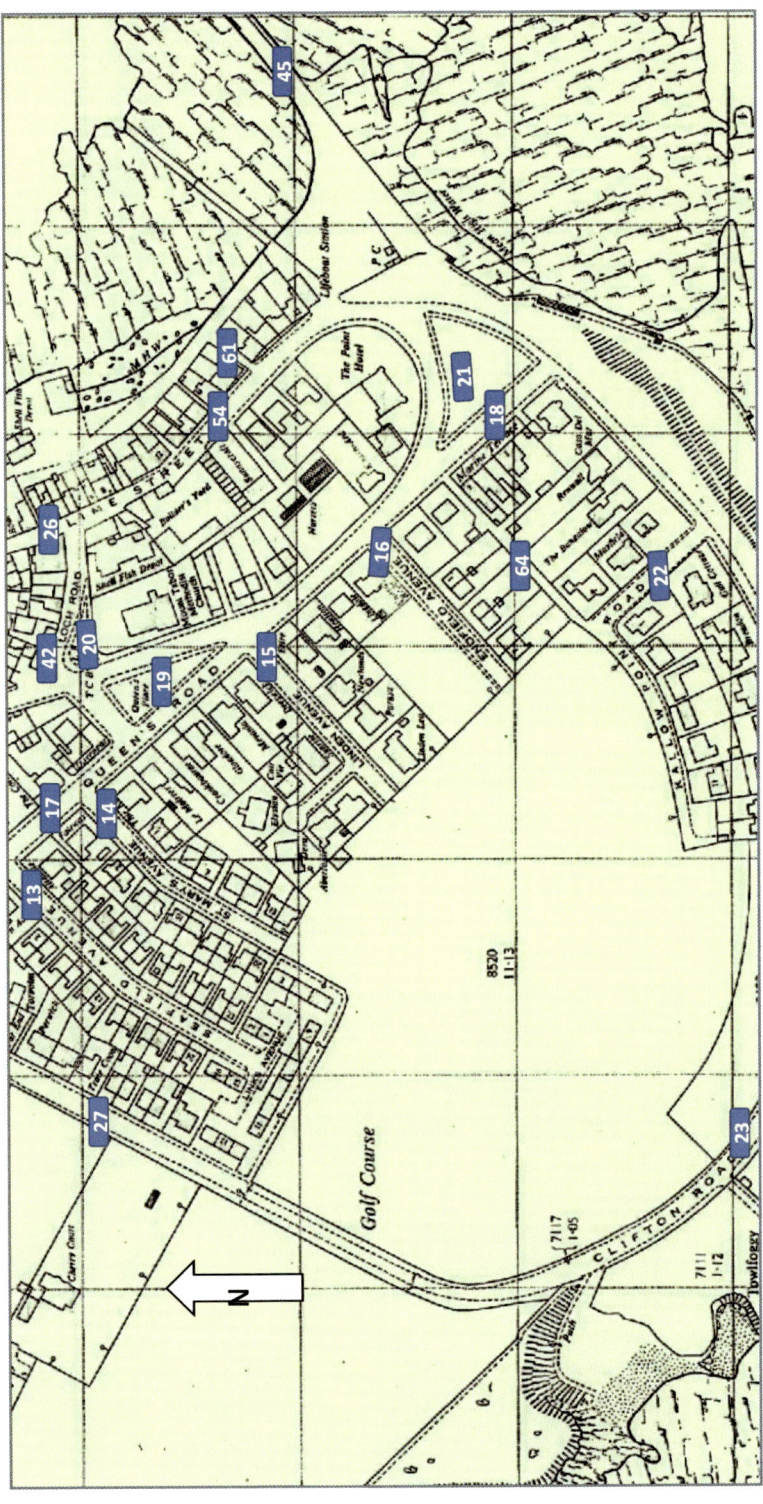

When looking at which name is the oldest, the likes of Fistard and Perwick have an Old Norse background which means they are least 1,000 years old. Beach Road and Cronk Road are probably old names, because a road to the beach and hill is reasonable. Surprisingly few names have some connection to the sea, fishing, ships and other marine themes.

Most streets have names, but not all. It has been tempting to suggest names for the missing ones. Some streets have more than one name, and it's not always easy to tell which is more accurate.

This chapter wouldn't have been possible without the help of Cathy Clucas, whose knowledge of Port St Mary has been invaluable, and Adrian Cain, for his assistance with the Manx Gaelic place names.

Translations below are from the Manx Gaelic unless indicated otherwise. See map for numbering of streets, roads, etc.

1. Howe Road – *Raad Yn Ow*
The road to the headland. Howe or Ow means headland in Manx Gaelic.

2. Plantation Road – *Raad ny Keylley*
This is the road to the plantation or forest on Cronk Skibbylt. The word 'keylley' means woodland or forest. The school, Scoill Phurt le Moirrey, at the junction of Bay View Road and Plantation Road, was built in 1994. Ballacreggan Farm is opposite the school.

3. Cronk Road – *Raad y Chrink*
The road arcs around Cronk Skybbylt, continuing to The Lhargan. It was on Skybbylt that the first golf course in Port St Mary was established in 1905. One of the quarries on Skybbylt had its own small railway to move stone. A standing stone is located on the lower slopes of Skybbylt, to the rear of one of the houses on Cronk Road. Skybbylt means 'nimble' and Cronk means 'hill'. Skybbylt could be a Scandinavian name meaning 'a lookout for ships', which you certainly can do on the Cronk.

4. Victoria Road – *Raad Victoria*
Named after Queen Victoria – and Lord of Mann – who reigned 1837-1901. The Royal yacht sailed past Port St Mary in 1847. At one point in the early 20th century, a road was planned between Victoria Road and Gellings Avenue but was never built.

5. Gellings Avenue – *Astyl Gelling*
Named in 1933 after Robert Gelling (1816-1895), who resided in High Street, a prosperous timber merchant who learned the trade from John Taubman and succeeded him in the business. Mr Gelling purchased land from the sale of the Holmes estate and acquired land from the port along to Chapel Bay – from the boundary wall parts, still seen at the back of Park Road, to where the railway line is, and down to the Smelt. The Abbeyland , the land which belonged to Rushen Abbey, was divided up and sold off.

Abbeyland was known as Ballavrara which was also marked on a map (Smythe, 1827) as Ballakilley and sometimes known as Ballacreggan. The area on today's Government map is known as Chapel Gate. Mr Gelling bought a field, from the sale of the Holmes estate, where the Wesleyan Chapel was built around 1835. Mr Gelling was a devoted member and superintendent of the church's Sunday school. The New Wesleyan Methodist Chapel was built around 1895 and demolished in 1970.

Between Gellings Avenue and Victoria Road a road was planned but never built; you can today see a lawn marking the proposed road.

6. Primrose Terrace – *Strane Sumark*

Named after William Primrose, an Inspector of lighthouses. At the end of the terrace is the Police Station, now residential. Opposite Primrose Terrace was Harley`s College. It was a Dame school, early private elementary school, often in the home of the teacher, usually taught by women.

Primrose Terrace is one of the routes leading through the heart of Port St Mary – from Bay View Road, which starts in the corner of The Promenade and continues south to the former police station (now residential); then Primrose Terrace as far as Bay View Hotel; High Street from the Bay View to Cumberland Square; and from there, Athol Street as far as Queens Road.

7. Park Road – *Raad y Phairk*

Park Road is located on a field known as the North Flat. The garden wall on the municipal properties was built with the stone from the so-called 'pop houses' (quickly built, affordable houses) on the Lower Promenade. The road was built and named in 1926.

8. Barna Beg – *Baarney Beg*

Baarney is Manx Gaelic for 'gap', so Baarney Beg is the Little Gap. Baarney Beg is also known as the Brows, from the Manx Gaelic 'brogh', meaning bank or brink.

9. Fistard Road – *Raad Fistard*
Fistard, or fisk-gaard in Old Norse, means fish garth, an enclosed yard, a place where fish were deposited. A garth can also be a farmstead, house, farm, cottage – most likely it can be translated to 'the road to the Fisherman's cottage'.

10. Perwick Bay – *Baie Pherwick*
This road leads down from Fistard Road to the old Perwick Bay Hotel. Perwick is Old Norse meaning a 'small bay in front' – if you are sailing to Port St Mary, then it is the 'front' of the village.

11. St Mary's Glebe – *Gleeb Voirrey*
This leads from Fistard Road and is mainly residential buildings. 'Glebe' means a land used to support the parish priest, although no evidence has been found to support the theory that this land was owned by the church.

12. Paddock lane – *Lhoan ny Faaieghyn*
In Manx Gaelic 'faaie' means field, green, lawn or paddock, where animals were kept at the nearby butchers. The meadow belonged to Port St Mary Farm, and was later allotments, before being built on.

13. Seafield Avenue – *Astyl Magher Marrey* &
14. St Mary's Avenue – *Astyl Keeil Voirrey*
Seafield Avenue and St Mary's Avenue were built on a field, known as the South Flat, which had belonged to Port St Mary Farm. The farm was bought by Port St Mary Commissioners in 1936, and in 1940 allotments were rented out in the field. In 1944 proposals were submitted for building social housing and in 1947 the first tenants moved into Seafield Avenue. The houses at the bottom, facing onto Queens Road, were built about the same time and sold as plots. On the side nearest the farm the original field wall makes up the back boundary of the gardens in Seafield Avenue.

15. Linden Avenue – *Astyl Biljyn Theiley*
Linden Avenue was built and named in 1948. Most likely there were linden trees in the area. Linden is a deciduous tree with large heart-shaped leaves and yellowish flowers.

16. Endfield Avenue – *Astyl y Vagher S'jerree*
Endfield Avenue was built and named in 1951. However, with it being on the site of Port St Mary Farm, the name could come from a path or road leading to the end of the field. Lace's rope walk (a long lane where long strands were twisted into a rope) was situated at the end of the avenue.

17. Queens Road – *Raad y Ven-Rein*

Named after Queen Victoria. Most towns have places or roads named after queens – Port St Mary has three; Queens Road, Queens Place and Victoria Road.

In the 1880s there was a proposed extensive expansion of the road to Perwick Bay, but only Queens Road and Clifton Road were constructed. Queens Road cut through Port St Mary Farm in the Treen of Fyshgarth, and converted outbuildings are still on Queens Road and Fistard Road. The road was earlier called Alfred Street.

18. Marine Terrace – *Ardane ny Marrey*

The continuation of Queens Road, at the end towards the sea. Opposite the Point Triangle.

19 Queens Place – *Boayl y Ven-Rein*

An open grass plot between Queens Road and Mount Tabor Methodist Chapel. Queens Place had railings around it once, but these were removed in 1937.

20. Corner Plot – *Ploht Corneil*

An open grass plot between Loch Road and Mount Tabor Methodist Chapel.

21. The Point Triangle – *Gob Troorane*

An open triangular-shaped grass plot between Marine Terrace and Clifton Road/Lime Street. The Point Triangle had railings around it once, but these were removed in 1937.

22. Kallow Point Road – *Raad Gob Kallow*

Kallow can be interpreted as Collowah – 'a creek in the cliff' – and on maps a spring can also be found. An alternative explanation suggests that the first part could be a Scandinavian name, Kal or Kolli – same as it is used in Colby (Kolli's Farm). Kallow Point has intertidal (the area between tides) carboniferous limestone ledges and one of the best rocky shores in the British Isles for marine ecological studies.

23. Clifton Road – *Raad Clifton*

The road to the house Strathallan Castle, built on an ancient fort at the promontory (levelled 1896), called Towl Foggy (Towl means 'hole'). The land was part of Port St Mary Farm, then sold by Port St Mary Building Estate Company to Dr George Jotham of Kidderminster, Doctor of Medicine, who built a property named Shag Rock House – an 'ultra-hygienic house', possibly designed by Baillie Scott – which was renamed Strathallan Castle. Latterly the famous pianist Ronnie Aldrich lived there until the late 1980s. Further around the shoreline, opposite Clifton Road, was a rope walk. Baillie Scott (1865-1945) was an architect and artist. Scott developed his own style of Arts and Crafts and was a friend of Archibald Knox.

24. The Quay – *Y Keiy*/Duke Street – *Straid Duke*

Originally known as Duke Street (after the Duke of Atholl), this road was renamed The Quay in 1939.

25. Duke's Corner – *Corneil Duke*

Duke's Corner, named alongside Duke Street (again after the Duke of Atholl), can be found at the junction with Lime Street.

26. Lime Street – *Straid Eayil*

At the southern end of Lime Street there was a sawmill, lime kilns and a quarry (known as the Big Quarry). Many people living in Lime Street worked at the quarry and lime kilns. The kilns, active from the 19th century, were owned by the Lace and Gawne families. Further around the shoreline, opposite Clifton Road, was Lace's rope walk. The quarry was owned by a Mr Jefferson. Lime Street was known as 'Moscow', although it's unclear why.

27. Clifton Road North – *Raad Clifton Twoaie*

Clifton Road and Clifton Road North were once connected, making it possible to cross over the golf course. There is still a path there today.

28. High Street – *Y Traid Vooar*

High Street was the village's primary business centre. On a map from 1869, High Street basically follows its current course. In earlier censuses it was also known as Main Street. It is one of the roads that leads through the heart of Port St Mary – from Bay View Road, which starts in the corner of The Promenade and continues south to the former police station (now residential); then Primrose Terrace as far as Bay View Hotel; High Street from the Bay View to Cumberland Square; and from there, Athol Street as far as Queens Road.

29. The Underway or Shore Road – *Y Fo-Raad or Raad y Trai*)

The Underway, or the Shore Road as it's also known, along with the sea wall in this area, was built in 1907. It runs from the New Quay, just below the Albert Hotel, to the former Carrick Hotel, which has been converted to flats. Before the Underway was built, there were cottages and paths for access. One of the cottages was owned by 'Maggie the Brooghs'. Brooghs means bank or brink.

Maggie the Brooghs cottage. The work being carried out is maintenance of the roof.

30. Karran-Quirk Footpath – *Cassan Karran-Quirk*

This is the continuation of The Underway (also Shore Road) and named after Harold Karran, the Commissioners clerk from 1936, and Harry Quirk, who was appointed foreman mason for the Commissioners in 1949. The path was designed by Wesley Gill, proposed in 1959, with work commencing in 1962. It was opened in 1964 and named Karran-Quirk Footpath in 1977, but it is commonly known as 'the Cat Walk'.

31. Willow Terrace – *Ardane Shellagh*

Willow Terrace is a terrace of houses, between The Underway and the Primrose Terrace.

32. Athol Street – *Straid Athol*

Named after the former Lords of Mann, the Dukes of Atholl. Over a period of time the Atholls sold the feudal rights pertaining to the Isle of Man to Great Britain, with the last sale in 1828. Athol Street, built in 1869, roughly follows the edge of a meadow field for Port St Mary Farm.

Athol Street is one of the roads that leads through the heart of Port St Mary – from Bay View Road, which starts in the corner of The Promenade and continues south to the former police station (now residential); then Primrose Terrace as far as Bay View Hotel; High Street from the Bay View to Cumberland Square; and from there, Athol Street as far as Queens Road.

33. Carrick Mews – *Close ny Carrick*

Carrick means cliff or rock. The area is named after the Carrick Rock in the middle of Baie Ny Carrickey (a volcanic plug), while the mews is named after the Carrick Hotel across the road. The mews was built on land formerly used for tennis and golf.

34. Bay View Road – *Reayrt y Vaie*

Formerly known as Church Road, the name was changed to Bay View Road in 1926. This is one of the roads that leads through the heart of Port St Mary – from Bay View Road, which starts in the corner of The Promenade and continues south to the former police station (now residential); then Primrose Terrace as far as Bay View Hotel; High Street from the Bay View to Cumberland Square; and from there, Athol Street as far as Queens Road.

35. Lewthwaites Way – *Bayr Lewthwaite*

Named after local doctor and chemist John Lester Lewthwaite, who was born in 1891 and who was later with Gelling Bros. in Douglas as a pharmacist. He lived in the house on the corner of Lewthwaites Way and Station Road.

36. Creggan Mooar

Running perpendicular from Station Road, Creggan means 'rocky place' and mooar means 'big' – the big rocky place. The road was built on the field Crouguilt, on the Ballacreggan Farm.

37. Creggan Beg

Leading from Creggan Mooar. Creggan means 'rocky place', beg means 'small' – the small rocky place.

38. Creggan Lheeah

The road leading from Beach Road. Creggan means 'rocky place', lheeah means 'grey' – the grey rocky place.

39. Cooil Veg

The road leading from Creggan Mooar. Cooil means 'nook' and veg means 'small'. This area was part of Ballacreggan Farm, known as Crouguilt.

40. Station Road – *Raad y Stashoon*

The road to the station from The Promenade. The railway opened in 1874, with the village only receiving a station following public outcry when the proposed route was announced, with a request to deviate the line also being submitted. This was not carried out, however, resulting in today's station being some distance from the heart of the village it serves. A standing stone, 10ft high and with no trace of decoration, can be found in the field opposite Ballacreggan Farm. The field is known as Clagh Ard. The road is close to the treen boundary between the Abbeyland and Edremony.

41. Truggan Road – *Raad y Truggan*

The origin of the name could be Struan, meaning 'stream', due to the stream close by Glendown Farm. Truggan Road is the 'road to the stream'.

42. Loch Road – *Raad Loch*

Named after Sir Henry Loch, who was Governor of the Isle of Man from 1863-1882. Under Lord Loch's Reform Act (1866), members of the House of Keys, the Island's parliament, were elected by the people – by public ballot. The road is also known as 'Flitter Street'.

43. The Promenade – *Y Shooylaghan*

The Promenade was originally called Cary`s Promenade after George Cary, who owned the land and gave Gansey and the Promenade to the people of Port St Mary. It was built in 1887 and mentioned in Commissioners minutes as Cary's Promenade in 1890. The Promenade area was part of the Ballacreggan Farm known as Crouguilt. An old cart track along part of this area, known as cass ny feie (the wild/natural path) or cass ny faaie (the flat path), went out to Rhenwyllan and Gansey.

44. The Lower Promenade – *Y Shooylaghan Heese*

The Lower Promenade was constructed as a winter works scheme in 1906. The extension of Lower Promenade is the Old Royal Road, formerly the main road into the Port, which came around Gansey.

45. Alfred Pier – *Peer y Alured*

The foundation stone for the pier was laid by Alfred, The Duke of Edinburgh on the 31st January 1882, but the pier was not completed until 1886. A guidebook from the time said: 'It was built of cut limestone and has lasted well – certainly better than the breakwater in Port Erin, which was constructed by the British Government.' The pier is almost 300 metres long and vastly increased the area of sheltered water in the harbour. The lighthouse that stood at the end of the pier is said to have come from the breakwater in Port Erin. However, it was swept away in a storm in 2009.

46. New Quay –*Keiy Noa*

Built in 1812, Inner Pier was home to shipyards and several blacksmiths and nail makers.

47. The Lhargan

This old road runs from behind the Bay View Hotel and leads to Cronk Road. The 1834 map of Port St Mary shows the road and a number of dwelling houses. Through most of the nineteenth century the name of the road appears in written records variously as Lagghan, Laggan, Laggan Street, Laghan and Largan. It was recorded as Mount Pleasant in Porter's 1889 Trade Directory and in the records of the Port St Mary Commissioners in 1891. The name Lhargan came to be used in the early twentieth century and Mount Pleasant became the name of one of the houses on The Lhargan. The Manx Gaelic origin of the present day Lhargan is unclear – it may derive from laggan, meaning hollow, or lhargagh meaning slope.

48. Bank Lane – *Lhoan y Vank*

Named after Parrs Bank – later Westminster and National Westminster – at the top of High Street. The lane was also called Corris`s Gut, as two brothers and a sister, named Corris, lived in a cottage there. It is the 'gut' leading to Purt Verk (likely means Timber Harbour in Old Norse).

49. Watterson Lane – *Lhoan Kodhere*

Known as Watterson Lane, but also Quillin's (Queelan's) Gut. It was named after Quillin, who had a butcher's shop at the top of the lane. At the top of this lane is a cellar under the road, which was used as an air raid shelter.

50. Carrick Steps – *Greeishyn ny Carrickey*

These lead from Bay View Road to The Underway. Down the steps, the gable end of what was the Port St. Mary National School, built in 1837, can be seen. When a new

Corri's cottage and the gut coming down to the left.

school was built in 1880, the building became the Rushen Hall and was used by the Commissioners for meetings and other community events. The first Commissioner's meeting was held on 28 April 1890.

51. Rhenwyllan Close – *Close Rheynn Wyllin*
Rhenwyllan Close – in Manx 'Ring Willen' – was built on Mill Division field; there was a mill at the bottom of Beach Road. Wyllin means 'mill'. During World War II it was used as a dummy village and assault course for the Officer Cadet Training Unit.

52. Four Roads – *Kione Ny Kiare Bayryn*
The road from Port St Mary Station to the roundabout where Four Roads, Castletown Road and Church Road converges. In the old days, people living around the roundabout claimed to be living at the 'Four Roads'.

53. Beach Road – *Raad Ny Traie*
Beach Road was named in 1933, first from the Shore Hotel to Gawne's Brewery (demolished after fire), then further to Station Road. The brewery – owned and operated by the Gawne family of Kentraugh – was located on the site of what was later the Shore Garage and is now detached houses. At the Port St Mary end of Brewery Beach (which is often wrongly referred to as 'Gansey Beach') was a smelting house for the local lead mines, located opposite what was Rhenwyllin Mill, a tall building built from Manx stone, which was originally a threshing mill, later a woollen mill, and which is now apartments. Rhenwyllin Mill was known locally as 'the Big Mill', while the one at Kentraugh was known was the 'Little Mill'.

54. Tom Mac's Gut – *Gut Hom*
Runs perpendicular to Lime Street. A man known as Tom Mac lived in the house to the left (as you're standing on Lime Street looking down to the Gut).

55. Cumberland Square – *Kerrin Cumberland*
The area in front of today's Quine & Cubbon Printers is Cumberland Square. The old butcher's shop, Quillins, was once the Cumberland Inn. Two proprietors of the inn were Edward Gale in 1850 and Mrs Elizabeth Cubbon in 1882. The village market was behind High Street.

56. Old Chapel Road – *Cass ny Faaie*
The old path Cass ny Faaie ('flat field path') was also called The Old Chapel Road. It was part of the Old Royal Road, the main road into the Port which came around Gansey. The road runs past the seaward side of the Town Hall, almost opposite Gellings Avenue.

57. Barney Smoo
A cul-de-sac from Fistard Road, Barney Smoo means 'big gap'. Older locals say Barney Moo, with the 's' having been dropped.

58. Promenade Back Road – *Raad Cooyl Y Chooylaghyn*
This road runs behind The Promenade.

59. Pound Lane – *Lhoan Croa*
This road leads from Beach Road to Castletown Road and follows the Pound River.

60. Ned Madrell Path – *Cassan Ned Maddrell*
Named after Edward Ned Maddrell (1877-1974), a fisherman and the last native speaker of Manx Gaelic. He lived and passed away in Cregneash.

61. Mullet's Gut – *Gut Vullet*
This leads off from Lime Street and down to the sea.

62. Clugston Gut – *Gut Clugston*
Charlie Clugston had his coal yard at the top of the lane for many years. The coal yard was originally on the New Quay and was owned by Richard Keig, who had two schooners, *Capricorn* and *St Saviour*. He moved the yard to the lane that links Primrose Terrace with The Lhargan in 1925 and sold it to Jimmy Clugston senior, who was a master on the schooners. The coal yard was taken over by his sons Jimmy Clugston junior and Billy Clugston They gave up through ill health and another son, Charlie Glugston, took over. The office at the coal yard was the old Port St Mary mortuary. The coal was tipped into the yard from an entrance in The Lhargan, now bricked up.

63. Crebbin's Workshop

This street has no name. The oldest building along the street is the old barn or plumber's workshop, owned by a Mr Crebbin.

64. Lane between Kallow Point Road and Queens Road

This lane has no name. It is in the area of Lace's rope walk and runs between Kallow Point Road and Queens Road. Did it at one time connect up to the lane that runs along the back of Lime Street and to Loch Road?

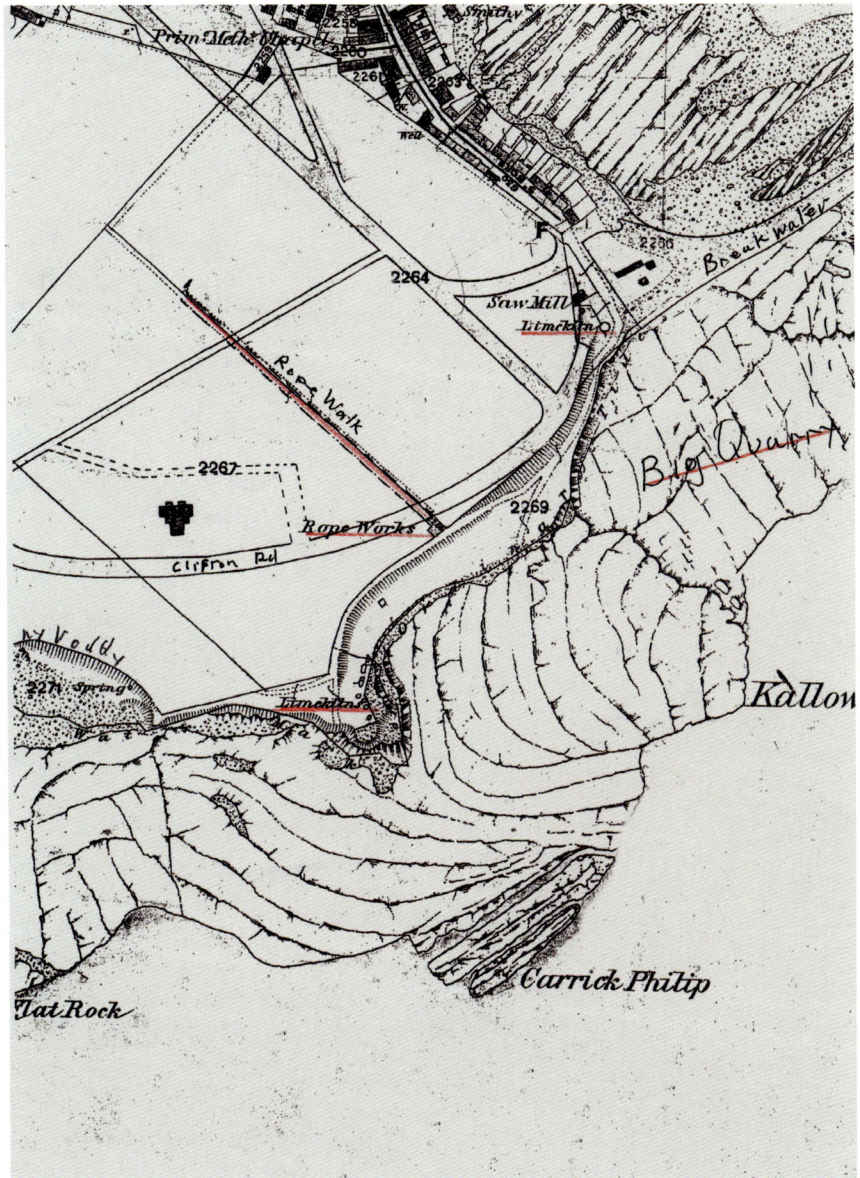

Location of Lace's rope walk.

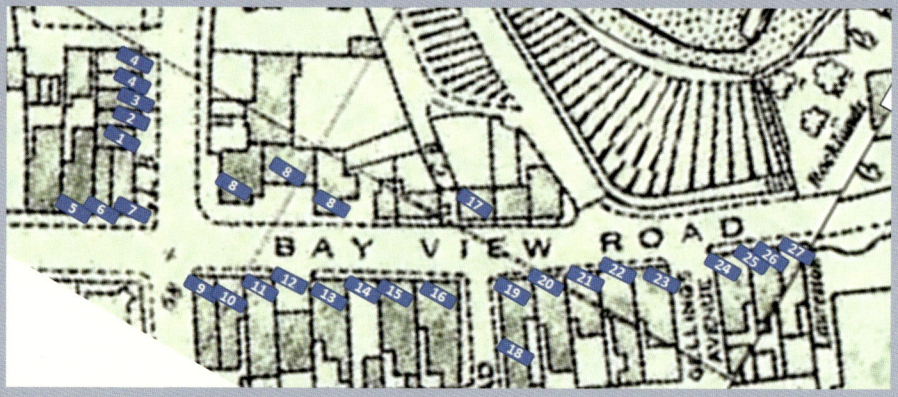

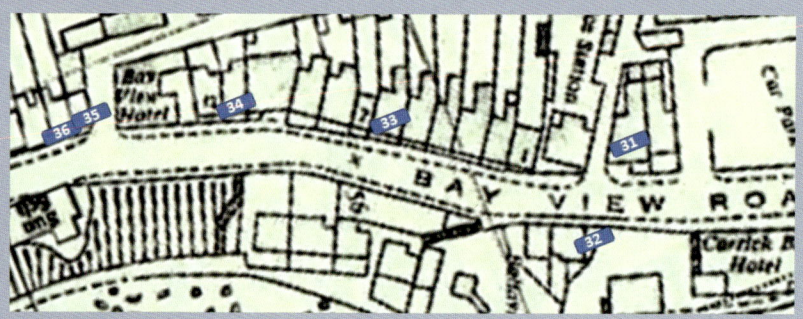

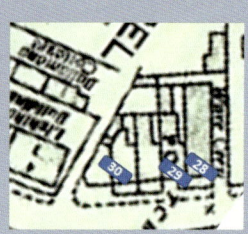

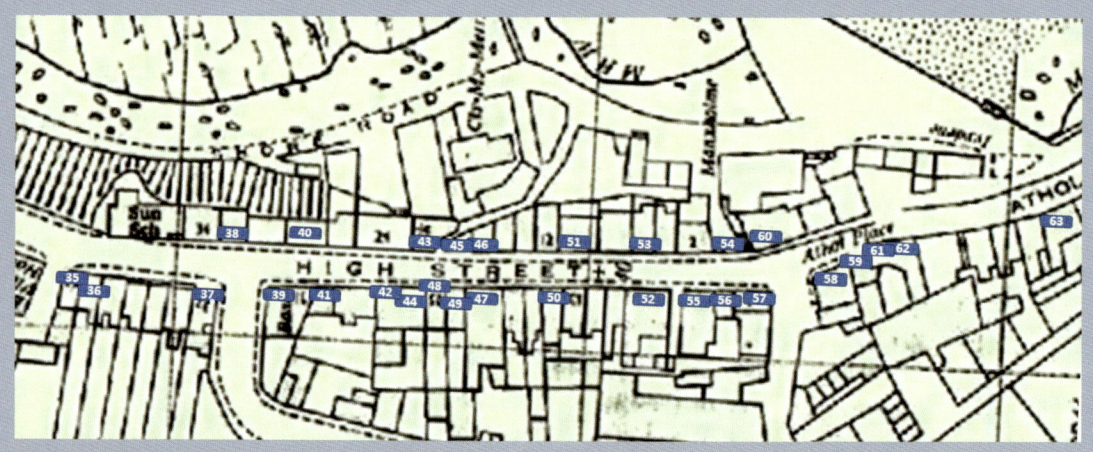

Knickerbocker Breeches for Golfing and Fishing

CHAPTER 9

STAFFAN OVERGAARD and JOHN W. QUALTROUGH

Decades ago, Port St Mary was something of a mercantile mecca, a 'shopping mall' for the south. That's all changed, of course, due to modern buying patterns. Today many Port St Mary residents might go to Port Erin for major food purchases, or if they work in Douglas, do their shopping there before returning home. And some will shop online. The bottom line is that the days when residents of Port St Mary had five grocery shops to choose between are long gone. In the past the tourism business asked for enormous supplies during a few months of the year and the suppliers had to be dormant to the next season, with the seasonal boom sustaining them during the quieter months.

The plan was to identify shops within the village and it seemed simple – find the address and research what kind of shop has operated from the site. But in many instances the same location has housed many shops over the years. Some shops were divided into two, and sometimes two shops were merged into one. We also have found shop owners who moved from location to location. The fact that sections of Station Road and Church Road were named Bay View Road in 1921 did not make it any easier.

Businesses were normally small and production the size of cottage industries. Some sites saw unlikely combinations of trades – such as a painter also selling toys, or another selling and producing sweets in the front of the shop while doing dressmaking from a room in the back.

We found eighty locations for 'shops', omitting the likes of coal yards, kipper houses, and shipyards. In those eighty locations we found 250 shopkeepers who were active during the last 120 years. But the true number of shopkeepers will be much higher – the residents of Port St Mary are very industrious.

We would like to thank Norman Collister and Linda Winstanley for supplying valuable information towards this chapter, and Adrian Cain's interviews with residents from fifteen years ago has also been a valuable source.

Years in brackets in the text are when we could find evidence of the shop. We have found reference to some shops but could not locate them, so the actual number of shops within the port is more than what is contained in the list below.

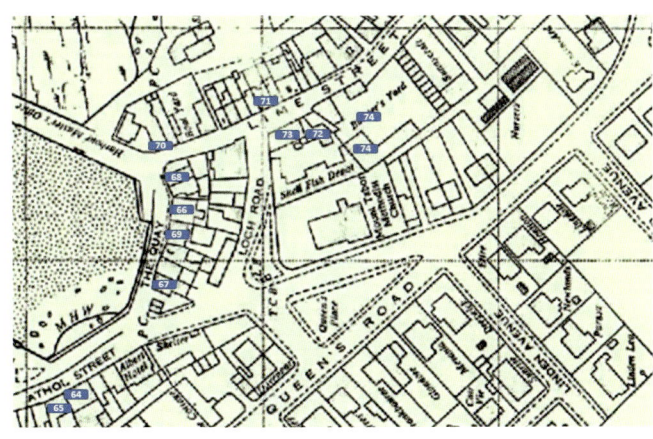

PROMENADE

1. Chips
The location for a few chip shops over the years, but today it is home to The Laundry Room launderette. The chip shops took only a part of the building, the left side of where the launderette is located today.

Shops in chronological order: Dodd chip shop, Columbine chip shop (had moved to High Street by 1926) glazier and The Laundry Room.

2. Sweets and batteries
Part of what is today The Laundry Room, it was once an electrical shop, taking in batteries for radios (or wireless, as some readers might remember them!). It was also home to two sweet shops.

Shops in chronological order: Maddrell W. Confectioners, Curphey's sweet shop, G.L. Maddrell Radio & Batteries, Maureen Richards Celtic Jeweler and The Laundry Room.

3. Chinaware and fish
One of an old row of four shops, which is now home to The Laundry Room.

Shops in chronological order: Annie Costain's China Ware, milk shop, cobblers, Jackson's fish and newsagency, Maureen's haberdashery and The Laundry Room.

4. Greengrocers and newspapers
One of an old row of four shops, which is now home to The Laundry Room. Mr. Prideau had a greengrocer's shop here and he now and then teased the children by flinging handfuls of broken biscuits over the shop floor – one of his young customers recalled, 'we all grabbed as much as we could!' Hygiene did not matter so much then. Mr. Prideau also sold tickets to coach trips and excursions with the Isle of Man Steam Packet Company. The shop also had a sugar supply license issued in 1917.

Harry Watterson was a tailor, clothier and outfitter and sold, as written in the ads, 'Walking and Golfing Costumes', 'Manx homespun Suits in Choice Designs at Moderate Prices', and 'Knickerbocker Breeches for Golfing and Fishing'.

Shops in chronological order: Prideau greengrocer, J. Hills Army surplus, ladies' hairdresser and barber, newsagents, and various tenants such as Harry Watterson, Wallace Jackson, Woodend's, Hawley's, Eaton S.G., Alan Quine and, finally, The Laundry Room.

STATION ROAD

5. Haberdashery and cycles

Miss Mary McNeill sold wool in large quantities when knitting and knitted products. The haberdashery also rented bicycles, and we are told it was cheaper to hire a cycle for a whole day than for a couple of hours.

From Miss McNeil's adverts – 'Ladies visiting Port St Mary during the Summer Months find a visit to this Establishment most interesting when in search of any materials or requisites for Fancy Work'.

Shops in chronological order: Miss McNeil haberdashery and wool shop (1926), Jack Downs electrical/cycles, Edith Cain's Snack Bar, travel agent, and Suzanne's Flowers.

6. Sweets

Miss Katie Skelly had a sweet shop at the premises and her sister did sewing for people from a room behind the shop. One young customer said: 'Where you stood with your nose to the window and that half penny went an awful long way for getting liquorish strips, do you remember those liquorish ribbons?'

Shops in chronological order: Katie Skelly Sweets (1926), Chapman Sweets and a private house.

7. Toys and cycles

This corner shop had many tenants over the years ranging from selling toys, cycles, wool, fish and even being the village Post Office. It could be that Thomas Rushton Painter and Toys had his establishment here in 1889.

Shops in chronological order: Eaton's Toys and Gifts (1926), Miles Walker's Toys and Radio (opened in 1938), W. R. Gelling electrical/cycles, café, wool shop, Post Office and The Fish House (restaurant).

BAY VIEW ROAD (previously Station Road)

8. Dress shop and advocates

A nine-year-old remembers that in the 1950s there was a toy & beach shop, 'selling buckets, rubber rings, beach balls plus loads of toys'. Today the building is home to an advocate's office.

Shops in chronological order: Port St Mary Boys' School (closed 1926), Cowley's Café, toy & beach shop, Manxonia dress shop and Judy Thornley Advocates.

9. Chemist and Indian restaurant

Today this site is home to Kitchen of India restaurant, and before that Rasoi restaurant. It was previously divided into two premises, one a chemist and one a greengrocer. The building dates from 1937.

Shops in chronological order: Johnnie Quine chemist, Walter Quillin chemist, Rasoi Indian restaurant, Kitchen of India.

10. Greengrocer, souvenirs and Indian restaurant
The other (left) half of what is now Kitchen of India. Earlier on this spot you could find a greengrocer, The Lobster Pot.

Shops in chronological order: Jimmy Hislop greengrocer, The Lobster Pot, and part of Rasoi Indian restaurant and Kitchen of India.

11. Co-op
The Co-op has been in Port St Mary since 1912 and this, its second (and current) site, was built in 1929.

12. Garage and a mall
This has been home to several garages – Stubbs (also called the Victoria Garage), Gorry's and, lastly, Millers. There was a garage and petrol pumps and all. In an advert, Stubbs said: '... haulage, repairs, accessories, cars for hire, motor coach tours, new cars and motorcycles supplied, second-hand cars bought, sold or exchanged'. Today it is a small shopping mall, with an Italian restaurant and dress shop, by the name of Ports of Call.

Shops in chronological order: Stubbs Garage (opened 1925), Gorry's Garage, Millers Garage and Ports of Call

W. H. GELL

GROCER, WINE AND SPIRIT MERCHANT.

Agent for W. & A. Gilbey.

THE STORES, STATION ROAD,
:: :: PORT ST. MARY. :: ::

Telephone 60.

NOTED FOR IRISH BACON.

13. Millinery

Shops in chronological order: Edith Qualtrough millinery and part of Ports of Call.

14. Open space
Empty. No house or shop. Today part of Ports of Call.

15. Café and bakery
The location for several cafés and bakeries. The building dates from 1902 and was called Café St Mary. It operated as Coole's Café for the mid-1900s and was then Good Life, a greengrocers and plant shop. It changed to a haberdashery called Patchwork, which converted into a café, and is today the Sugarloaf Café. Miss Coole marketed her establishment with 'Pastry a specialty. Tea baskets loaned for shorter picnics. En route for shore, caves, chasms, druid circle and coast road to Port Erin'.

Shops in chronological order: Café St Mary/Coole's Café and Confectioners (1926), Kelly's Café, Good Life, Metaxa & various, Patchwork Café and The Sugarloaf Café.

16. Grocer and art gallery
The grocer was in the left part of what is today's Gallery 42.

Shops in chronological order: Kneen's (type of business unknown), Prideau grocer, Tom Kelly grocer, Chinese café and Art Shop Gallery 42.

17. Cobbler
Teddy Collister had a cobbler business at the right-hand side of the Old Road, opposite where Gallery 42 is today.

Shops in chronological order: Teddy Collister cobbler, today a private house.

18. Watches and records
On Victoria Road, Bashforth's had an establishment selling watches and records, located on the left-hand side as you come from Bay View Road.

Shops in chronological order: Bashforth watchmaker & records (1926) and now a private house.

19. Grocer and lingerie
Words from an eyewitness, about the establishment Darnill & Keig grocers: '… they kept a lovely cake shop there… you could smell the cakes, oh, they were beautiful, they were lovely. And they were awful nice the people that were there …' The advert for Gell's grocer said: 'Best Danish Butter & Irish Bacon, Fresh Ground Coffee'. They had a sugar supply license issued in 1917. This area used to be part of Station Road, until it was changed to Bay View Road in 1926.

Shops in chronological order: W. H. Gell grocer, Darnill & Keig grocer, Homemaker DIY and Chantilly Lace ladies lingerie.

20. Newsagents
Newsagents and a printer by the name Broadbent S K. B. Co Ltd were located here from 1926.

Shops in chronological order: Broadbent (1926), Isle of Man Examiner Shop, various tenants before today's Calvert Newsagent.

21. Shoes and pharmacy
All sort of businesses operated from this shop – draper's, antiques, and hairdressers and today it's a pharmacy.

Shops in chronological order: Collister shoes, Hollis's shoe shop, Miss Newton shoe shop, Mrs Sheard shoe shop, Isle of Man Bank, ladies hairdressers and Clear Pharmacy.

22. Drapers

Shops in chronological order: Qualtrough draper, Mrs Eslick antiques, John Kneen painter, Costain Pharmacy, Pharmacy Worthing and now Hair Traffic.

23. Ironmongers and coffee
The left side of today's Cornershop Coffee. Previously home to Kara Café, for which an advert promoted '…teas, luncheons and homemade chocolate…'

Shops in chronological order: Willie Watterson baker, Kara Café, Jack Christian ironmonger, Clague clothes, John Kneen painter, Pindelfin antiques, Barbara Malin greengrocer and Cornershop Coffee.

24. Butcher and diving

TRY

Thomas Clague

BAY VIEW ROAD, PORT ST. MARY,

For Prime Beef and Lamb, Pork & Veal.

: :   : :   All Home Killed.   : :   : :

❖▮▮▮▮▮❖▮▮▮▮▮❖

Corned Beef and Pickled Tongue, etc.

Home to a diving shop today, a stark contrast to its previous long life as a butcher's.

Shops in chronological order: Thomas Clague (1889 and 1926), Alec Maddrell, Arthur Corkhill, E.G. Jones, Alan Radcliffe, and John Corrin – all butchers – and Discover Diving.

25. Hairdressing and photography
The shop was a part of Discover Diving shop, the left-hand side if standing in front of the shop. The Clague

sisters (Madge and Winnie) were the daughters of the butcher, Tom Clague, in the neighboring shop. The family was doing butchery in one part and hair styling in the other – a very capable family. It has been said that Lawrence in the photography shop would 'go on the beach and to local events and take photos which would be displayed on boards in the shop and you would order the photos you wanted'.

Lawrence Photographers, left-hand side of today's Discover Diving shop.

Shops in chronological order: Clague sisters' hairdressers, Lawrence Photographers and the left side of today's Discover Diving.

26. Greengrocer and hairdressing

Shops in chronological order: Costain chinaware & postcards, Nicholls greengrocer, ladies' hairdressers

27. Butchery and takeaway

This was Laureston Snack Bar and ice cream parlour in the 1950s, with adverts promoting 'Homemade ice creams, homemade cakes & scones. tea & coffee, ice cream sundaes and knickerbocker glories'. The shop, which opened in 1947, was also known as Smokey Joe's.

Shops in chronological order: Willy Watterson tailor, Quillin and Maddrell butchers, Laureston Snack Bar (Smokey Joe's Snack Bar) and Chinese takeaway, the Good Luck.

28. Grocer and heating

A young visitor remembers Maddrell's grocer shop here: '... they used to have lovely syrup... Mother would send us down with a jar to get this syrup and they just poured it out of a tub and it was a dark colour.' Frank Maddrell had a sugar supply license issued in 1917.

Shops in chronological order: Frank Maddrell's grocer (1926), Joughin's grocer, Hansen's grocer, Hair Traffic, Falcon Heating and Port St Mary Sports Injury and Rehabilitation Clinic.

29. Post Office

Port St Mary has had three locations for its Post Office, this one opening in 1907. In 1926 the shop was near the Bay Hotel.

Shops in chronological order: Post Office, doctors' surgery, Hair Traffic, Falcon Heating and Port St Mary Sports Injury and Rehabilitation Clinic.

30. Chemist and painter

Shops in chronological order: R.K. Kermode's chemist (1889, 1926), John Kneen painter and decorator, Hospice Shop and office.

PREVIOUSLY CHURCH ROAD

31. Greengrocer
This house is in the corner of the lane, and according to an advert (1930-1940s) proprietor Maggie Gawne was selling '… fruit, vegetables and flowers'.

Shops in chronological order: Maggie Gawne greengrocer, L.T. Peak Radio and Television, and today a private house.

32. Cobbler and shoe shop
The shop was located on the other side of the road, on a lane leading up to the Clugston coal yard.

Shops in chronological order: Harry Maddrell shoe shop, Miss Newton shoe shop and now a private house.

33. Optician
This house is located in the centre of today's Primrose Terrace.

Shops in chronological order: Harborough optician.

34. Post Office
This was a post office in the 1940s and in the 1950s the Manx Electricity Board shop could be found here, '… selling ovens, electric kettles, and the new and very expensive refrigerators only a very few people could have them…', as one customer explained. Later it became David Glovers Upholsterers, which moved to Foxdale in 2017.

Shops in chronological order: Post Office, Manx Electricity Board, greengrocer (unknown), insurance broker and David Glovers upholsterers.

HIGH STREET

35. Painter and greengrocer
The corner house is today a private home.

Shops in chronological order: John Oliver Painter, Ted Swales greengrocer, Eaton greengrocer, Nash greengrocer, Enoch Mellor greengrocer, Aspinal greengrocer, Quillin sisters greengrocers and now a private house

36. Barber and estate agent
Private house today, this was a men's barbershop in the 1940s.

Shops in chronological order: Billy Cubbon barber (1926), Cowell estate agent and now a private house.

W. TURNBULL
— Family Butcher. —
A Trial Order Solicited.

Families & Shipping supplied on Special Terms

For the Finest Quality of Manx Meat
of Guaranteed Freshness you cannot
do better than visit this Establishment.

HIGH STREET, PORT ST. MARY.

33

On some of the facades you can still see the hooks from where the meat hanged.

37. Butcher
The corner house, in the local adverts you could read that Turnbull butchers was a 'family and shipping butcher'. The slaughterhouse was nearby and the schoolchildren sneaked down there to have a look in at the animals and were terrified.

Shops in chronological order: Willie Turnbull butcher, Tommy Little butcher and now a private house.

38. Millinery

Shops in chronological order: Miss Collister greengrocer, Annie May Bridson milliner, Mrs Carine Milliner and now a private house.

39. Isle of Man Bank
Ashton Cannell and later Bob Lawson were two of the managers of what was at one time the Isle of Man Bank.

Shops in chronological order: Isle of Man Bank (1889), now a private house.

40. Sweets
This shop was located opposite the Isle of Man Bank. A visitor told, '… they used to make these long sticks of cinnamon toffee, Manx knobs, twisted sticks of toffee, Manx toffee, it was lovely…'.

Shops in chronological order: Ollie & Addy Kermode boiled sweets and now a private house.

41. Kippers
J.J. Qualtrough's kipper shop (1926) was located here, a small shop between J.J. Qualtrough's house and the bank.

Shops in chronological order: J.J. Qualtrough kipper shop, John Watterson greengrocer and now a private house.

42. Confectioner and millinery

Shops in chronological order: Miss Helm confectioner, Miss Miles millinery, Miss Mary Quirk millinery, Mrs Harrison shoes, and today a private house.

43. Bank
The Parrs and later Westminster had a bank at the top of High Street. One of the names of a nearby lane is Bank Lane/Corries Gut.

Shops in chronological order: Dumbells, Parrs Bank, Westminster Bank and now a private house.

44. Bakers

A visitor said of one of the bakers: "…used to make the big sea biscuits that the lighthouse people had, a big flat biscuit, sort of, if you ran out of food you'd always have those in. The lighthouse-keepers always had them… they were very hard but they were good… The baker lived above the shop … then there was another confectioner's next door, Miss Helm's…".

Shops in chronological order: Johnnie Collister baker (1889), Ronan's baker, Martin's baker and Herbert Elliot souvenirs and now a private house.

45. Greengrocer and painter

Shops in chronological order: J. Hills greengrocer, unknown greengrocer, Jack Kinvig painter and today a private house.

46. Greengrocer and watchmaker

Shops in chronological order: Unknown greengrocer, Gales greengrocer (they had sugar supply license issued in 1917), Miss Miles millinery, Alan Quillin watchmaker and today a private house.

47. Bakers

W. Watterson was selling 'bread, pies, cakes etc' says a customer, who continued '… he had one of the old-fashioned carts, up high, a bread cart, and a rail round the top …'.

Shops in chronological order: J. Skillicorn baker (1889, 1926), W. Watterson Baker, clothing, fisherman's shop and today a private house.

48. The People's Store

Shops in chronological order: The People Store (1881, 1889), managed by a Mr Gawne. The People Store was a grocer.

49. Watchmaker

Swales Watchmaker and Photographer. Adverts from Swales (established 1896) said: 'Visitors requiring MEMENTOS of their visit to Port St Mary, would do well to call on V. L. Swales, Watchmaker, Jeweler and Photographer…" and "Outdoor Photography a Specialty".

Shops in chronological order: Swales photographer (1926).

50. Greengrocer and toys

Shops in chronological order: Miss Gawne Greengrocer, Jack McCrimmin toys/blinds, Jim Oliver painter and now a private house.

51. Chip shops

Not only a shop but also with a couple of eat-in tables.

Shops in chronological order: Columbine's Chip Shop (1926), Gold's Chip Shop (1948), Hudson's Chip Shop, Best's Chip Shop and now a private house.

A view of High Street, with The People's Store on the left.

52. Draper and shoes
Shops in chronological order: Tom Kelly draper (T. Kelly grocer's father) (1926), Fred Watterson draper, Boyd's shoes, Marine shop, Manx Gas showroom and now a private house.

53. Shoes and Dressmaker
Shops in chronological order: James Crebbin shoes (in 1889 on The Quay), Jack Downs Electrical, Mrs Allen dressmaker and now a private house.

54. The first Co-op
Located close to Watterson Lane, this was the first Co-op in Port St Mary.

Shops in chronological order: Co-op and now a private house.

55. Grocer and restaurant
A customer recalls '... big block of cheese and they had a... like a wire thing, and they'd pull this wire down through and cut a wedge, a perfect wedge of cheese'. Alfie Moore the grocer had a public phone box in his shop.

Shops in chronological order: Kneen draper (1903), Qualtrough Bakery (1904), Kinte Baker (1905), Alfie Moore grocer (1889, 1926), Maddrell & Woodruff grocers, Anchorage Restaurant and now a private house.

J.J. Qualtrough Shoe and Bootmaker on High Street.

56. Butcher
This property was rebuilt in 1934-35 and was then a part of Qualtrough's shoe shop.

Shops in chronological order: Alfie Gawne plumber (1926), Eddie Woods butcher (1934-35), Harrison butcher, Tommy Little butcher and now a private house.

57. Shoemaker
This was previously one shop, but in the 2000s was split – to the right it was a beauty salon and to the left a fish and chips shop. From the Qualtrough adverts: "An up-to-date and select stock of Ladies' Gents' and Children's Boots and Slippers of the best and most Noted Makes, suitable for all seasons, to select from. The oldest established House in Port St Mary and Port Erin. Our goods are noted for Fitting, Style, Durability and Value."

Shops in chronological order: J.J. Qualtrough shoe and bootmaker (1889, 1926), H.J. Qualtrough bootmaker, Dick Kneen fishmonger, Latham fishmonger, café & chip shop and today a private house.

ATHOL STREET

58. Grocer and printer
One customer recalls: '… the greengrocer's used to have a big sack full of figs or nuts … ham hanging up in the ceiling, there'd be legs of ham, hanging up, it was all spotlessly clean … buy butter … and get it cut up, however much, they'd weigh it for you…'. The 1926 Port St Mary Guidebook mentioned an Edward Gale grocer at this address.

Shops in chronological order: Edwin Qualtrough grocer (1881, 1889) and net manufacturer (1889), John Skelly grocer, café (1976), souvenir shop and today Quine & Cubbon Printers.

59. Garage

Shops in chronological order: Miller's garage, Cardale's garage, Metalco and today Talco ENG Ltd.

60. Inn and butcher
Located just besides Watterson Lane.

Shops in chronological order: Cumberland Inn, Brockley butcher, Moorhouse butcher, Eddie Woods butcher, Willie Quillin butcher and now a private house.

61. Fishmongers
This was a fishmonger's before it was joined with next door (#62, below) and became The General Store.

Shops in chronological order: Aldritts fishmonger (1926), Dick Kneen fishmonger, The General Store and now a private house.

62. Bazaar
This was home to Robert's Bazaar, a hairdresser and tobacconist. It sold a wide variety of postcards, fishing tackle, cycles, and model boats.
In the adverts they said: 'Original maker of Manx Clipper Model Yachts, all guaranteed fast sailors.' They had cycles for sale and hire, they were agents for 'Triumph, Sparkbrook, Premier, Bradbury, Humber, Iris, Star, and Robin Hood Cycles.' Robert's Bazaar was located both on Athol Street and the Promenade.

Shops in chronological order: Robert's Bazaar (barber and tobacco) (1926), Roberts F.W. Newsagents and Stationers, The General Store, and now a private house.

63. Paint shop
Reggie Cregeen had a wallpaper and paint shop, and he would also come and decorate your home.

Shops in chronological order: Reggie Cregeen painter, paint shop and today Guy Thompson architect. The house is called 'The Old Paint Shop'.

64. Bakers
A customer recalls: 'Bread and cakes of all descriptions, from potato cakes to wedding cakes, baked and iced on the premises and delivered daily.' When Princess Alexandra came to the Isle of Man in 1983, she visited the shop and bought a loaf of bread.

Shops in chronological order: W. Watterson baker (1926), A.J. Faragher baker and now a private house.

65. Butcher
Shops in chronological order: Clague butcher (1881) and now a private house.

The Quay [Duke St]

66. Ironmonger

Shops in chronological order: Thos. Coole ironmonger and now a private house.

The Compton building demolished (1976) and replaced with private houses.

67. Mrs Evans sweets

Shops in chronological order: Mrs Evans sweets and pop, and now a private house.

68. Compton building
The old Compton building was demolished (1976) and replaced with private houses.

Shops in chronological order: Compton Buildings: Various shops, emptied in the 1940s. Now private houses.

69. Grocer

Shops in chronological order: Qualtrough grocer (1881, 1889) (with a sugar supply license issued in 1917), café, launderette and now a private house.

70. Fish shop

Shops in chronological order: Arthur Neild Fish Shop

Lime Street

71. Greengrocer

Shops in chronological order: Bridson greengrocer and now a private house.

72. Mineral waters
Rushen Mineral Water Co. produced here, alongside the warehouse in Lime Street. The well was in the house. Another mineral water supplier was located in the pop-houses down from the Promenade, the proprietor was Samuel Waterson, who also a baker and confectioner.

73. Merchant warehouse

Shops in chronological order: Hampson's Paper merchant warehouse.

74. Timber yard

Shops in chronological order: Qualtrough's Kipper House, Gelling's Timber Yard and Qualtrough's Timber Yard (now in Castletown).

Millennium Minesweepers, Glamorous Grannies and Boney M

CHAPTER 10

PAMELA CROWE

The tourist trade in Port St Mary had been declining gradually for many years and in 1978 tourism was at a low point in the port. With the Millennium Year of 1979 approaching, the Isle of Man Government was planning events to celebrate 1,000 years of Tynwald, the oldest continuous parliament in the world.

A local Traders' Association was established to look at ways to promote the village and attract more visitors. Graham and I owned the Examiner Shop and we were keen to support this initiative.

One of the suggestions was for traders to wear Manx dress one day of the week, with Tuesday identified as the poorest trading day. I was asked to coordinate some activities on costume days and encourage folk to join in to promote the village, and I quickly got into the spirit. I rang any dance groups, choirs and bands that were scheduled to visit the Island. I rang the Grenadier Guards, who were to be the official escort at Tynwald. I even

Pamela Crowe in costume, with (above) the Millennium Medal she was awarded for her efforts during the year. (Courtesy of Southern Photographic Society)

*Costume days -
spinning and sheep
shearing on Station
Road. (Courtesy of
Southern
Photographic
Society)*

*One of the many bands which played on
the costume days. (Courtesy of Southern
Photographic Society)*

rang the BBC, which televised a Seaside Special show, a prime time show broadcast from seaside venues. I was surprised at the positive response from most groups, but heard nothing from the BBC. I was a member of Port St Mary Women's Institute and we embraced the idea as it fitted in with the Festival of Women that the then Tourism Department was organising, and our Southern Agricultural Show WI competition.

An old bonnet was picked apart to make an authentic pattern and to our surprise we found that it had been repaired with embroidered tape from the *Clan MacMaster*, a ship that foundered on the Thusla Rock in 1923, with a cargo of Singer sewing machines, many of which found good homes in the village. I even secured the pipes and drums of the ceremonial guards who were attending the Tynwald Day celebrations that year, so decided we should have an Alternative Tynwald Day in Port St Mary.

Our first costume day was on May 4th, with the public as well as shopkeepers embracing the idea, and it saw a little group of strolling players entertaining visitors – seeing twice the number of tourist coaches in the village was a great encouragement to us all. The President of Iceland made a flying visit to Port St Mary, but his popularity did not compare with Geoff Joughin, landlord of the Bay Hotel, and his yard of ale competition!

One of the most fascinating initiatives for Millennium Year saw a team of photographers from the Southern Photographic Society, led by Mike Goldie and Donald Gellion, meticulously plan a whole day – May 26th – recording every aspect of life in the village, with each member of the team assigned a particular project. A Day in the Life of Port St Mary is a remarkable historical document, still preserved to this day in the Manx Museum. From bin lorries and a birth, to drains and a death, every aspect of life was recorded.

Members of Port St Mary WI with their children during one of the costume days. (Courtesy of Southern Photographic Society)

As the year wore on, the number of tourist coaches and trains increased week on week, with visitors filling the streets each Tuesday. Bands, choirs and dancers were brought in to increase the appeal and more villagers were joining in, including a postmaster in his top hat, and the children of Port St Mary had great fun joining in the activities.

As July 5th approached, plans were finalised for Port St Mary's Alternative Tynwald Day – a Manx 'wedding', a fair on the harbour, trade stalls, sheep shearing, Manx dancing, food vendors and the pipes and drums of the ceremonial guards. But one thing we hadn't planned for was the vast crowds that turned up on the day. Traffic was backed up all the way along Bay Ny Carrickey. The police were all deployed at St John's where Queen Elizabeth II was presiding over the Island's Tynwald ceremony. Into the breach – well, at least into the road – stepped Cynthia Gelling, arms akimbo. The band marched and the spectators cheered as the procession walked from the Town Hall to the harbour.

Rosemary Bartlett had agreed to be the Manx 'bride', but unfortunately we forgot to mention the horse she would be riding! She went by horse to the Mount Tabor Church, where she 'married' Kevin Keig. So convincing were they, many visitors thought the re-enactment was a real marriage – and the newlyweds did not disappoint them, much to the amusement of the locals!

The wedding was more popular the the *Ceres*, a French minesweeper that was open to the public on the day. The festivities ended with a Scandinavian choir singing from the balcony of the Isle of Man Yacht Club.

Later in July, there were Irish dancers, a youth band, and, as usual, the popular regatta week that we held each year, which celebrated everything from bonny babies to glamorous grannies, and included the bay swim – in short, a week of community fun, which culminated in a wonderful, colourful fancy dress parade.

August saw the arrival of the tall ships, and what a wonderful sight it was to watch them sail into the harbour, every boat resplendent in flags. I recall the harbour master sending one of the ships out to sea again to get cleaned up. I think it was the *Winston Churchill*, with an all-girl crew, who had not been too well on the voyage to the Island.

King Olaf V of Norway arrived on August 1st and stayed until the 5th, on the Royal Yacht, the *KS Norge*. He reviewed the tall ships before they took part in the Round-the-Island race and many residents chatted to him as he strolled around the village each day.

Something incredible had happened – in a few short months, Port St Mary had become *the* go-to destination for tourists and islanders every Tuesday. There was always some attraction: the local Girl Guides learned Manx dances and performed outside the Manxonia department store, spinners brought their wheels into the streets, a Welsh male voice choir sang outside the Isle of Man Bank, much to the consternation of the manager, who complained that the crowds of people listening were blocking the doorway.

It was then that we heard from the BBC – they were coming to scout the village. The success of what we had been doing had caught their attention and they later confirmed that the Seaside Special of the BBC Show of the Week was coming to film our costume days. Michael Hurll, who had previously produced the Eurovision Song Contest, arrived in the village in early September. Boney M, who had sold eighty million records around the world, were to star in the show.

Opposite:

(top left and right) 'Bride' Rosemary Bartlett and 'groom' Kevin Keig at the Manx wedding, part of the Alternative Tynwald Day. (Courtesy of Southern Photographic Society)

(bottom left of the four) Vast crowds flocked to Port St Mary for the Alternative Tynwald Day. (Courtesy of Southern Photographic Society)

(bottom right of four) Youngsters being entertained by a Punch and Judy Show. (Courtesy of Southern Photographic Society)

(bottom pic) Tall ship Sir Winston Churchill visited the port in September 1979. (Courtesy of Southern Photographic Society)

In costume at Port St Mary Railway Station, for the Chattanooga Choo-Choo routine. (Courtesy of Southern Photographic Society)

King Olaf V of Norway arrives on the royal barge. (Courtesy of Southern Photographic Society)

In costume at Cregneash. (Courtesy of Southern Photographic Society)

It was an onerous task, to provide everything that the producer demanded – Loaghtan sheep, Manx cats, everyone in costume – but the community pulled together and the result was televised around the world, and indeed lives on today on Youtube.

The charming singers of Boney M, dressed in stunning white and silver outfits, sang outside Harry Kelly's cottage surrounded by villagers and their children, all in Manx costume. The Wurzels, a rustic singing duo, sang their hit song *Combine Harvester* in the adjacent field. We were all amazed at the length of time it took to complete the filming, with take after take of the same action, but by the time we reassembled two days later (in 1940s costumes as requested by the producer) on the railway station to be part of the Chattanooga Choo-Choo routine, we were accustomed to the take after take after take, as the Seaside Special dancers leapt from the steam train onto Port St Mary Station, time after time.

When the BBC team left the village, they telephoned to say they had forgotten to leave tickets for all the people who had taken part in the filming to attend the live show, which would be in a huge big top tent on Rushen School playing fields. I suggested they leave the tickets in Douglas for me to collect. I drove into Douglas to collect them… only to find that they had given them away.

However, that was only a minor blip on what was the most incredible and memorable year for the village, and it had the desired result – Millennium Year and the decision to have costume days revived trade in Port St Mary for a number of years following 1979.

Superstar band Boney M performed outside Harry Kelly's cottage in Cregneash. (Courtesy of Southern Photographic Society)

INTRODUCTION NOTES

1. A sheading is an administrative division, of which there are six on the Isle of Man.
2. One who issues summons to courts.
3. I thank Breesha Maddrell for the allusion to the 'space between'.
4. Rushen Heritage Trust, 2018.
5. A strict comparison of population is not possible since census boundaries changed over time. In 1881 there were 167 households and 699 persons listed as living in the Port St Mary census district. By 1968, but with boundaries extended now to include the Howe, Fistard and the Four Roads, the population was c.1400.
6. Moore, 1901, Kelly, 1996.

Introduction References:

Kelly, D. (Ed.) (1996) New Manx Worthies, Douglas: Manx Heritage Foundation.
Moore, A.W. (1901) *Manx Worthies*, Douglas: S.K.Broadbent and Company.
Rushen Heritage Trust *(2018) Friend or Foe?*, Douglas: Rushen Heritage Trust.

Chapter 1 sources of information:

Captain Harry Watterson's lists of Port St Mary fishing vessels as in 1879 and 1886, Published by the Manx Heritage Foundation 1979 and 1986.
Manx Museum Folk Life Surveys, contributions from John Gawne, Martin Woods, Henry Cooper.
Manx Museum Castletown Ship and Fishing Vessel registers, Manx Museum newspaper records online.
Irish Sea Herring Fisheries, W.C. Smith, Curator of Port Erin Biological Station, University Press of Liverpool, 1923.
Early Manx Fishing Craft, B.& E. Megaw.
Quarterly Journal of the Society for Nautical Research, Vol.27, No.2, 1941.
The Development of Manx Fishing Craft, B. & E. Megaw.
Proceedings of the Isle of Man Natural History and Antiquarian Society, Vol.V, N.111, 1952.
Sailing Drifters, Edgar J. March. First published in 1952 by Percival Marshall & Co. Ltd. Reissued in 1969 by David & Charles (Publishers) Ltd.
Our Heritage – Memories of the Past in Rushen, Books one to four, Kate Rodgers 1986.
Manx Sea Fishing, Resource Book, Manx Heritage Foundation 1991.
Fish & Ships, Angela Kneale, The Manx Experience 1995
For the Love of Manx Kippers, Mike Smylie, Lily Publications 2018.
CLIP – the Crew List Index Project online – Ship records
Northern Lights Board online records, Port St Mary Lifeboat records, Isle of Man Yacht Club records.
Irish Sea Schooner Twilight, Richard J Scott, Black Dwarf Publications 2012.

CHAPTER 2 NOTES

1. Slack S, 2003, *Manx Milestones*.
2. J.J. Bagley, 1985, The Earls of Derby 1385–1985, 130-134 Genealogical details have been taken from *Burke's Peerage* 106th Edition. Edited C Moseley, 199 Vol I 133-139.
3. C.W. Gawne, 2009. *Controversy, 1651-1895*, 57-80; Winterbottom, D., 2012. Governors of the Isle of Man since 1765, 12-25.
4. Most of these issues are documented in Murray-Stewart, J. (Ed.), 1908 *Chronicles of Atholl and Tullibardine*, Vol. IV.
5. Gelling, J, D 1998, History of the Manx Church 1698-1911, 52-58 for the Duke's patronage and Bishop Murray's episcopate.
6. L.S. Garrard et.al. *Industrial Archaeology of the Isle of Man* 1972, pp 232-234.
7. MNHL SSS May 1823-65.
8. MNHL dated 9th April 1822.
9. MNHL Deed dated 2nd June 1832.
10. Sale to Duke dated Nov 1822. MNHL May 1823-65. Mortgage to Gawne dated August 1832. MNHL Oct 1832-45.
11. *Chronicles of Atholl and Tullibardine*, Vol. IV (as above).
12. Nothing but unpopularity Spencer Walpole, *Land of Home Rule*. £60,000 *Chronicles*, Vol 4, p. 346.
13. Little has been written on the Duke's massive borrowings but on the authority of the *Chronicles* his overall indebtedness prior to his sale of his Manx interests was in the region of £500,000.
14. Gelling, Canon John, 1998, *A history of the Manx Church*, The Manx Heritage Foundation, Chapter 5, 52-58. Craine MA, CP, David *Manannan's Isle*, Chapter XIV, 197, 1955, Moore, A.W., *A History of the Isle of Man*, Vol II, 1900, 659 onwards.
15. *Chronicles of Atholl and Tullibardine*, Vol. IV (as above).
16. Gill, J F (ed) In accordance with the Boundary Walls Act of 1763, Statutes Vol I, 1883.
17. MNHL Enquest File 1726. I am obliged to William Kelly for this reference.
18. Material on the Gawne family is included in the Manx Notebook website.
19. An account by Frances Coakley appears under "Breweries" in her Manx Notebook website.
20. Made over to Edward Gawne Junior by a document dated 25th October 1790. SSS May 1794 No. 138.
21. *Manx Sun,* 23rd March 1823.
22. *Manx Advertiser* 1st November 1821.
23. I am obliged to William Kelly for a copy of the relevant document dated 2nd July 1803 recorded 5th February 1810
24. *Manx Advertiser* 24th October 1837 for the large fortune. Patricia Tutt (2013), 279-81, provides a beautifully illustrated account of the house. See also account of the house in the Introduction to the present volume page 8.
25. MNHL Registered Deed SSS Oct 1795 – 57.
26. MNHL Registered Deed SSS Oct 1795 – 57.
27. IOM PRO – Lib.Plit.1888/14 – Cary v Taylor.
28. Talbot T, 1924, *The Manorial Roll of the Isle of Man,* 1511-1515, 3.

29. See Article by J.K. Qualtrough, 'An Introduction to Manx Water Mills', Proceedings IOMNHS Vol VII No. 2, 256-259. This should be read in conjunction with his later writings on the topic in Garrad, L.S. et al, 1969, *Industrial Archaeology of the Isle of Man*, pp 155 & 245, and in his own 2008 Volume on Port St Mary.

30. Megaw B R S, 1940 & 1944 JMM Vol IV, 199-202 and V, 147-8, for the main account of "little mills" in a Manx context.

31. Deed dated 23rd October 1753 MNHL N/SSS October 1753-62.

32. Deed of sale dated 8th June 1793 – MNHL SSS October 1795-57a.

33. Qualtrough J K, *op cit*, p10.

34. *Manx Sun*, 30 August 1862.

35. R.P. Kelly; *IOM Newspapers* Millennium Supplement, Issue 4, p.15.

36. MNHL, MS, 10723, Clucas Notebook.

37. The early mining endeavours generally are discussed in A Scarffe, 2004, "The Great Laxey Mine", 1-2. More detail on Glen Chass appears in J Rimington, 2000, "Features and History of the Meayll Peninsula", 60-65.

38. *IOM Times* 27th August 1898.

39. MNHL, D151/18X and IOM PRO SOG 1904 – 25 & 140; 1905 – 13 & 147.

40. IOM PRO, SOG, 1930 – 5 & 195.

41. S. Slack in Cringle and others1992, 56.

42. J.C. Curwen, 1810, Presidential Report – Isle of Man Section. 'The Rules & Proceedings of the Workington Agricultural Society'.

43. *Manx Patriot*, 16th April 1825, 2.

44. A series of sales of property on the west side of the High Street by Thomas Clucas begins in that year.

45. Quayle quoted in J W Birch, 1964, *The Isle of Man – A Study in Economic Geography*, 161.

46. Ibid.

47. MNHL AP 50-38 dated 6th October 1827 McCrone to Carrington.

48. SSS Oct 1819-61.

49. SSS O1814(28).

50. *Woods Atlas.*

51. IOMPRO SOG 1904 140 and 1905 13.

52. Readers may make strange of a reference to *brooghs* at this location, but in fact this Manx term can refer to any steeply sloping land.

53. Registry of Deeds, December 1919-226, Harriet Kissack to Henry P Kelly.

54. Registry of Deeds, July 1986 – 484. Administrators of M K Kelly to Mr & Mrs S Bradshaw.

55. An *Isle of Man Examiner* article 19th May 1939 entitled 'Altruism of 1897' details the contribution of Judge Jones and his family to the building.

56. See J. K. Qualtrough, 2008, 25.

57. Qualtrough J. K, 2008, 18.

58. The description appeared in *IOM Examiner*, 23rd June 1894.

59. The auction of Gelling's property is described in the Manx Sun, 7th September 1895.

60. *IOM Examiner,* 5th December 1908.

61. *Ramsey Chronicle*, 28th June 1927.

62. Clarence Horatio was born in Madeira in 1813, the second surviving son of Capt. William Cary & Susannah his wife. His father owned an estate, Doogary, in the parish of Tynan west of Armagh in the north of Ireland.

63. The Woods family later changed their name back to Stevenson and the Goldies became the Goldie-Taubmans. For details of the Cuninghames of Lorne House, see Patricia Tutt's book *Lorne House – A Manx Survivor* (2010).

64. The main sources for the family history are the late Stowell Kenyon's Drinkwater family tree deposited at MNHL. MS. MD 971 and the family history at MD 12540.

65. The use of name *Lucius Cary* hints at a relationship to the Viscounts Falkland.

66. KWC Register, Ed. K S S Henderson, 1928, 60, 70 & 459. *Alumni Cantebrigiensis* available online.

67. Extracts from John Drinkwater's correspondence in V. L. Drinkwater's TS account of the family: *The Drinkwaters of the Isle of Man*, assumed the surname Lawe in addition to Drinkwater in 1879. The intended recipient has previously been identified as George Drinkwater of Kirby (b. 1852).

68. The Cary family's association with the Calf is comprehensively discussed in John Wright's article on the Calf of Man, Its Owners & Tenants (1800-1910). Proceedings of IOMNHAS vol IX number 4 page 459. W.L. Marshall *The Calf of Man* (1978).

69. *Isle of Man Times*, 28th August 1886.

70. Summarised by C K Radcliffe "Shining by the Sea", 1989, 112/113. For further details refer to the reports of the debates of the Manx Legislature.

71. IOM PRO *Lib Plit.* 1888 – 14, Section F for the depositions

72. Details of deaths derived from publications of the Isle of Man Family History Society, Rushen Burial Registers and MIs.

CHAPTER 3 NOTES

1. *Land of Britain* part 44: the Isle of Man 1941 Elwyn Davies.

2. *History of the Isle of Man* 1900, A.W. Moore.

3. Commonly known as Liber Assed and Liber Vast.

4. www.manxmanorialroll.com 19/04/19.

5. www.manxmanorialroll.com 19/04/19.

6. Belchem, John (Editor). 2000 *A New History of the Isle of Man, Volume 5: The Modern Period, 1830-1999*, Liverpool University Press pages 18-22.

7. A quarterland: an agricultural land division usually subdivided by four within a treen varying in size from 50 to 180 acres, most large farms were about a quarterland.

8. A treen: a division of agricultural land varying in size from 200 to 600 acres usually with boundaries formed by natural land features. PSM is a coastal plateau treen from coast to hill.

9. There are various spellings for this abbeyland: Ballavrara/Ballavraarey. Most sources say it means farm of the brethren/brothers'.

10. *The Manorial Roll of the Isle of Man* by T. Talbot 1924 Oxford University Press.

11. John Clucas 1795-c1853 son of Thomas Clucas and Isabel Nelson of Ballakilley, Rushen. He married Margaret Gell of Kenaa, German in 1819 their son John Thomas Clucas 1827-1887 JP, Captain of the Parish of Rushen, Clerk of the Rolls, secretary to Governor Loch, the first treasurer of the IOM plus many other roles.

12. 25th November 1822 Rushen Enrolled deeds page 11.

13. John Murray 1755-1830.

14. Plan of Port St Mary belonging to his Grace the Duke of Atholl by J. Taggart Douglas June 1827.

15. Margery Forbes 1761-1842.

16. There has been more research done by Nigel Crowe on the 4th Duke further references and information within Nigel's chapter in this publication. And: Frank Cowin 1972 IOMNHAS VOL Pages 100-115 paper on Holmes's Bank.

17. John Welch Six-day tour of the Isle of Man 1836.

18. 1837 directory farmer and limeburner Port st Mary noted in 1832 shipping out limestone to Ardglass in shipping news in the Manx newspapers.

19. William Barwise Jefferson 1814-1892 and Isabella Jane Moore of the Abbey, Malew 1816-1886.

20. Thomas Jefferson 1775-1861 married to Jane Kelly 1779-1836.

21. 1841 Teare's Butchers, Duke Street, Douglas 1840-1850 snippets in all Manx Newspapers.

22. 1851 census at Ballahott Farm, Malew.

23. J.K. Qualtrough *Port st Mary* 2008 reprint, in appendix transcript of reminiscences of PSM c1850 by John Watterson, PSM Station Master.

24. 1752 the year the date changed from the Gregorian to the Julian Calendar, the same reason why Tynwald day is celebrated on Old Midsummer's Day.

25. John Kermode 1818-1908 Manx Speaker and historian three wives and ten surviving children.

26. Brig Lily of Liverpool bound for the west coast of Africa, more information within other chapters.

27. James Holmes c1778-1853 banker, fish curer, ship owner, merchant and landowner. Last business partner to die, the others being John and Henry Holmes.

28. Frank Cowin *Holmes Affairs* IOMNHAS Proceedings Vol: VIII, 1972 P100-115.

29. Captain Peter Petrie 1789-1870 married to Elizabeth Blyth Grindley 1800-1873.

30. Deed Ref March 31st: sale Harris to Petrie MS 09494/1858/04/109.

31. Deed Ref April 30th: sale Avison & Boardman to Petrie MD 09494/1858/05/091.

32. Deed Ref June 22nd: sale Avison & others to Petrie MS 09494/1858/08/066.

33. John Kermode and Catherine Shimmin's children: Catherine Ann 1843, John Thomas and Eleanor 1846, James 1848-1915, William 1850, Elizabeth 1852-1877, Thomas Richard 1854, Henry Shimmin 1855.

34. Catherine Ann Shimmin was from Ballacross, German, died 1857 aged thirty-three.

35. Caroline Green, of Ballaugh, died 1860 aged twenty-one; she had one daughter, Emma Amelia Kermode, baptised 1860 Rushen.

36. Catherine Costain married John Kermode 1865 Rushen; their children were Anna Isabella Kermode, baptised 1869, and George Costain Kermode 1872-1951.

37. 1895-1898 In her Majesty's High Court of Justice of the Isle of Man Common Law Division case between George William Jotham (plaintiff) v Joseph Kelly & Thomas Moore (defendants).

38. 1896 part of John Kermode's evidence in the rights of way dispute in endnote xxviii.

39. Walter Grindley Petrie 1822-1862 died at Ronaldsway Farm farmed by his brother-in-law John Blyth.

40. 1871 Census: Agnes Thomson (neé Petrie) married to John Thomson sugar refiner married 1869 Rushen, Isabel Thomson (neé Petrie) married to John Thomson Esq photographer 1837-1921 married 1868 Hong Kong.

41. *Mona's Herald,* 03 August 1870, Manx Sun 01 October 1870.

42. Deed Ref 1st June 1864: bond and security Petrie to Blyth MS 09494/1873/08/076.

43. Deed Ref 17th Jan 1871: appointment of trustees Blyth will of Peter Petrie MS 09494/1880/04/097.

44. David Petrie and family immigrated to America in 1877 by 1880 they were living in Frederick, Virginia, David died in 1907 he had changed his name to Cruickshank sometime after 1900 on the condition so he could inherit a fortune from a relative in Scotland.

45. *Isle of Times*, 9th December 1871.

46. Deed Ref 1st June 1864: bond and security Petrie to Blyth MS 09494/1873/08/076.

47. PDF of Transcription of will: 8th December 1866 Testament of Sir James Young Simpson, Vide Record of Inventories Vol 149, page 433 ref SC70/4/127.

48. Deed Ref 12th Nov: sale for D. Petrie by Coroner of Rushen to Alexander Magnus Retzius Simpson MS 09494/1874/01/72.

49. Deed Ref 10th January: Alexander M.R. Simpson to John Blyth MS 09494/1874/01/073 John Blyth of Ronaldsway Farm, Malew was married to Margaret Grindley Petrie 1850 Patrick.

50. Adverts for worker with horses 10th Feburary 1872, farm sale October 1873, baptism of Eliza Patterson daughter of David Patterson farmer October 1873 Rushen.

51. John Blyth Senior 1777-1839 born Fifeshire, Scotland buried Malew, Isle of Man.

52. Margaret Grindley Petrie 1824-1899 daughter of Captain Peter Petrie and Elizabeth Blyth Grindley of the Raggart, Patrick.

53. Elizabeth Robertson Petrie c1837-1884 keen supporter and student of the Douglas School of Art.

54. 1880 at Bolton, England, William Carine eldest son of Edward/Edmund Carine, farmer Port st Mary House to Eleanor Letitia Raby; 1880 at Castletown Wesleyan Chapel,

Sarah Carine, 4th daughter of Edward Carine, Port St Mary House to William Goldsmith watchmaker, Castletown. Other Carine offspring: Thomas, Annie and Frederick, a pharmacist. He emigrated to Johannesburg, South Africa in 1903.

55. 16th May 1887 at Port St Mary Farm Edward Carine aged 75.

56. William Carine 1860-1924 died at the Four Roads, ex-managing director of the Fishermen's Supply Association PSM, Superintendent of the Wesleyan Sunday School PSM, member of Harbour of Peace PSM.

57. 30th July 1887 *IOM Times* page 1.

58. 27th August 1887 *IOM Times* Mr. Sparrow of Sparrow & Hardwicke of 10 Major Street and 107 Piccadilly, Manchester, textiles manufacturing company.

59. 31st August 1887 *Mona's Herald* page 5.

60. 1882 Aug 12 *Manx Sun* 12, 1889 26 Jan *IOM Times*; 21st May 1937 *IOM Examiner* page 11, it mentions the discovery of a stone coffin with a skeleton when drains were being dug to the farmhouse in c1903.

61. Deed Ref 14th June 1889: sale Woodworth to Port St Mary Estate Company Limited MS 09494/06/167 dwelling house in Port St Mary. Work commenced early September 1889, a Mr Caudle was the foreman.

62. 1887 *IOM Examiner* 3rd September page 5.

63. 'Port st Mary two ghosts' 21st May 1937 *IOM Examiner* page 11.

64. 1901 Census Thomas Clague butcher, Effie T. Clague wife and Effie M. Clague four months in farmhouse; Henry Nelson, Martha Nelson and Annie aged five months; Joseph Crellin 51, Elizabeth Crellin 57, Annie M. Crellin 15, both families in houses connected to the farm.

65. Converted into houses and holding areas built on. 1911 Thomas Clague Junior and family lived above his butcher shop in Station Road, Port St Mary; the sign can still be seen on the ground to the entrance of the shop 2019. The dive shop is there in 2019.

66. Thomas Clague Junior 1869-1944 farmer, butcher, hotelier of Perwick Bay Hotel, Fistard, only son of Thomas Clague Senior 1850-1915 and Margaret Catherine Moore 1846-1922 lived Athol Street, Port St Mary. Married Effie Theresa Gelling in September 1899, Douglas.

67. Port St Mary Estate Company Limited 1887-1904 some of the directors were already landowners in the Port, interconnected through marriage and blood, and at some point, with Port St Mary Commissioners. Involved in developing the Port for the tourist industry. Also involved in negotiations with the Isle of Man Steam Packet Company to bring steamers to Port st Mary having a deep enough dock because of the newly built Alfred Pier.

68. Reports of the Board of Advertising numbers of visitors landed in Douglas in 1889:229,312; 1890:260,786; 1895: 292,525; 1897: 314,667;1901:418,000; 1913:634,512 to give a sense of how many people were coming to the Isle of Man and needing accommodating and feeding.

69. William Taylor of Ballakilley, Rushen 1870-1952 and Eleanor Catherine Corrin of Scholaby,Rushen 1875-1949.

70. *IOM Examiner* 5th March 1904 page 6, at the newly built Mount Tabor Primitive Methodist Church and meeting rooms.

71. The Taylor's five daughters were: Meta Kathleen 1905-1987, Isalen Jane 1906-1959, Edith Mabel 1908, Rita Emily 1910-1975, Eleanor Winifred 1912-1976.

72. Thomas Cannell of Lime Street, Port St Mary had worked on the farm as an agricultural labourer since 1905.

73. Haviland, Dr A. *Port st Mary Health Resort* 1891.MML Ref M 07836/ F.76/3(5) The pamphlet was distributed throughout England and included a plan of Port St Mary Estate later publications have sketches included.

74. Deed Ref 1904: sale Port st Mary Estate Company Limited in liquidation & William Henderson Walker to Edward Clague MS 09494/12/108; sale Edward Clague to Edward Qualtrough MS 09494/12/102.

75. William Faragher 1830-1929 married to Jane Moore 1845-1932 both from Ballafesson/Surby. Faragher children: Frederick James 1866-1933; William 1867-1946; Thomas Moore 1870-1951; John 1872; Lizzie Jane 1874-1952 (Cormode); Margaret Julia 1875-1961 (Keggin); Charles Joshua (1877-1940); Esther Annie 1879-1950 (Callow); Eleanor Catherine c1881 (Costain); Edward 1884-1947; Emily Isobel 1889-1943 (Scarffe). Source *IOM Times* 29th January 1938 page 19.

76. *IOM Times* 29th March 1916.

77. Edward Faragher 1884-1947 President of the Farmers Club Ltd; Director of the Agricultural Show at the Nunnery in August 1947 among many other roles.

78. Edward was in the Rifles 3rd Battalion 1915-1921 Document ref: National Archives Kew. http://discovery.nationalarchives.gov.uk/details/r/ C1090530?descriptiontype =Full&ref=WO+339/36631.

79. 7th November 1924 *IOM Examiner*.

80. 1952 Edward retired to Surrey and died at New Malden. Source obituaries.

81. 1923 the first residents were allocated housing in Park Road. Port St Mary Commissioners edited minutes from meetings.

82. 1929 *IOM Examiner* 8th November page 14, 12th December fields for let.

83. Plans submitted to Port St Mary Commissioners for planning approval 1931; September conversion of stables to dwelling house, April 1932 April erection of a garage, August 1932 two new dwelling houses, October 1932 for a bungalow.

84. 16th November 1934 architect J. L. Clague.

85. 2002 Harvey Briggs, *A Harvest of Memories*, published by The Manx Experience

86. 2002 Harvey Briggs, *A Harvest of Memories*, published by The Manx Experience

87. 1935 – *IOM Examiner* 11th January page 3 and IOM Examiner 18th January page 7.

88. 1935 *IOM Examiner* 5th April page 6; create golf course, tennis courts, bowling green, café, garden allotments and sale of building plots; and Mona Herald 16th April page 5.

89. 1936 April 19 page 12 – after much initial debate the Port St Mary Estate Bill was passed and carried by Tynwald; 5th

June page 6 – course opened by Lieutenant Governor Butler on the first official visit to the Port of a Governor since the Commissioners had been formed.

90. Willie Clucas, sailmaker 1877-1960 married to Rhoda Rivers 1878-1952 they had three daughters: Inez Edna Clucas 1910 –? (married Thomas Collister) in photograph, and Mona Lilian Clucas 1905-1987 (married a Costain) and Irene Rivers Clucas 1906-1927. Willie Clucas's parents were John Clucas, sailmaker 1834-1901 and Eliza Coffey 1847-1920.

91. My uncle (Ronald C. Clucas) was a grocery delivery boy in the early 1960s for Darnill & Keig Grocers, Bay View Road and he remembers delivering groceries to the Faulkners at the Old Farmhouse. I remember the Gueudres living there up to the 1980s, Jacques worked for Port St Mary Commissioners and Maureen had a hairdresser's shop, later a wool shop where the new laundrette is built now. Jacques 1929-2008, Maureen c1930s-2018.

92. In the Gleton in the 1511 Manorial Roll, includes quarterlands of Ballahane and Ballacreggan.

93. *A Dictionary of Manx Place-Names*, George Broderick 2006, map of treens and quarterland of Rushen XLVII.

94. Daniel Callister 1682-1732 son of Daniel Callister born c1655 and Mary Mcylvorrey 1660-1743, his sister Jane Callister 1699-1739 was married to William Clucas 1693-1764 of Port St Mary Farm. Daniel's daughter Isobel 1710-1788 married John Nelson 1711-1795 of Ballakilley, Rushen.

95. 1844 largest ever ox.

96. 1845 *Manx Sun* 25th June.

97. 1861 census William Kneen farm steward at Ballacreggan with four other labourers, 1871 census living in Malew Street, Castletown working as a butcher.

98. William Kneen Senior, IOM Newspapers, August show results from 1876-1887, William Kneen Junior 1888-1900 possibly showing stock in the same agricultural shows in the late 1880s.

99. His brother John had died in July 1878 at Ronaldsway Farm, Malew.

100. 1886 *IOM Times* 28th August page 12 – Valuable estate sold astonishing price of land.

101. 1900 *IOM Examiner* 2nd June page 5 – 'Sudden Death of Mr Cary' – George Drinkwater Lucius Cary 1845-1900 married to Sarah Ann, son of Clarence Horatio Cary 1813-1900 and Elinor Drinkwater 1814-1884.

102. 1888 *Manx Sun* 3rd March page 13 – The building extensions complimentary dinner.

103. As above, purchasers at the dinner were Edward Qualtrough, T. Crennell, M. Pollard, W.J. Cannell (banker), Daniel Lace, Thomas Clague, W.E. Qualtrough, J. Moore, Thomas Qualtrough, J. Costain, B. Pulkinhorn, J.J. Qualtrough, William Kneen, Thomas Taylor, W. Skillicorn, Samuel Keggen, G. Gelling, W.J. Merritt, and J & T. Costain.

104. 1900 *IOM Examiner* 2nd June page 5 – Sudden Death of Mr Cary, found dead in a railway carriage at Port St Mary station on a journey from Ballabeg, he had heart disease.

105. As above.

106. 1900 *IOM Times* 13th October page 2, 1905 *IOM Examiner* 16th September page 7.

107. 1919 *IOM Examiner* 9th August – a plot offered for sale that 'belonged to Mrs Cary'. Mrs Cary does not appear to be on the Island by 1911, before 1935 she died and left her will to John Frissell Crellin and George Parsons Crellin and after their death to go to their children, a sale of land goes through in Port St Mary from the Crellins estate in 1935.

108. Sarah Anne Cary, 28 Bowling Green Road, Castletown with two servants; WDL Cary and Eva Cary (born Illinois), Beach House, Douglas Road, Castletown with two servants and a visitor from New York.

109. Annie Kneen (1857-1937) married to Samuel Watterson 1842-1916 baker, flour dealer, one of the first Port St Mary Commissioners, owner of the Smelt Corn Mill, IOM Insurance Company agent, landowner and farmer, Fistard and Port St Mary Estate, ran a mineral water company at the Pop Houses, Chapel Bay with his brother Daniel and owner of bakeries in PSM and Douglas.

110. Elizabeth Kneen 1860-1902 married John Clague 1854-1926 a joiner, builder, grocery and bakery shop proprietor, hotelier of The Hydro in Port Erin. (Youngest brother of Thomas Clague 1850-1915 butcher, Belle Vue, Port Erin and Perwick Hydro, Fistard) 1881 Mona's Herald 8th June described their marriage as the most fashionable wedding that had taken place for 'some time past', honeymooned on the continent.

111. William died in 'Kimberly', Cary's Promenade in 1895, buried Malew, a younger son Robert Charles Kneen was involved with Mylcreeshts diamond mines in South Africa. I suspect that may be something to do with why the house was called 'Kimberly'.

112. Sources deeds for Rushen with William Kneen, J.J. Kneen's shop advertised in newspapers from 1897, 1901 census. William Kneen Junior 1865-1925 married to Margaret Ann Watterson died 1935, they lived at 8, Victoria. Road, Port St Mary, their daughter Miss Annie Kneen contributor to Manx Folklife Survey FLS K/134 in 1976 about Ballacreggan and Port St Mary.

113. Henry Alfred Cooil c1870-1960 (son of John Cooil Ballagawne, Arbory) married Isalen Janie Corrin 27th November 1900 Arbory. Cooil sons: John Corrin Cooil 1902-1994, Henry Ewan Cooil 1907-1967, William George Cooil born 1909.

114. 1956 *IOM Examiner* 18th May – Port St Mary Commissioners apply for a grant from Tynwald to widen the road for £3,055 giving twenty men twelve weeks' work over the winter, 1956 IOM Examiner 05 Port St Mary Commissioners requested an additional grant of £2,349 for the scheme. Widened from 4 feet 6 inches to 27 feet and 10 feet wide pavements for pedestrians.

115. On old postcards and photos, the barn can be seen, to the east of the main farm today.

116. 1919 *IOM Times* 26th July page 8 – Sale of one the largest and best farms on the Island.

117. Interviews with Johnny Corkish for Rushen Heritage Trust 2017 & 2018.

118. personal recollection of the author of this chapter.
119. MML:MS 13646 Isabel Kathleen Combe (neé Keggin) 1923-2013.
120. Other Corkish siblings: Walter 1923, Kathleen Anna c1925, Robert Henry 1928, James Albert 1930, Margaret 1932, John David 1934, Leslie and another girl (two of the girls had died as infants).
121. Information taken from the transcription of Johnny Corkish's interview 02/11/2017.
122. as above.
123. as 110.
124. as 110.
125. as 110.
126. John Donald Clucas 1869-1939 barrister, MHK Rushen & Ayre, Captain of the parish of Rushen, director of various companies: IOM Bank, IOMSPC, Manx Salt & Alkali, IOMR. Son of John Thomas Clucas 1827-1887 and Margaret Callister 1839-1913.
127. *A Dictionary of Manx Placenames* George Broderick 2006 page 110.
128. More research required about the farmstead at Gansey, the area has been discussed further in Nigel Crowe's chapter on roads and buildings.

CHAPTER 4 NOTES:

1. eds Lynch & Davey 2017, 92-93.
2. Bruce, 1968, 55-62.
3   Bruce, 1968, 55-60; Kelly, A W 1986; Johnson & Fox 2017, 214-5.
4. Bruce, 1968, 60-62; Watterson, J. 1903, 42; Qualtrough, J.K. 2001 15).
5. Gelling 1998, 44.
6. Curry 1906, 897; Chapman, 1971, 4.
7. Chapman, 1971, 13.
8. Curry 1907, 155.
9. Chapman, 1971, 9.
10. Chapman, 1971, 6
11. Chapman 1971, 9, 21; Harrison, A 2000a 361 quoting Coakley.
12. Harrison, A 2000b 396-8.
13. Cowin, F 2015.
14. *Manx Sun*, Tuesday 22 May 1832, 3; Qualtrough, J.K. 2001, 19, 31.
15. Watterson, J 1903, 42.
16. *Manx Sun*, Tuesday 9 August 1831.
17. anon 1986, 56.
18. Harrison 2000a, 360.
19. Gelling 1998, 177.
20. Gelling, 1998, 153.
21. Gelling 1998, 122, 176.
22. Gelling 1998, 177.
23. Gelling 1998, 177.
24. *Manx Sun*, Saturday December 10,1892; *Mona's Herald*, Wednesday July 18, 1894.
25. Manx Wesleyan Methodist Church Record 2 (1894), 27.

26. MNH MS 09494/1895/08/158.
27. Anon 1986, 56; Qualtrough J.K. 2001, 20-21,
28. Curry, 1907, 155, 218; Qualtrough, J.K. 2001, 19.
29. Manx Wesleyan Methodist Church Record 1 (1893), 46.
30. Manx Wesleyan Methodist Church Record 6 (1898), 48.
31. Manx Wesleyan Methodist Church Record 7 (1899), 45-46.
32. Squire 1984, 9; Qualtrough, J.K. 2001, 18.
33. Dalheim 2011, 295, 313.
34. Squire, 1984, 9.
35. D & K Gellion pers comm; Anon 1986, 56; Qualtrough, J.K. 2001, 21.

Chapter 4 References:

Anon 1986 *Old Wesleyan Chapel.* in ed Rodgers, K 1986b, 56.

Ed Belchem, J *A New History of the Isle of Man Volume V: The Modern Period 1830 – 1999.* Liverpool. Liverpool University Press.

Bruce, J.R. 1968 *The Manx Archaeological Survey: Sixth Report 1966: Keeills and burial grounds in the Sheading of Rushen.* Glasgow. The Manx Museum and National Trust.

Chapman, E.V. 1971 *The Story of Methodism in the Isle of Man: interim report.* Typescript. MNH M 11370.

Cowin, F 2015 Methodist Heritage: Isle of Man reproduced at www.methodistheritage.org.uk/isleofman.htm 06/09/2018.

Curry, W 1906 – 1907 *The Story of the Primitive Methodist Church in the Isle of Man* (extracts from Primitive Methodist World 1906–1907).

Dalheim, R. 2011 *The Sunny Hours.* Brighton. Pen Press.

Feltham, J 1798 *A Tour through the Island of Mann, in 1797 and 1798.* Bath. R Crutwell.

Gelling, J.D. 1998 *A History of the Manx Church (1698–1911).* Douglas. The Manx Heritage Foundation.

Harrison, A 2000a *Religion in the Nineteenth Century* in ed Belchem, J 2000 *The Modern Period 1830 – 1999*, 357-64 = *A New History of the Isle of Man Volume V.* Liverpool. Liverpool University Press.

Harrison, A 2000b *Associational Culture, 1830 – 1914* in ed. Belchem, J 2000 *The Modern Period 1830 – 1999*, 393-406 = *A New History of the Isle of Man Volume V.* Liverpool. Liverpool University Press.

eds. Lynch, F & Davey, P 2017 *The Chambered Tombs of the Isle of Man: a study by Audrey Henshall 1969-1978.* Oxford. Manx National Heritage & Archaeopress.

Johnson, A. & Fox, A *A Guide to the Archaeological Sites of the Isle of Man up to AD 1500.* Douglas. Culture Vannin.

Kelly, A.W. 1986 Ballaqueeny (sic), *Port St Mary. A Heritage for Seven Thousand Years.* In ed. Rodgers, K 1986a, 13 – 15

Qualtrough, J.K. 2001 *Port St Mary.* Port St Mary. J.K. Qualtrough.

ed. Rodgers, K 1986a *Our Heritage: Memories of the Past in Rushen Book One.* Port St Mary. Quine & Cubbon.

ed. Rodgers, K 1986b *Our Heritage: Memories of the Past in Rushen Book Three.* Douglas. Norris Modern Press Ltd.

Speed, J 1610 *The Isle of Man Exactly described, and into several parishes divided, with every Towne, Village, Baye, Creke and River therein conteyned. The bordring Coasts wherewith it is circulated in their situations sett, and by the Compass accordingly shewed, with their true distance from every place unto this Island by a severall scale observed. Described by Tho Durham Ano. 1595.*

Squire, L.S. 1984 *St Mary's Church 1884-1984 Parish of Kirk Christ Rushen.* Port St Mary. Parish of Kirk Christ, Rushen.

Watterson, J 1903 *Port St. Mary in 1850* in Qualtrough, J.K. 2001 40 – 44.

Port St Mary Beach Mission:

Watkinson, Peter and Watts, Andrew: '*Yesterday, Today and …. The Story of Port St Mary Beach Mission 1901 – 2000*' – Port St Mary Scripture Union Beach Mission

Acknowledgements: Evelyn and David Stewart – Team Leaders (2017) Port St Mary SU Beach Mission

CHAPTER 5 NOTES

1. Moore, 1900, Cameron-Jones and Kelly, 1973, Bird, 1995, Clamp, 1985, Hoy, 2015.
2. Barrow, quoted in Butler, 1799.
3. Qualtrough, 2005.
4. Rushen Parish Red Files 11.10.1822.
5. Hoy 2015.
6. Jackson, 1906 p.18.
7. *The Manx Church Magazine*, 5, p1-3, January 1895, quoted in Heaton 2019, p.59
8. Heaton, 2019, p.45 and Bird, 1995 Vol 1, p.173
9. Killip, 1975.
10. Otherwise known as the British and Foreign School Society
11. Little, 2006.
12. Clamp, 1991, p. 4
13. Watterson, 1903, MFLS.
14. Interview 2002
15. MFLS, 1972.
16. Kneale, 1897.
17. Committee of the Isle of Man Educational Library, 1847.
18. Kelly, 1996.
19. Rodgers, 1995.
20. *Manx Sun* 11.10.1831.
21. 'from across' is a Manx expression referring to people who travel to the island from other parts of the British Isles, mostly from England.
22. Bird, 1995 Vol 1 p 198.
23. Christopher, 1905.
24. Council of Education, 1921.
25. RSCM 1872-1907.
26. RSCM, p.41.
27. Census, 1881.
28. RSCM, 1879, p. 119.
29. Watterson, 1962 MFLS.
30. Clamp, 1986.
31. Interview 2002.
32. Interview 2003.
33. Minutes of Evidence, 1896.
34. *IOM Times*, 10.06.1911.

35. *IOM Times* 10.06.1911.
36. *IOM Examiner* 11.11.1911.
37. Rodgers, 1995.
38. RSLBs.
39. RSLB, 30th June 1941.
40. RSLB 26th June 1944.
41. Moule et al, 2018.
42. The school was in transition and expanding year on year. Greeba Creer was in the 'top' year for several years: hence her long tenure as Head Girl. Information supplied by Ian Cottier.
43. CRHS, 1998 p 11. Also see *The Manx Experience*, 1999, p 240-241.
44. *IOM Examiner* 09.12. 1949.
45. Skillicorn, 2006.
46. Pedley, 1963.
47. *IOM Times*, 21.08.1959.
48. *IOM Examiner*, 27.11.1958.
49. Interview.
50. Mr Tom Thompson became head of Rushen Primary School in 1997, retiring in 2018. Ms Carol Best was the first head of the new primary school in Port St. Mary.

Chapter 5 References

Bird, H. (1995) *An Island that Led: the History of Manx Education*, 2 Vols, Isle of Man: Manx Heritage Foundation.

Board of Education Annual Report (1946/7).

Butler, W. (1799) *Memoir of Mark Hildesley*, D.D. Bishop of Sodor and Man, London.

Cameron-Jones, M. and Kelly, D. (1973) Education in the Isle of Man, in Bell, R., Fowler, G. and Little, K. (Eds.) *Education in Great Britain and Ireland: a source book*, London: Routledge and Kegan Paul and Open University.

Christopher, H. S. (1905) *King William's College Register, 1833-1904*, https://archive.org/stream/kingwilliamscol00mangoog/ kingwilliamscol00mangoog_djvu.txt Accessed 07.03.2018.

Clamp, P.G. (1986) *Schooling in the Isle of Man, 1650-1950*, (Doctoral Dissertation) University of Alberta, Edmonton

Clamp, P. G. (1991) A question of education: class, language and schooling in the Isle of Man, 1800-1833, *Journal of Educational Administration and History*, Vol XX111 (1), 1-14.

Committee of the Isle of Man Educational Library (1847) *A Statistical View of the State of Education in the Isle of Man*, 1847.

CRHS (1998) *Castle Rushen High School 50th Anniversary Booklet, 1948-1998*, Port St. Mary, Quine and Cubbon.

Heaton, J. (2019) *Kirk Christ: a brief history*.

Hoy, M. J. (2015) *Isaac Barrow: builder of foundations for a modern nation*, (Doctoral Dissertation) Liverpool: University of Liverpool.

Interviews (various years) by Adrian Cain for the Manx Heritage Foundation and the author.

Jackson, C. (1906) *Report on Secondary and Higher Education in the Island, including the Training of Teachers for Public*

Education Schools, Douglas: Isle of Man Council of Education.

Killip, M. (1975) *The Folklore of the Isle of Man*, London: Batsford.

Kneale, W. (1897) *Oddfellows Companion and Guide to Douglas, Isle of Man* http://www.isle-of-man.com/manxnotebook/history/socs/odf_hist.htm Accessed 08.03.2018.

Little, A.W. (2006) *Education for All: multigrade realities and histories*, in Little, A W (Ed.) *Education for All and Multigrade Teaching: challenges and opportunities*, Dordrecht, Netherlands: Springer.

MFLS (various years) *The Manx Folk Life Survey*, Manx Museum

Moore, A.W. (1900) *A History of the Isle of Man*, London, T.Fisher Unwin.

Moore, R.B. (1926) *History of Education in the Isle of Man*, *Education Week*, May 8-15, pp. 9-14.

Mona's Herald, obituary 12.11.13.

Moule, D., Crowe, P., Graham, A., Saywell, J., Wertheim, D. Davidson, H, Davidson, S. (2018) *Friend or Foe? The fascinating story of women's internment during WWII in Port Erin and Port St.Mary*, Isle of Man, Rushen Heritage Trust.

Pedley, R. (1963) *The Comprehensive School*, London, Penguin

Population Census, 1831, 1841, 1851, 1881.

Qualtrough, J. (2005) http://www.telusplanet.net/lawson/twill/1810_019.html Accessed 26.02.2018.

Qualtrough, J.K. (2001) *Port St. Mary* http://www.qualtrough.org/ history/Port-St-Mary.pdf Accessed 27 02 2018.

Rodgers, K. (Ed.) (1995) *Our Heritage: more memories of the past in Rushen. Book Two*, Printed by Quine and Cubbon.

RSCM Rushen School Committee Minutes, various dates.

RSLB, Rushen School Log Books, various dates.

Rushen Parish Red Files, Manx Museum Library.

Skillicorn, P. ((2006) *Wave to your Daddy: the life of a family in the Isle of Man*, Onchan: The Manx Experience.

Statistical Annex in Belchem J (Ed.) (2000), *A New History of the Isle of Man, Vol V The Modern Period 1830-1999*, Liverpool: Liverpool University Press.

The Manx Experience (1999) A Chronicle of the 20th Century, 1905-1950, Douglas.

CHAPTER 6 NOTES

1. *Port St Mary Guide*, 1909.
2. Waugh, Edwin: *A Guide to the South*, 1869.
3. Broadbent; *Guide to Port St Mary* 1882.
4. *Port St Mary Guide*, 1909.
5. Havilland, Alfred: "Report on Port St Mary as a Health Resort", 1891.
6. Ibid i.
7. *Port St Mary Guide*, 1955.
8. Ibid.
9. Note from Mr Peter Kelly, MBE.
10. Conversation with Chris & Avrile Bramson.
11. Ibid x.

12. Much of the Perwick Bay Hotel section is based on research conducted by Jonathan Latimer in 2015, and used in Rushen Heritage Trust's 2015 exhibition 'Five Places and their People'. Hugh Davidson also stayed at this hotel in 1940s.
13. Ibid.
14. Interview with Lisa Walster (Ken & Margaret Ives' daughter) by Alan Jackson and Drew Herdman, 2015.
15. The Balqueen section owes much to multiple interviews with Betty Kelly (wife of Walter Kelly) by Hugh Davidson (3 in 2015), Beth Espey (1 in 2015) and Rosemary Walters (1 in 1994). Other significant interviews on the Balqueen by Hugh Davidson in 2015 were with Jane Fargher (daughter of Charlie and Ivy Ward), and Barbara Guy (waitress at Balqueen in 1969-70).
16. Ibid.
17. At this time, the Waldorf Astoria was the largest hotel in the world, with 1500 rooms. It is now owned by a Chinese company.
18. Alec Davidson (1902-1986), father of Hugh Davidson.
19. Isobel Baillie, the famous soprano, stayed at the Balqueen as did Violet Carson, one of the early super stars of ITV's 'Coronation Street' who played Ena Sharples.
20. Sir David Wilson, later Director of the British Museum, worked at the Balqueen in university vacations.
21. Interview with Adrian Bashforth by Hugh Davidson, 15 September 2017.
22. Mary Eslick was the mother of Joan Eslick (see page 182 below), and grandmother of Ali Graham and Jane Saywell, key members of Rushen Heritage Trusts' WWII Internment Team.
23. Conversation with Graham Shaw, September 2017, interviews with Daphne Murray, Lilian's daughter, 2018.
24. Ibid iii.
25. Information on scenic attractions below taken from the *Port St Mary Guide*, 1950.
26. Alexander Alec, *History of Port St Mary Golf Club*, 1903–2003.
27. Information on Mr & Mrs W A Kelly and Walter Kelly OBE, JP, mainly from Betty Kelly, Walter's wife. Also, reminiscences of Balqueen Hydro by Robert Kneale 22 October 1998 (unpublished). Conversation with Marian and Tony Morfett (former guests), Brian & Carole Cooill.
28. Interview with Aileen Swales (Mr Scrimgeour's daughter) by Hugh Davidson and Drew Herdman 2015. Memories of John Qualtrough.
29. Information from Jane Fargher in interview with Hugh Davidson, 2015.
30. Memoir by May Addison.
31. Interviews with Mona Quillin by Hugh Davidson and Beth Espey 30th July 2015. Conversation with Brian & Carole Cooil, 21 March 2015.
32. Ibid xxxi.
33. Sources: interview with Betty Kelly, conversations with Graham Shaw, Ali Graham, Sir Miles Walker, Edwin Looney, Barbara Guy.

Acknowledgements:

We would like to acknowledge the funding support provided by the Trustees of the Manx Museum and National Trust, Culture Vannin and Gough Ritchie Trust.

The following archives, biographies, surveys and memories have been of great value to our research.

The John W. Qualtrough collection of images of more than 160,000 photographs, maps and other artefacts, collected across many decades, has been immensely helpful to all of us at Rushen Heritage Trust. John is the first holder of the Rushen Heritage Silver Medal awarded in 2017 for outstanding achievement in local heritage.

In 1996 Dollin Kelly edited *New Manx Worthies*, a substantial update of Manx Worthies edited by the Manx historian, A W Moore in 1901. Both contain profiles of Port St Mary people.

During the 1980s and 1990s Kate Rogers edited a series of collected memories of Port St Mary, titled *Our Heritage*. In 2000, John Rimington published *Features and History of the Meayll Peninsula* on behalf of the Rushen Parish Commissioners. In 2001 and 2008, John K. Qualtrough, with support from Port St Mary Commissioners, published *Port St Mary, a brief history of key places and people in the port*. This includes a detailed description of the people and places of the 1850s as recalled by John Watterson, a former Port St Mary station master.

The ever-helpful staff of the Manx National Heritage Library and the Public Records Office have sourced a range of material, including maps, newspapers, Manx folk-life surveys, government reports and John Gawne's *Port St Mary and the Fishing Fleets* (1950).

Internet sources have also been important, including the Port St Mary draft appraisal for conservation status (2009), available from www.gov.im and *A Manx Notebook*, edited by Frances Coakley, www.isle-of-man.com/manxnotebook/

Additional acknowledgements:
- Allan Kelly, of Mannin Collections, Peel, for supplying the cover image.

Chapter 1
- Yvonne Kneen for allowing us to use her Kipper House memories.
- Annie Kneale for proofreading the chapter.

Chapter 2
- The many individuals and groups who assisted in the research for this chapter.
- Janet and Guy Thompson and Gill Pause for facilitating access to properties and providing documentation concerning them.
- Vanessa and Richard Drinkwater for permission to quote from their family papers.
- Port St Mary Commissioners for allowing access to their holdings of maps and plans and giving permission to publish extracts from the Kaye material and the 1904/5 boundary extension map.
- Cathy Clucas and Alex Maddrell for the discussion of obscure points concerning the evolution of the road network.
- Chris Callow for providing details of his Callow forebears.
- William J. C. Kelly for his enthusiastic encouragement and assistance and providing mapping and other materials.
- Hugh Davidson for his suggestions about the structure of the chapter, Angela Little for her valued guidance and Doreen Moule for transcribing a crucial document.

Chapter 3
- Johnny Corkish, Richard Baker, Nigel Crowe and the late Harvey Briggs for their invaluable assistance.

Chapter 4
- Rosemary Cooil, Donald and Kathleen Gellion and Reverend Joe Heaton for their knowledge and support in developing this chapter.
- Grateful thanks to Evelyn and David Stewart, leaders of Port St Mary Beach Misssion.

Chapter 5
- Heartfelt thanks to the following people for their comments on draft chapters and in many other ways: Audrey Barker, Hinton Bird, John Bowers, Lalage Bown, Edythe Bridson, Adrian Cain, Francis Coakley, Norman Collister, Ian Cottier, Dorothy Hook, Helen Leigh, Keith Lewin, Brenda Little, Breesha Maddrell, Gary McCulloch, Judy Sille, Tom Thompson, Jamys O'Meara.

Chapter 7
- National Portrait Gallery for the use of the photograph of Dame Joanna Cruickshank.
- Betty Kelly for the use of photographs and information.
- Alison Graham and Jane Saywell for the use of photographs and information about their grandmother and mother.

Chapter 8
- Geoff Pickles for his help with this chapter.

Chapter 9
- Norman Collister and Linda Winstanley for their knowledge about Port St Mary's shops.

Our book has addressed some but not all of the important aspects of Living with the Sea in Port St Mary. There are many themes and questions that others may wish to research in the future. We look forward to collaborating with you all.

All material in this book has been credited to the original copyright holder where possible. If we have inadvertently misascribed or have been unable to trace the original copyright holder, please accept our sincere apologies – contact the publisher so that this can be rectified in any future edition of this book.

INDEX